Being and Contingency

Being and Contingency

Decrypting Heidegger's Terminology

Ricardo Sanín-Restrepo

ROWMAN & LITTLEFIELD
Lanham • Boulder • New York • London

Published by Rowman & Littlefield
An imprint of The Rowman & Littlefield Publishing Group, Inc.
4501 Forbes Boulevard, Suite 200, Lanham, Maryland 20706
www.rowman.com

6 Tinworth Street, London SE11 5AL, United Kingdom

Copyright © 2021 by The Rowman & Littlefield Publishing Group, Inc.

All rights reserved. No part of this book may be reproduced in any form or by any electronic or mechanical means, including information storage and retrieval systems, without written permission from the publisher, except by a reviewer who may quote passages in a review.

British Library Cataloguing in Publication Information Available

ISBN: HB 978-1-53814-767-2

Library of Congress Cataloging-in-Publication Data

Library of Congress Control Number: 2020945994

ISBN 978-1-5381-4767-2 (cloth)
ISBN 978-1-5381-4769-6 (paperback)
ISBN 978-1-5381-4768-9 (Electronic)

Contents

Introduction	1
1 The "X Game of Language"	7
2 Definition of the Ready to Hand	27
3 That "Thing" with the They and the Hinges of Signification	35
4 Naming and Difference: Multiple Worlds and the Power Play	71
5 Objects and Social Performances: Seeing as Gathering	97
6 Resoluteness (*Entschlossenheit*), Discourse, and Disclosedness	129
Conclusion	147
Bibliography	149
Index	153

Introduction

We feel as if we had to repair a torn spider's
web with our fingers.

Ludwig Wittgenstein (1986, 106)

INTRODUCTION

Is another world possible? If the answer is no, could it not be that the tyranny of necessity spools inside us and we are but voluntary servants of its horrors? If the answer is yes, then it is possible that of all the worlds that it takes to make a world we have chosen none so we could become them all.[1]

Let me begin with an invitation that is a warning as well. This book is about contingent difference and the possibility of another world. Henceforth, it pursues difference not as a contrived or exotic form that remains retracted and hidden somewhere but as the very form of the world that domination (power as potestas) occludes and plunders. We will be patient and let difference emerge from itself. Writing, in this book, is simply setting the right environment, the stage, for difference to become and show itself in all its variations, in all its infinite splendor. We will not force it or bend it, but let difference wrap itself around us, penetrate us, steep itself through every pore, and lift us from our intellectual illness that only asks for unrepentant truths and readymade formulas. As in any search for and through difference, it must not precipitate its findings; they are not objects or trophies; they cannot be shown in one triumphal pedestal; rather difference guides the sight out of the darkness of identity into the color of life. We will have to let go of everything and slide into difference, the most difficult, yet the most urgent of all political and spiritual tasks. For the impatient reader who needs thick plotlines, who demands that heritage be sacralized and poetics banalized, who cannot see the ropes handed to them unless they can pull back a comfortable philosophical tradition where to rest their guilt and despair, I must say wait. Be patient and read this book as a mystery that slowly and delicately unfolds, not through shocking revelations or violent twists but though subterranean passages that connect with each other subtly and silently. Let things appear and come into presence by themselves, not in our invoking them from a sterile exterior but through their own form and corporality. Let us simply set the scene for the titanic confrontation between potestas (domination) and potentia (difference), but let the contest unravel in itself; only there can we truly appreciate the magnitude of power. Therefore, we cannot draw a silhouette or anticipate a formula of power that does not, as yet, exist and only comes forth as the exercise of intense difference. If it were to be understood as a film, there is no Computer Generated Imagery (CGI) in this work, but only special forms of lighting, of representing things and acts that illuminate truths without touching upon them, without making propaganda out of our conclusions. We are not erecting truths as islands in the middle of a silent ocean but as surrounding scenes, opening them up as we turn away from them. The style of the book is better understood as a poem (or a poetics in its utmost Aristotelean sense). The book conducts a fierce defense of difference and thus purports that only true radical difference can determine the world; hence it steers away from any form of imposition; it disbeliefs in the possibility of singular truths and particular forms of observation; hence it does not impose its views but rather paints them; it leaves them unpronounced; it does not invade the "visual room" of the reader to dictate what should be seen or understood. Here the answers are not served in happy meals to be devoured in one chomp but rather are an invitation to join the beautiful struggle of becoming other as the only possibility of life. If I wrote "Decolonizing Democracy" under the influence of my teenage self, piercing though the hypocrisy of the powerful, relentlessly set against authority, and unbending against injustice, this one is written under the spell of my child-self as children know no hierarchies among beings or languages of the world, as representation is infinite and has no end point, and everything can stand in the place of everything; thus the child knows only difference and difference is the world.

We propose the "X" game of language as a hypothesis that allows us a radical reconsideration of being and nothingness, of identity and multiplicity, of existence and meaningfulness, of contingency and necessity, and of potentia and actuality that will reveal a new and unsuspected relation between being and power, shattering the binarity in which these terms stand upon. Through contingency, we will reinstitute power as the very limit of what is possible and impossible, of what can be, what cannot be, and, fundamentally, what may become to be from "feigned" regimes of impossibility.

Working the premises of "the X game of language" through the theory of decryption of power, the book decrypts the pillars of the philosophy of being. Mainly Heidegger's construction of the "ready to hand," thus proposing a novel theory of being where the only necessity is contingency and thus where a being can only be deemed as a becoming from immanent collective difference. Heidegger's construction of being is paramount in Western philosophy, seemingly, the most innovative, riveting, and enduring effort to construct a presupposition free ontology. Nevertheless, using the theory of encryption of power, we discover that the said effort is simply a very sophisticated perpetuation of a kind of knowing (epistemology), of counting (politics), and of doing (ethics) that alienates the possibility of any kind of politics as a commonality of differences. Henceforth, we will harness not only the shortcomings of Heidegger's theory but what is not only salvageable but also fecund in his theoretical complex in order to take aim at our most relevant theoretical game, the idea of democracy as the permanent exercise of immanent difference set against power as domination (or potestas). Hereafter, we will connect the theory of encryption of power with an array of ground-breaking philosophical, spiritual, artistic, and scientific traditions of the last hundred years in order to perforate and depose Heidegger's metaphysics (through his construction of the ready to hand).[2] Thus, through an alliance of the theory of encryption, mainly not only with Wittgenstein's philosophy of language, but also with the likes of Kripke's theories of naming, Latin American literature, Actor Network Theory, Deleuze's and Guattari's Assemblages, Quentin Meillassoux's speculative turn, and Hugh Everett's Multiple World Interpretation (quantum mechanics), we will push "being" to its political and phenomenological limits, revealing, in the very same act, a new way of considering being and difference. However, the aforementioned theories will not remain immune to decryption; on the contrary, they will be deeply pressed and filtered through and through in order to obtain a theory of being that is not merely political but where politics (as the immanent and collective order of difference) defines being.[3]

Difference is always contingent, and thus any quilting point of it in necessity is its primal disavowal. Allow us to rapidly pose the central question of contingency and necessity that will resolve the question of power in this book: "Change can be contingent or necessary, or it can be possible or impossible. Contingent refers to what can happen without it being necessary that it happens. Necessary refers to that for which it is impossible not to happen. Impossible is that which cannot, under any circumstance happen" (Sanín-Restrepo 2016, 85). It is in between contingency and necessity where the drama of power unfolds and attains its full meaning. As we have clarified before,

> While contingency is the unleashing of immanence, generation, transitions, and creativity; necessity is the sovereign grip of every definition of time and space from a predefined point zero. While in necessity, the contingency of the future is captured in what is presently actual; contingency is the edge where possible and impossible are to be decided. Contingency is always the unbound multiplicity of becoming. Hence, there is no expression of difference that is not contingent as there is no negation of difference that does not always fall back into necessity. Contingency and necessity are then the gridlocks of power, that is, of what is possible and impossible. (Sanín-Restrepo 2018, xi)

As we will prove, only in contingency is the world possible; when the world is harnessed in necessity, it is simply a simulacrum of the world through a simulacrum of power.

Necessity is the world of potestas (power as domination, the denial of difference). Thus, we open the door to all doors, contingency. Only in contingency is the world possible. Difference and multiplicity are tantamount to contingency as much as potestas is to necessity. A fundamental imbrication between multiple world interpretation (MWI), the problematic of naming, and decryption of power serves as the steppingstone to thwart Leibniz "best of possible worlds" as the dream of he who teaches us conformity to power as potestas through necessity. The idea is not to oppose MWI with the power of poetics but to poetize it, so we can clearly prove that no present is actual, no future is predestined, and no past is irrevocable.

The poetization allows us to fix a powerful paradox of actuality and necessity (potestas) that will serve as the epicenter of our findings. We can stipulate it as follows: if there is an infinity of multiple parallel universes, then it is absolutely necessary that there is a universe where multiple parallel universes are impossible; hence the infinity of multiple parallel universes is limited and thus finite. As we will discover, this paradox will lead us to a critical conclusion, that "this," the world of potestas, the very world we live in, is but a mere simulation. Potestas (this very world we live in) is the only world that is unreal, immaterial, and impossible. Precisely the most hideous and effective feature of potestas is that it has no reflection and no double side; it is a frozen state of identity and oppression. Potestas is thus the paradox of existence, a sheer simulacrum of world, the utter denial of difference, and multiplicity. The world of potestas (of the simulacrum of difference) is that which cannot exist outside itself, that which is not even different in itself. Consequently, contingency (whose name in politics is democracy), as the infinite extension of intense difference, is necessary for all possible worlds.

Power is created in its exercise; all power is manifested in a relationship of forces and affections. A kiss, a bomb, a decree are all expressions of power; they alter the world in its conditions of possibility and recognition. Power can vary its intensity, dispositionality, and formula as the act is inserted within ethical and aesthetic webs of significance. Such insertion is also an expression of power. What is paramount, in order to understand power structures, is not their corporality but their expressions. As Michel Foucault proved, the description of their structures will always be superficial and nimble compared to the fields of reality they create and the cartographies they design (Foucault 1978). Power as potestas is the heinous game of luring the multiplicity of power, its abundance and horizontal production into structures of uniformity that solidify it into a rachitic form of language.

One of the fundamental efforts of the book is to be consistent with the material dimensions of the world purported by power as domination (or potestas). Without traversing potestas, or the negation of difference, the world remains wrapped in a cloud of vapor; it is but a mere simulacrum. The problem we have to acutely attend to is that potestas, despite its horrors, or better because of them, does constitute the dimensions of our world; it generates an awful truth of race and gender, but a truth altogether, one we cannot leap over or close our eyes to in order to wish it away. Rather well we must lock horns with the creature until it shows us its full colors. Thus, we propose a novel way to understand power. Threading in between potentiality and actuality, and actuality as a division between *Energeia* and *Entelecheia*, the theory of decryption of power will create a chain reaction in ontology, metaphysics, and phenomenology, proving that contingency is the only order of difference and that the very possibility to communicate lies in the infinitude of difference. Decryption of the ready to hand means no unity or identity of the things but the possibility to create new forms of involvements in disobedience of every transcendent order.

The creed at the heart of the book, in reference to being and difference, is but one: "flatter." Flatter ontologies, flatter worlds, and flatter lines of communication, which do not mean monotony or uniformity, but the liberation of the profusion of life through flatter surfaces where no hierarchy or model can take the upper hand of the world, and hence where all the fertility and exuberance of being can come to life and reproduce difference infinitely.

Throughout the book, I am introducing a new concept that is germane to the theory of the encryption of power. Based on Wittgenstein's "language games" and understanding their emancipative and subversive potential, I am ascertaining that in order for power "as potestas" to create a simulated language game (to hold on to a false construction of power) it requires a "power play." The tendency of power as potestas to construct ideal languages, to detach meaning from ordinary language, to create forms of knowing and doing that are outside of any possible game where the rules are said to anticipate the move (transcendent) but are only knowable in their application after the move (*ex post facto*) is what I call a "power play". A power play consists of a method designed to jump out of a language game altogether and into transcendent models of power that deny every form of difference. A power play reveals an ontological gap in any consideration of politics. If the political question is who or what can participate in a language game, then the game is politically flawed if not be the case that everyone or everything can participate in it.

At the end of the game, we may discover a form of power that is beyond both actuality and potentiality—a horizontal and immanent power that is the order of both. A third order of power where everything is contingent and contingency means that only when beings exist, not as a necessity, is the meaning of being *necessary*.

NOTES

1. I would like to ask the reader that when and if they finish the book to come back, "reloaded" to read this introduction anew, as a form of epilogue.

2. We are not holding that Heidegger's construction of the ready to hand is a part of Heidegger's metaphysics, or that Heidegger's analysis of readiness-to-hand offers a metaphysical theory. Our wager, and this constitutes the justification of why we chose Heidegger's ready to hand, is that Heidegger intends to depose of all Western metaphysics and that the ready to hand is a mainstay to such undertaking. What we try to prove throughout the book is that by doing so he installs a new form of (undetected, encrypted) metaphysics. Of course Heidegger and his scholars would deny that Heidegger is doing metaphysics through the ready to hand, one of the most ambitious processes of this book is to prove otherwise, that is, to demonstrate how in the sense that the ready to hand is not decrypted it falls into the pit of metaphysics that it rejects in the first place.

3. For an introduction and differentiation of all the topics here imbued, see Sanín-Restrepo (2016 and 2018).

Chapter 1

The "X Game of Language"

Imagine that tomorrow every single written sign of every written language is transformed into the letter "x" (all scripts = the extensive combination of x's). This includes all written words in books, statutes and statues, constitutions and databases, instruction manuals, signposts, screens, keyboards, etc. The x "changeling" also applies to every written sign ever recorded in the form of stone, facsimile, photographs, movies, binary codes, photocopies, etc. A total collapse of the written word. All written signs disappear but not our ability to remember them and their connection to sound (phonetics). We should have no trouble remembering and speaking our name, the number of our address, or where every single letter corresponds to a keyboard, as well as the first words of "A Hundred Years of Solitude," and the rules of this game. When you call your dog, it is prompt to respond as any other day (and when you call your cat it is prompt to ignore you as any other day). In short, the memory of the written word remains intact. If we hit the old keyboards with the letter r, a letter x would be irremediably reproduced. However, we could produce new keyboards with the letters we remember, and "r" would correspond with "r" and so on; that is, the ink would still flow and the wax, as well as the electronic tablet, would still be docile for our indentations of language. Numerals and ampersand, as well as binary arrangements, will all collapse. As numerals disappear, the clock still moves its hands; there would be movement but not representation! However, the hands of the clock would have the dashes but not the digits. The clock would still track tomorrow the same motion as it did today, the same exact pathway as yesterday (but we already knew that the clock itself is nothing but space).

As we know, the number is independent of everything except its symbol. Hence try this experiment: can you think "3" without its sign? No? Only if you think of three things? Can we think of 3 without three things? Yes, but then are we not thinking of the sign 3? Try to avoid thinking of three, picture independent unities (numerals) between 2 and 4 . . . can you?

A total collapse of the written word. As if everything ever written was written in the sand and the "Great Wave of Kanagawa" washed it all away in an instant.

BOUNDARIES OF THE GAME

It is difficult to give a sole description of what a written system is. For the sake of this game, it is hedged in the following attributes. First, it is any visual or tactile method of representation of verbal communication (the intimate relation between the spoken and the written word is what defines written language and excludes drawings, paintings and other forms of symbolic systems from our little foray). For example, a stop sign that has the word "stop" written on it will become a red octagon with four x's written on it, while the stop sign with a hand in the position of stop will remain unaltered. In our game, "written language must also refer to artificial graphic marks on a more or less durable medium and at least one set of defined base elements or symbols, individually termed *signs* and collectively called a *script*" (Coulmas 2003, 34). Finally, at least one set of rules loosely shared by a community, which assigns meaning to its elementary particles (graphemes). In short, a script through a medium as the representation of the spoken that may be decipherable by a reader of the said language.

The game includes all systems of written language (Daniels and Bright 1996): alphabets, syllabaries, pictographic or ideographic writing systems, segmental scripts, logosyllabaries, and every logographic system. That is, it comprises any glyph as a building block within a settled set of symbols, intended to represent the possibilities of reading and writing (Borgwalt and Joyce 2013). This includes every language based on pictograms, indicative icons, hieroglyphics, or ideograms, that is, what we roughly understand and use as the written language that is able to convey the meaning of phonetic complexes.

The game applies to everything that is a written symbol or a grapheme, as elementary particles that use marks that relate conventionally to articulate speech (the systematic arrangement of significant vocal sounds) or electronic programming in such a way that communication is achieved (Fischer 2001, 12).

We will not consider an emoji a writing system; hence the happy and sad faces of Sock and Buskin will not disappear.

CLUES THAT ARE QUESTIONS AND QUESTIONS THAT ARE CLUES

X marks every spot.

Don't think of this game as an outcome of winning or losing.

What changes would the game x bring about to concepts such as hierarchy, order and orders, samples, totality, principles and axioms, obedience, becoming, necessity, and contingency?

First possible answer: written language has not disappeared; it is impossible; it is simply concealed by something else that stands in its place. But can there be something in the place of language that is not linguistic in itself?

There is no hiding without a narrative to justify the hiding. The need of a narrative is germane to the act of hiding.

Is there a new relation between logic and thinking?

What will become of the relation between signifier and signified?

What would happen with structure and agency?

What would we understand by constituent power?

How profound would the change of the relationship between names, identity and multiplicity be?

How is the relationship between naming and baptizing altered?

Would the meaning of a name be informed by the relation of the thing to itself? Or rather the thing within a medium that defines its cluster of meanings?

Would there be a new relation sprouting between the real and the virtual, and between the virtual, actuality and potentiality?

Is a reconstitution between price and value necessary?

What would transmission, transportation, tradition, and hearsay mean in this new world?

Would the assertions "it's cold" or "it's hot" lose all reference to temperature?

Would the model meter in Paris lose all its meaning?

Could a GPS speak? Can it guide you? Does it know where to go?

To what extent would we need to alter the meaning of the concept of symbol?

What could we localize and what would be evasive in a map, moreover, what would simply disappear from a map?

Have we all gone crazy? Ahh, but can people delude themselves beyond language?

Could we rely on some variation of the solution rendered in Fahrenheit 451?

What would Quentin Meillassoux's (2008) "arche fossil" tell us anew?

Can writing have any reference beyond our memory? And what would memory become?

Would there be a new relation between *langue* and *parole*?

What would happen to Austin's Illocutionary acts?

What would happen to Bakhtin heteroglossia?

What would the meaning of *Corpus* become?

How would we appreciate Basquiat's "Hollywood Africans in Front of the Chinese?" (Would the face to the right of the picture have teeth?)

Utopia or dystopia?

Do the rules and clues determine the content of this book?

And so it goes . . .

There are countless ways to play this game. You can play it as a detective mystery, a whodunnit of kinds. Or, you can try to play it as a scavenger hunt or a caper in order to recover written language, that is, try to determine how a thing like this could happen. If a treasure (language) has been hidden, what is the difference between the treasure and the methods to unearth it? Or, among many more, simply take at face value what has been set out as a hypothesis and ask what could happen to the world after the fact, this, I believe, is the most enticing way to play this game.

In what follows, I will propose a way to play this game, one way among innumerable, one way among infinite ways. For reasons that will become evident, I am proposing that the way to drill through the rock of the game is through a reconsideration of the relation of being within Western philosophy that delivers a genuine form to consider immanent difference and democracy as the sole order of the world. I have already advanced in this path through my previous work, specifically in "The People vs Hegel," an article that is part of the collective book *Decrypting Power* (Sanín-Restrepo 2018). Notwithstanding, Heidegger's concept of the "ready to hand" seems to me a fundamental alternative as a major key to wiggle in the lock of the game. I have not chosen Heidegger as the pick that seems to unlock the game; rather Heidegger has been imposed onto the game. His work is set upon an uncanny crossline that makes it an obstacle and a swift passage to engage the game. Heidegger has promised to deliver us from transcendence and representationism, the two bitter illnesses of this thing called "the West." And he has delivered this promise providing a picture of the world that thinks being and "being in the world" without suppositions. The ready to hand is thus not a capricious election but the downright and logical confrontation between the theory of decryption of power with the apparent coronation of the struggle against metaphysical eminence. Thus, through decryption we will test the validity of not only Heidegger's, but his epigones claim that being, as a presupposition has been destroyed utterly, for if it has not, if it still survives it is then encrypted in its worst of forms, as a supposition.

I am not holding back the fact that I put all my chips in my theory of the "encryption of power" as a true ground breaker for the solution of the enigma purported by the game. In order to hit the ground running, we will deploy the theory of encryption of power with all its theoretical and pragmatic advances, within a cluster of theories that will potentialize its clarifying strength. I am referring here to Wittgenstein's concept of "rule following," Kripke's naming as causality corrected through the likes of Rorty and Peirce; Deleuze and Guattari's concept of "intensity" drawn from Bergson, who in turn drew it from Reinman and corrected here, among others by Quentin Meillassoux's "speculative turn" and the Actor Network Theory of Bruno Latour. A key element that I have been working from sun to sun is the intimate and reverberating intersections between potentia and actuality, contingency and necessity, *Energeia* and *Entelecheia*, the "hidden people" and the simulacrum, and thus the advances purported here should be read as a follow up of to my book *Decolonizing Democracy: Power in a Solid State* (Sanín-Restrepo 2016), specifically the fourth chapter of said book. The final question is thus posed: the fundamental, perhaps the only, question of politics is if there can be a non-qualified (immanent) actuality (as *Energeia*) whose acts and base are contingent. Hence, if this question can be given a positive answer, we have a world; otherwise we are stuck in a simulation of a world.

If the reader is familiar with the theory of encryption of power and specifically to the definitions of potentia, actuality, *Energeia*, *Entelecheia*, contingency, and necessity as developed in the books *Decolonizing Democracy: Power in a Solid State* (2016) and *Decrypting Power* (2018), they may want to jump to chapter 2 entitled "Definition of the Ready to Hand."

FUNDAMENTAL PRE-DEFINITIONS

The Theory of Encryption of Power[1]

In its most uneventful textual definition, encryption consists of hiding a message at plain sight. The encrypted text is in the open through a medium that appears transparent, built on an objectivity that is exposed and supple. Nevertheless, there is no access to the meanings of the symbols that are inscribed in it as they are obscure and puzzling, utterly evading our understanding. The message is intended to be understood (decrypted) by someone else who either possesses the same knowledge of the encryptor or at least holds the codes to decrypt the message (Sanín-Restrepo 2020). In architectural terms, the crypt conceals a dead body while being a site of reverence to it. The body becomes sublimed in stone as the representation of a soul that is elusive as it is only itself a representation of a cadaver that lays hidden.

The body is a nonfunctional object, a no-object that gets enshrined through an artifact that stands in its place as a symbol. The body does not speak, the crypt speaks for it, the crypt represents the libidinal link of adoration.[2] Representation, adoration, and hiddenness mark the architectural appraisal of the crypt (Sanín-Restrepo 2020).

Encryption, as the intentional way of hiding or confounding the meanings of a symbolic system, is a characteristic proper to any language that is what allows every language to be elastic, creative, and resilient; this is a fact that is not in dispute here. Nevertheless, we are before a whole unlike kind of creature when we deal with the "encryption of power." Here, we are before a primordial prohibition (political, legal, and racial) to access the programming and uses of language (as the first common difference) through permanent qualifications and conditions for the exercise of power and therefore a rigid stratification for the belonging of any possible world (Sanín-Restrepo 2016, xiii).

What we see; what we think, build, and destroy in time and space; where we live, love, suffer, name, struggle, reproduce, prevail, fade and die, and live again; be it material or immaterial, made out of intensity or extensity, virtuality or reality, in short everything that can exist and communicate its difference, we call *the world* (Sanín-Restrepo 2020). There is the only world when it is made up of all the differences that can produce and communicate difference. Insofar, power is either the exercise of immanent difference or its privation. What the encryption of power inhibits is the possibility of communicating meanings that are not defined in advance by a transcendent model, where the political lexicon is hierarchized, and the possibility of its engagement is predetermined and reserved for a few that hold the codes of its uses. Where there is encryption of lexicons, there is a hierarchy of beings and objects in the world. Nevertheless, what is occluded by encryption is not the language itself but the process of its transmission, the norms by which it operates, and the means by which it is distributed, but primordially, the reality to which it refers (Sanín-Restrepo 2018, xviii). What encryption guarantees is an absolute hierarchical social and political control over the areas of conflict that are debatable, and the empirical and normative bases that can arise in any discourse. Henceforth, reality becomes what the expert at hand (encryptor) says the reality is. That is why, for the encryption of language, it is fundamental to create the idea of a totality (the nation state and the constitution) that is previous and superior to any interaction that may emerge. The totality holds within it the design of parts that are integral to it, creating simultaneously the mechanism to calculate every emergence of possible relations. A regime of encryption anticipates the emergence of difference and tries to paralyze the formation of truths trough difference. Within a totality, the possibility of meaning is already distributed among centers of significance. Encryption is thus the negation of democracy (the order of difference) from the impossibility of politics through the alienation of language that makes the world possible. In the end, the impenetrability of language becomes the impenetrability of the political (Sanín-Restrepo 2018, xviii).

*De*crypting power is then the fundamental rejection of politics as any finality (*Entelecheia*) established by invisible and untouchable models. What *finality* denies is the very possibility of a relation of power. Politics is therefore a question that we have not allowed to be formulated among us creatures that produce difference as the form of existing. As Angus McDonald has recently noted, "What is encrypted by the constitution of liberalism are the people of democracy" (McDonald in Sanín-Restrepo 2018, 31). The concept of the people becomes a synecdoche, where a false totality (the people of human rights and constitutions, the included) incarnates (symbolizes and falsely represent) an impossible infinity (the excluded, the hidden people). The people as a totality is a *pars pro toto* synecdoche; that is, an arbitrarily determined part (white people and the debtor within a nation state) defines an unattainable infinity (the marginalized people and the forced migrant). The people as a synecdoche conjoin a part that is an excrement of the totality and what the totality lacks in order to become a true totality.

Hence, there is only a world (as an infinite multiplicity of beings) when it is made up of all the differences that can produce and communicate difference. Insofar, power is either the exercise of immanent difference or its privation. When power is the privation of difference, it is domination—a primordial denial of power, a false construct of existence, and its potentialities that we name "potestas." Any and every denial of difference is thus a denial of the world. Potestas is the negation of power (as difference) through the stratification of the conditions to exercise it. This denial produces a simulacrum of the world. Politics is the world that is alive, swarmed, and bustling in the conflict bearing all the differences that produce difference.

What will become evident in the crosshairs of the theory of Encryption and Wittgenstein's "language games" is that encryption means surreptitiously establishing sturdy rules that invade the games from nowhere to determine the aesthetical, the poetical, and the religious; to determine once and for all what language is and how it can be assessed. To encrypt is to colonize the rest of the world with rules whose creator is outside the language game. It is to control utterly any language game through power plays that control every possible move. Encryption is to establish possible games where the rules are said to anticipate the move but are only knowable in their application after the move (*ex post facto*). This is the beating heart of liberalism.

Encrypting as an act of hiding always leaves a trace, a mark on the topsoil of language. There is no hiding that is not followed immediately by a narrative, an alibi for those who do the hiding. In the alibi something stands in the place of the hiding, a justification of a new bifurcation in the myth of the origin.

POTESTAS, POTENTIA AND ACTUALITY, ENERGEIA AND ENTELECHEIA[3]

In *Decolonizing Democracy: Power in a Solid State* (2016) we went through Aristotle's configuration of potentiality and actuality, and the latter as a division between *Entelecheia* and *Energeia* as the lever that helped us to eject Agamben's privation and Negri's impotence out of the folly of political inaction. There, through a reconsideration of the concept of *Energeia*, we proved there was another comprehension of actuality (an actualization of difference) that brought action into difference and unconditioned difference into the world. Accordingly, we proved that despite all their liberating efforts, Agamben (1998, 2015) and Negri (2003) fall prey to the preeminent game of Western philosophy, which consists of neutralizing contingency, favoring what exists as necessary over what may come to be. We revealed that through *Energeia* as power (as potentiality) without transcendent finality, contingency, as the order of the political, would be unleashed and with it the possibility of the new. Consequently, we proved that life is an end in itself and bare existence is the only condition for politics (becoming just for the sake of becoming). Let us return to this fundamental discussion in order to synthesize what we proved there, this new theory of power, so we may set the path for the rest of our book.

Potentia and actuality are the core substance of power. In between these two concepts hinges not only the definition of power[4] but also its sheer possibility. We have called the relation of potentiality and actuality the "dyad." Understanding what is at play in the dyad is grasping the very possibility of existence, being and becoming, final and efficient cause, possible and impossible, causality, ethics, logical necessity and contingency, and time.

Let us paint various pictures in order to clutch on to the consequences we are after as we define the differences and intermingling of potentiality and actuality. Think of a statue, a song, a movie, a person, a people, a plum cake (Alice in *Through the Looking Glass*), a shredded vegetable, yellow wings breaking from a cocoon, an arrow in flight, the death of a galaxy, the birth of a cell, a kettle heating water and the vapor that it produces, a foal splashing in the mud after falling from the womb, the first stroke on a mural by Siqueiros (and the wall before it), or a person operating a blowtorch welding two metal parts together. Think of all these things from the perspective of generation and transitions, of identity and multiplicity. Potential is what a thing may come to be without it being as yet the thing, although it can be, at the time, another thing (an example is a colt that is not yet a full-grown horse; its actuality is being a colt, and its potentiality is being a full-grown horse). When can we say that the thing is authentically the thing, and when is it potentially the thing? When is the thing the "actual" thing and when is it "potentially" the thing?

The Aristotelean definition of the dyad stands the test of time as the definition of what exists, what does not exist, and what could exist. The question for Aristotle is twofold and stems from a unique concern. First, how does anything (be it called substance, being, or *Ousia*) come about (generation) and perish in time? And, second, how can an object persist in its being (the thing that makes it what it is) through the transformations it suffers in the crux of time and space? This is the terrain of potentia and actuality. The dyad is not only the passage from inexistence to existence but also the index of its possibility; it offers the point of discernibility between being and coming to being, and the exact determination of its possibility in time.

Logics and existence, or rather the logical possibility of existence, are decided in the dyad. The dyad defines what is possible, what may be possible, and what is not possible at all. Nevertheless, the central operation of the dyad is the explosive and constitutive relation between being and non-being. Non-being—the negative, the vacuum, the lack—is essential to the equilibrium of ontology but is also its breaking point. Non-being is the extreme and unaccountable force that can destroy any certainty and predictability when confronting being; it is the precipice of being, its utter contingency. Non-being is the agent of destruction of any regime of predictability. Western philosophy exists as a permanent effort to expulse non-being from existence, and to convert non-being as a synonym of nothingness, and Aristotle, through the dyad, is the great conjurer of the explosivity of becoming. What has to be conjured? Contingency. How? Through the primacy of actuality over potentiality.

Potentia is the solution of the enigma of non-being as the possibility of the becoming of being; it is what grants supremacy of what already exists to what can eventually exist. It brings a precise account of becoming, where in every being there is what the being already is and how it became to be as such in a straightforward and unbreakable relation. Aristotle tries to appease the unappeasable—movement, transformation, or, in a word, the transition that pushes every existence to the void of nothingness and necessity to the threshold of contingency.

Aristotle uses one word to describe potentia—dunamis (δύναμις)—while he uses two to describe actuality: *Energeia* (ενέργεια) and *Entelecheia* (εντελέχεια). Both terms (*Energeia* and *Entelecheia*) are far from being transposable to each other; they mark a deep contrast that is central to our construction of power as the unlimited exercise of immanent difference.

What the division between actuality and potentiality creates is a neutralization between contingency and necessity, in the sense that non-being is ordered entirely as a consequence of being. Accordingly, when being comes to be, it is necessary that it came to be from a given potentiality. While what is now potential reflects the contingency of its becoming, the contingency of the future is captured in the necessity of what is presently actual. Nonetheless, it is not that potentia is contingent; what is contingent is the coming to be of what is potential: what is in potentia may come to be or it may not. Contingency is reduced to this precise operation within the dyad. A seed may blossom into a flower (becoming a flower is contingent), but when the seed comes to be *this* flower, actuality is necessary as a retrospection from actuality to potentia. Contingency thus functions not as a causal force but merely as the possibility of the becoming of what is already programmed as actuality.

For Aristotle, potentia is a source of movement or change that is in another thing than the thing moved or in the same thing *qua* other (Aristotle. Met. 1046a). As we can observe, here a fundamental distinction can be drawn. There are some things that possess potentia in themselves, while others require an external agent to execute the change. According to Aristotle, a boy has the potential to become a man, but he also has the potential to become a great musician. We have a first and provisional division of potentia between natural and acquired. In the latter, potentia is tied directly to actuality more than to movement. Hence, it does not depend on a natural progression that is encapsulated in some sort of natural womb and would then extend its becoming as its extension but on the intervention of a rational formula to fulfill adequately what is potential.

But the cauterization of contingency through the dyad does not stop here. Through potentia, Aristotle has found two ways to give primacy to what exists. The first is to explain potentia as a kind of privation, and the second (that we will tackle further later in this chapter) is the structuring of the primacy of actuality in regard to potentiality through a theory of causes.

In between natural and acquired potentiality, privation means that while natural potentia is only capable of deploying itself, acquired potentia is capable of both itself and its contrary. The flame is capable only of burning, but the medical arts can produce both disease and health. Thus, while the potentia of a rational formula includes the possibility of its contrary (the potential of the *pharmakon* to produce either health or illness), this is not a possibility regarding natural potentialities that can only produce themselves.

The primacy of actuality over potentia refers directly to the loss of contingency and thus the possibility of the new; this is what stuns authors of the likes of Negri and Agamben. As we have remarked, in order to break the shackles of necessity, we propose to actualize difference, a maneuver that is no less than a heresy for the vanguard political thinkers of our era. What Antonio Negri and Giorgio Agamben[5] see in the actualization of potentia is the irremediable loss of contingency and with it the forfeiture of the opportunity of creation from the nihil. They see the death of politics as the becoming of the new at the hands of actuality. Their answer is to take refuge in utter impotence. To prevent the exhaustion of potential, Agamben fixes its force, its true powerful gesture in passivity, in the passion of impotence. The model is Melville's Bartleby the scrivener as the modern holder of power, as he is capable but does not want. In this sense, potentiality is achieved and preserved only in not being, in preserving its instance permanently as a passion of not being.

Nevertheless, I believe that the true problem is elsewhere, not in the definition of potentia but of actuality. As we proved, they (Agamben and Negri) are identifying actuality with one of its forms and neglecting the other, and consequently they are sinking in a false construction of the problem.

Complimentary to privation, a theory of causes is the second tool Aristotle uses to neutralize contingency within the dyad. It is here where we prove the wrong construction of power in both Agamben and Negri. For Aristotle the present measures all possibilities, and hence the existent is given priority over the inexistent as the latter is possible only if it reaches existence. As Aristotle puts it:

> That actuality is prior in formula is evident; for it is because it can be actualized that the potential, in the primary sense, is potential, I mean, e.g., that the potentially constructive is that which can construct, the potentially seeing that which can see, and the potentially visible that which can be seen. The same principle holds in all other cases too, so that the formula and knowledge of the actual must precede the knowledge of the potential. (Aristotle. Met. 1050a)

Through this line of thinking Aristotle proves that actuality is prior not only in time but also in logos to potentiality, so actuality is the material, formal, and efficient cause of potentiality. Nevertheless, in the theory of causes, Aristotle gives priority to one particular cause over the rest as the defining element of the superiority of actuality over potentia, as the definition of what is actual in reality: the final cause. Aristotle characterizes the final cause as the end (*telos*) for which a thing is done. Achieving such an end is pure actuality and thus the perfection of being.

A crucial distinction is made at this point. What is the difference between the finality of something natural (the baby that became a man, a woman, or a they) and finality as a rational formula (the virtuoso having executed his potentia to play an instrument)? Aristotle called actuality both Entelecheia (ἐντελέχεια) and Energeia (ενέργεια). The root of *Energeia* is *ergonó*, which can be translated as activity, action, or an operation, from which derives the adjective *energon*, meaning "active" or "worker." The etymological compound brings us *Energeia*, from *en* (in or within) + *ergon* (work). In this first approximation, we have a first meaning not only of actuality but also of a very specific finality of actuality, which is the work required to maintain the state of a substance through the being-at-work of the substance. The being-at-work that is the result of a precise capacity implies directly that the capacity qualifies the work and the work the capacity, not as a tautology but as a necessity.[6]

The second form of actuality is *Entelecheia*, attained by combining *entelēs* (ἐντελής, "complete, full-grown") with *echein (hexis)*, which means to be a certain way by the continuing effort of holding on to that condition. But a third and defining block of significance is put into the composite when Aristotle plays with the more usual word *endelecheia* (ἐντελέχεια, "persistence") by inserting *telos* (τέλος, completion) as the definite component of the concept (Sachs 2005). Etymologically, *Entelecheia* is thus composed of *en* (within) + *telos* (end or perfection) + *ekhein* (to be in a certain state).

There is, then, a fundamental addition in the construction of *Entelecheia*, something that is well beyond *Energeia* and that announces that which can only become when it is perfected. Hence, preservation is no longer the finality but is something that, while being outside of work, defines what work must strive for: completion. This is the subtle, almost invisible ingredient that launches being on the hunt of an ideal of perfection. *Telos* is thus introduced as the fulcrum between *en-telēs* (being within), and *echein (hexis)*, turning the plain meaning of holding on to into a more qualified being in possession of an end.

We are thus faced with a fundamental split within actuality, a split anchored in teleology. Natural, or rather "existential" final, causes pose no problem, for they are involved directly in *Energeia*: it is the being-at-work to preserve substance that defines being. For natural things, formal, efficient, and final cause are one and the same: the actualization of being *qua* being. *Energeia* is thus immanent as the principle of generation is already included; hence, "One thing is potentially another when, if nothing external hinders it, it will of itself become the other" (Aristotle. Met. 1049a). Being a butterfly, a piece of wood, or a neutrino possesses no negation of itself or the fact of being a certain something contrary to what it is; there is no qualification of its actuality. In *Energeia*, perfection (as a final cause, a *telos*) is already constitutive of being; it is never outside of it. This is our key point, for if what we are seeking is the meaning of politics and the composition of the body politic, we are thus asking the question of who belongs to it and under what conditions. The answer, through radical nonliberal democracy, is everyone and everything, with no further condition than life itself and no exception that can be imposed beyond the production of difference. To be is to exist with no further specification of the modes in which being is defined as being; the end (*telos*) of being is already a constitutive part of being.

The key is that potency engaged as *Entelecheia* is capable of its contrary and, thus, it is defined by privation (as Agamben correctly maintains). The fundamental feature is this: insofar as rational potentia can produce effects contrary to its finality, then it follows that to be a true actuality it must produce those effects well. The pharmacist must mix the matter in a certain proportion if it is to achieve health; otherwise, he will produce the contrary effects. As we have shown, natural potentiality (irrational potency-*Energeia*) is actualized directly in its generation and perseverance, while rational potentialities (*Entelecheia*) must not only produce a given effect but also produce it well.

Consequently, and this is what is relevant for politics, all rational potentialities are so called because they do so well: they demand a certain technique, a definite know-how. Hence, the fundamental concatenation is this: if the very definition of politics depends on *Entelecheia*, life as its precondition logically becomes a qualified life and thus politics is denied at its core. Politics would depend solely on a condition, and thus democracy would become impossible.

Agamben and Negri take to heart a connection between *Entelecheia* and power and thus establish a prohibitive barrier to actuality because they identify it only with potestas and domination. Only those who acquire the possession of a certain know-how could be part of the political. In *Entelecheia*, the condition of actualizing a rational potentia is already qualified—a condition that comes about from the transformation of a subject to a qualified subject who dominates a rational science. The problem is if the definition of the political falls under a rational *telos* (*Entelecheia*) or an *Energeia* as a being-at-work. This is the vortex of politics as ontology; it is the definition of the political that tilts any balance of power and of beingness.

What would the *telos* of a polity be according to Aristotle? The answer is not given in the Metaphysics but in the Nicomachean Ethics: virtue is the *telos* of a polity, the one that defines whether it has achieved the finality of actuality and thus beingness. Virtue (the doing well of politics) is the fulfillment of the perfect exercise of reason, men's distinctive and highest feature. Hence, the traditional interpretations that run through the infected veins of the West, in line with Aristotle, consider that politics follows *Entelecheia*, and so Plato's virtue (*areté*) and Aristotle's *Eudaimonia* demand that politics be defined as a question of refinement, perfection, and excellence. The perfect polity is as such because it has achieved an actuality through virtue as a telos.

Even though he rightfully understands that the aforementioned qualifies life into a certain life (*zoe tis*), as the rational actualization of potentia, Agamben plays right into Aristotle's division. Politics, then, can only be determined as such by a certain finality that involves a stringent qualification of life: a division between the rational and irrational, the virtuous and the vile, of the *oikos* and the *politikos*, and of life (*bios*) and bare life (*zoe*).

The passage from potentia to actuality in Aristotle, then, is defined by perfection, by a qualification of potentia in the final result of the work. Consequently, to safeguard potentia, Agamben withdraws labor to passive potentia, and, moreover, to impotence. Accordingly, ethics and politics will be defined for "men" through their participation in such an operation according to virtue. But curiously enough, for Plato and Aristotle, the belonging to politics is defined by natural conditions. Politics is defined by a doing well, but the very confines of the description of doing well can only be posited by those who are already inside politics! Politics is thus reduced to the level of a *techné*: if to play the harp is to play it to perfection, then to live means to live to perfection according to a logos. But the logos cannot define an abstract, a priori and universal property of perfection, and thus the power to define perfection is deferred to those already belonging to the political body. Power in its natural plasticity congeals into the power to define the finality of the polity even before the polity comes into being—this is the pitfall of *Entelecheia*.

The true order of politics lies in its construction as a non-qualified actuality. *Energeia*, as work, is the sign of the people; this will prove that Agamben's dominant interpretation of actuality as a synonym with the qualification of life is wrong. The hidden people, as the being of democracy, are in fact pure actuality as *Energeia* or being-at-work. Politics can only be considered when every being that makes a difference is considered as the condition of the existence of politics, with no further qualification. Hence, the ontological condition of politics is *Energeia*.

Agamben is stuck on the Aristotelian idea of form as the accomplishment of labor (work) where the finished work would define retrospectively a vocation and thus a prefigured nature of humanity, a finished work defining a nature. But defined from *Energeia*, humanity's work is to relate power to power; it is before all *synergy* (Συνεργία), it means to communicate. Agamben confuses history with ontology and then goes on to endorse the official history as the only history. The classic Greek definition of politics as qualification (*telos*) is but the historical fact that runs untrammeled through the construction of the West and that coloniality simply intensifies and globalizes, but that politics can only ensue when there is an infinite opening for difference is the ontological definition of politics.

The conditions under which we may actualize difference must meet the following: (a) that actuality is not seen as a finality, as the end of being-at-work, but simply as being-at-work, where all finality beyond constituting politics is severed from the commencement; and (b) that the creation of the common language of politics does not function as privation. This is where our interpretation of *Energeia* breaks the dead matter of politics. Staying the same through work brings a necessary redundancy to politics wherein whatever changes, changes into that into which it changes; this means the possibility of transitions of power and the possibility of overcoming the thick and decrepit cluster of potestas, but it basically means that contingency and immanence are at the heart of power. The argument favoring privation as the root of the legitimate exercise of a technique falls apart when we define politics through no particular virtue. It does not imply a naturalization of politics but understanding the very simple fact that existence (and existence alone) is the very condition of politics. Politics—if understood not as a qualified exercise but as being under the condition of being a common—leads us directly to work not as qualified work, but as work producing the conditions of life on its own (living labor), with life understood as an integration of difference through difference.

What is cast in *Energeia* is a composition as perfection, with no further qualification, transcendence or finalism than the composition of the common of politics: pure *Synergia*. And what would this composition look like? As an open infinity, an open constitution of being where every difference is included as its own topic of enunciation.

One thing must be crystal clear; we are not defending the thesis that power in itself is an actuality; this would be a physical impossibility. The nuclear thesis is that the people of the hidden people[7] are the actuality, as the very condition for their power to always remain in potentia. Power is always opaque, modal, and diffuse; it cannot be an object of direct knowledge. Why not simply understand the ontological tissue of politics as potentia? Simply because potestas exists! It is a whole disposition of power that already divides the people as its constituent disposition. The people are already its creation as its hidden component of operability. Hence, confronting potestas, potentia would be impotent on its own. Instead, the power of the hidden people must be actualized if the division of the people in the simulacrum of democracy is ever to be overturned.

Consequently, what is the difference between our reading of potentia/potestas and Agamben's? While Agamben retracts life into impotence, ours de-qualifies life, makes immanence an extension of life that cannot be severed by any qualification that thus sees immanence as a fully equipped form of life to do away with power as potestas. The order of immanence is difference in itself, which does not inhibit, *ipso facto*, the crossing lines of potencies within a relation, but rather well it presupposes them. However, Agamben is indifferent to the constituent power of relations of power. For him, the Aristotelian question is not "what is it?" but through what process does a thing belong to another? Yet, power is weightless, a-physical, and ultimately inconceivable without affections, without relation. Power and relation are a tautological formation; the world can only be seen and touched in the intertwining of powers, as communication. Proximity and effusion are only predicates of a relation that can only be through power. But while in Nietzsche this power of affection is multilateral, from appearance to being as an indefinite but constitutive relation of reciprocal exercise of power, for Agamben it is an exclusive feature of the passion of the self. It is only in the relation where potentia becomes its own actualization. To give to itself the passion of potency then must be to risk all extension in a relation. Furthermore, potentia, as we have shown, is inconceivable without the contact, the friction of a relation, here then lies politics in all its splendor. Conflict must then be defined as all the possibilities brought about as a sharing of power. There is no possibility for knowledge to describe and understand an individual, a subject, a being, a plurality, a system, or a structure if it is not in a relation of power; rather well it is "in" the relation of power where such things are produced and where they can be measured or put asunder. In Agamben the word "passion" is etymologically and logically fermented way too close to poison.

DECRYPTING AS A DECOLONIAL TOOL[8].

As we made clear in the immediate publication leading up to this book, the theory of decryption blooms from "creolization . . . Insofar, it denudes and overcomes the seemingly unbreakable broods spawned between liberalism and colonialism, capitalism and sovereignty, and constitutions and economics, which in themselves seem to devour all reality and permanently reflect the image of an unchangeable and insurmountable state of things" (Sanín-Restrepo 2018, x). Henceforth, the theory only makes sense when it is considered as an integral part of the studies of decoloniality and its basic findings regarding power and the shifts between colonialism and coloniality.

When the "theory of encryption of power" takes its footing as a conceptual weapon proper to political philosophy within the world of coloniality, it exposes something unique. Globalization through the hegemony of capital based on coloniality exists as a solid unit because it creates a specific form of power—a form of power that has only existed within these planes of reality, within this proper history that only theories of decoloniality were able to unveil; the said form of power is encryption. Strictly speaking, "encryption" is the formula of power of coloniality. Coloniality as the very form of modernity exist only because it encrypts power. As we held recently "The theory of encryption of power is thus not (only) a strategy or a tool to approximate and clarify the entanglements of power in our times, but rather, it unveils the essence of power (as domination) of our time" (Sanín-Restrepo 2020).

As we adamantly stated,

> The problem of language that decryption targets and which fashions its capacity and reach is, first and foremost, a political problem entrenched in language. Encryption is not a simple problem of one type of struggle among others, but is

instead the core problem of politics. Another way to say this is that coloniality depends absolutely on its power to deny language as the first common of politics. Therefore, coloniality exists because it encrypts. (Sanín-Restrepo 2016, 9)

The theory of encryption is thus the natural crystallization of the unstoppable advances of studies of decoloniality. Let us see. Power in all its incubations and incarnations is today and historically unthinkable without the dyad coloniality/modernity. The Americas were not incorporated into a pre-existing capitalist system; there simply would not have been capitalism without the Americas (Tlostanova and Mignolo 2009, 85). With a steady hand, Aníbal Quijano (2001) explains how the hegemonic idea of the West stands on two foundational myths: First, the idea that the history of human civilization is a linear and necessary path that flowers from a state of nature and culminates in Europe as its only and thus perfect model, a model that is imposed with all the brutality of physical and symbolic violence upon non-European worlds that, therefore, are considered as non-worlds, as aberrations. And second that the differences between Europeans and non-Europeans are fitted in a stable genetic pool of ideas, the Platonic *Eidos*, the Greek inception of Logos, as Heidegger (2000) tells us. Therefore, any and every difference between the European (model) and the non-European are natural-racial and make themselves present in a simple form of contrast between the model and its copies. Hence, the whole game of shadows of differences and identities, of simulacra and deviations, are not the consequence of history and power but are natural results of the application of the model to feral forms of singularities. This second idea is grounded in an epistemology that is called humanism and later liberalism within Europe, but that operates outside as a racial line of exclusion and submission that is shielded in projects that call themselves scientific, rational and Enlightened. Thus, evolutionism and what Nelson Maldonado calls "misanthropic Manichaeism" are the essence of Eurocentrism (Maldonado-Torres 2007).

Walter Mignolo demonstrates how conceptually coloniality is the "hidden side" of modernity (Mignolo 2001, 86). The dyad modernity/coloniality implies that coloniality is constitutive of modernity, and therefore there is no modernity without coloniality; they are in a state of pure symbiosis and cannot be disentangled. This uncanny duality allows modernity to have two faces. Within the slim boundaries of the West, an effective evolution of what Boaventura de Sousa Santos (2010) has dubbed the logic of "regulation/emancipation," a world infused with freedoms and prosperity, held together by the magic glue of democracy and the rule of law. However, its reverse, the underbelly that makes the first logic operational, in the colonial worlds is extraction and racism, domination, and exclusion. The vital thing to grasp is that there is no dividing these categories as they involve each other and are necessary for their concurrent operation. What happens in the inner workings of the colonial metropole is made possible because of the misery and extraction of the colonized world (even though neoliberalism is blurring the lines and making the core of the metropole a thing of dispossession as well, as the "Global South" is everywhere).

Theology and Christian evangelization covered in their lethal mist the first period of domination, at the end of the seventeenth century a new and monumental shift is performed emerging swiftly from a secular and commercial language that arises from England based fundamentally in profit and the supposedly free traffic of goods. A highly mobile and shifting animal is born out of the womb of colonization that will embrace the world until every last single one of its pores is smothered, gentrified, commodified, and racialized by it. Henceforth, it may well be said that while Spain considered the world, in its heavy colonizing enterprise, as a Church, England enters the scene and considers the world as a market. This second stage is marked by an Anglo-French combination of economic growth, secularization, and rationalism that underpins the civilizing mission of the Western world (Wallerstein 1999). The United States then enters the scene as the largest military and economic power known to humankind. It is but the refinement and improvement of the English imperialist-capitalist apparatus since, on a short side, it cuts ties with the hierarchies of English vernacular feudalism and it supersedes the problem of land expansion. This new monster polices the world in the name of democracy and freedom while it brings to fruition the dire dreams of a military-industrial and informatic conglomerate through a mixture of an expansionist constitution, pervasive spectacle, and heavy-duty military and economic interventions. Thus, the third stage focuses on developing the underdeveloped and modernizing the archaic.

As Aimé Césaire proves, when Cortés bleeds out Mexico and Pizarro carnages el Cuzco, they do not plant the flag of a superior identity; they bring spears, germs, havoc, and death. It is only when the science jurists of Christianity arrive that the "constitution" of violence is laid down as the paramount legal model. In it, Christianity is equated with civilization and paganism with savagery (Césaire 2000, 33). Evangelization and civilizing have given way to developmentism. Nevertheless, the heart of it all is still the violent imposition of a model of what it means to be human. In our times, the concept of development is a permanent companion of modernity (Mignolo 2001). However, underdevelopment is not equivalent to coloniality; it is attached to the backwardness of societies that refuse to embrace the model that are lagging off the pace of history by their own volition and incapacity to perform better. It is assumed that underdevelopment is what development promises to overcome, but in contrast, modernity never promises to overcome coloniality; on the contrary, it promises the overcoming of "tradition," "unsound beliefs," and "peripherical praxes"; that is, it promises to deepen coloniality (Tlostanova and Mignolo 2009). Coloniality is the magnificent weapon behind all the rhetoric of modernity. It is what justifies any type of action, including war, as a formula to overcome barbarism and ignorance. Napalm constitutionalism in the name of freedom. Drone strikes in the name of democracy. It is what enables the developmental and civilizing mission of modernity. Without coloniality, these projects lack any internal justification at all.

The first phase of colonization is linked to the theological extension of Europe to America or "Westernization." The second is tied to the relay of colonial powers and the Orientalization of the rest of the world (Said 1978). The third is the final solution of both. The first deals primarily with blood cleansing through theological normative statuses; the second, with the rise of the bourgeoisie and the planetary implementation of the free market; and the third supposes its magnifying scales of division of labor and the total rule of coloniality over the world in a blend of violent interventions (wars) perpetuated by soft interventions (constitutional traditions and academia).

Nelson Maldonado-Torres has developed a hard concept, the imperial "misanthropic Manichaeism" that governs the relations of coloniality and weaves together all of the phases of colonialism and coloniality. The Cartesian idea of the division between mind and matter (*res cogitans res extensa*) is preceded and built on top of a deeper ethnological difference of the conquering ego and conquered ego (Maldonado-Torres 2007). Thus, the Cartesian formulation "I think therefore I exist" became "I think therefore the others do not think, or do not think correctly, then I am when the others are not, or are dispensable." The Cartesian formulation privileges an epistemology that simultaneously hides the "coloniality of knowledge" that is equivalent to saying the others do not think. And the "coloniality of being" that is equivalent to saying the others are not (Maldonado-Torres 2007, 89), and both are related to potestas, that is, power as exploitation, domination, and control of knowledge and being.

It is in this situation that we refer to coloniality, and the ways in which the world is formed by an excess correlated with the systematic annihilation of otherness. Coloniality survives colonialism and is kept alive in constitutions, common sense; in the criteria of academic performance; in cultural patterns; in lipsticks, Instagram, moot law courts, and intelligent bombs launched from arcades. As Maldonado-Torres maintains, as modern subjects, we breathe coloniality all the time, every day (2007). Coloniality is not simply the consequence or residual form of a colonialist relationship, coloniality continues to be an inevitable product of modern discourses.

And thus, we lay our scene for the X game of language . . .

NOTES

1. For a complete definition, see Sanín-Restrepo, Ricardo (editor). 2018. *Decrypting Power*. London & New York: Rowman and Littlefield International.

2. A beautiful metaphor of encryption and architecture may be found in McDonald, Angus, The Equivocation That Lies Like Truth, in *Decrypting Power*. London & New York: Rowman and Littlefield International.

3. This subtitle is a brief synthesis of the fourth chapter of *Decolonizing Democracy: Power in a Solid State* (Sanín-Restrepo 2016).

4. For a comprehensive layout of power and its relations within coloniality and colonialism, see Sanín-Restrepo (2016 and 2018)

5. In *Decolonizing Democracy*, I make a thorough critique of both authors; nevertheless in this synthesis I will focus almost exclusively in Agamben's work.

6. This is not Spinoza's god but more relevantly Kurt Vonnegut's god in *Slaughterhouse Five*, a perfect nobody.

7. Here are two conjoined definitions of the hidden people in contrast with the orthodox functionality of the people in liberalism. "In modernity, but specifically with the advent of liberal constitutions, the concept of the people is not simply another category adjoined into a uniform structure that shares its attributes with another series of elements within a homogeneous group with which it forms a unit of meaning. Since Hobbes, but especially with the inauguration of liberal constitutionalism, when we invoke the people we call forth the materialization of nothing less than the origin and irreplaceable source of legitimacy of liberal modernity. The concept of the people in modernity is not just a part of a whole, but its binding element, the element that brings meaning and texture to the rest of the elements that are thus in a state of subordination to it. However, and this is the great simulacrum of democracy, modernity as an idea, as an economic, historical, cultural, and political organization can only function as it does under one inexorable condition: the annihilation of the people" (Sanín-Restrepo 2016, 34). "In liberalism, the totality of the people is the norm and the hidden people are the exception where law is suspended, and therefore absolutely anything can be brought upon it. A new legal structure arises from the shadows of the formal constitutions and legal practices where the aim is to maintain the hidden people in a legal vegetative state. In the analytic of power of modernity, the hidden people inhabit the paradox of sovereignty. The hidden people are at the same time the regime of the possibility of sovereignty and what must remain paradoxically outside of what the sovereign declares as normality. The decision of the sovereign regarding the norm and its outside—normality and abnormality, order and chaos—is made possible only when the sovereign is outside the norm and declares the exception that constitutes the norm. Hence, the hidden people are constructed in a constituent act of exclusion from normality and inclusion as the reverse of the law. The vital point is that the sovereign, in order to declare the taxonomy of inside/outside, cannot be inside or outside the norm, but only in the state of exception may he declare the norm and its suspension" (Sanín-Restrepo 2016, 36).

8. For a complete explanation and description of the ties between decryption and colonialism and coloniality, please refer to the first chapter of Sanín-Restrepo 2016 and the introduction of Sanín-Restrepo 2018.

Chapter 2

Definition of the Ready to Hand

As we made clear from the get-go, we did not choose Heidegger but rather Heidegger's construction of the ready to hand was imposed by the mainstream Western philosophical tradition that sees in it the final and definite bid for the liberation of being from the chains of metaphysical eminence and the fallacy of presuppositions. The Heideggerian "turn" means that Aristotle's convention of being and becoming has finally met its match beyond Descartes and Kant. Let us think first of the ready to hand as the things we use for there to be any connection of ourselves to the world, for there to be world upon ourselves. Without the things in the world, we are blind, deaf, and mute; we meet the others and ourselves in the world through things, and through the shaping of the things we bring significance to each relation. Hence, before any consideration, the ready to hand means work; it means the ways in which being not only gets around but the ways through which it constructs itself and the world of significance. It is the fundamental structure of *Dasein* being-in-the-world through the use of the things of the world. What is left unanswered is if the ready to hand is exclusively living labor or if it can be bent and turned into dead labor, if we meet the other in planes of equivalence or if the ready to hand serves to turn the world into a crypt of potestas (power as domination). We must determine if *Dasein* is alone in this world and what place does work have in it but specifically what is the place of the "other" within this landscape. The other we are asking for is not the (racial or gender) equal other, nor the unauthentic other (das Man), but the other deprived of beingness who is only perceived by being through a very specific configuration of the things in the world.

Let us lead off with a classic Heideggerian definition of the "worldhood" of the world.

> Being-in-the-world shall first be made visible with regard to that item of its structure which is the "world" itself. To accomplish this task seems easy and so trivial as to make one keep taking for granted that it may be dispensed with. What can be meant by describing "the world" as a phenomenon? It means to let us see what shows itself in "entities" within the world. Here the first step is to enumerate the things that are "in" the world: houses, trees, people, mountains, stars. We can depict the way such entities "look," and we can give an account of occurrences in them and with them. This, however, is obviously a pre-phenomenological "business" which cannot be at all relevant phenomenologically. Such a description is always confined to entities. It is ontical. But what we are seeking is Being. And we have formally defined "phenomenon" in the phenomenological sense as that which shows itself as Being and as a structure of Being. (Heidegger 2001, 91/63[1])

What Heidegger investigates is not meaningful things but their meaningfulness, not classical "*Sein*" but "*Anwesen*." If, for Aristotle, things exist insofar as they are real, and the real is enclosed in the relation between substance-presence, which gives us whatever is not nothing "*to-on*"; for Heidegger they exist insofar as they are meaningful. The fundamental question is therefore not the classical "why are there things instead of nothing" but rather "why is there meaning instead of no meaning." Buttressed in Husserl's phenomenology, where no object is meaningful in itself isolated in nature, nor in a solitary synthetizing ego (subjectivity), Heidegger follows the phenomenological creed "to the things themselves." We understand things as meaningful and the constitution of their meaningfulness through the bestowal of sense upon the objects (*sinnegebung*). Nevertheless, a "u" turn is performed by Heidegger, and the key to all of it lies in time, or rather "temporality" as the horizon of all understanding of being, a temporality that can only be attained by the being that constructs all meaning and that is itself the limit of every meaning: *Dasein*.

After dislodging the ontic (properties and categories) from the ontological (ways of modes of beings), Heidegger offers us three ontological ways or modes of being: (a) *Dasein*, (b) the available or *ready to hand*, and (c) the occurrent or *present at hand*. The ready to hand is the existential preparation—the only path—to reach *Dasein*; it marks the ontological "being with in the world" of the becoming of *Dasein*. For Heidegger, there are two ontological modes as to how being gets involved "with the world" (Heidegger 2001) that mark its existential attitudes: (a) the available or "ready to hand" (*Zuhandensein*) and (b) the occurrent or present at hand (*Vorhandene*).

Definition of the Ready to Hand

However, what we have to wrap our minds around is that the ready to hand is the existential preparation for *Dasein*.

Robert Brandom clarifies that "*Vorhandensein* (presence-at-hand), things are roughly the objective, person-independent, causally interacting subjects of natural scientific inquiry. *Zuhandene* (ready to hand) things are those that a neo-Kantian would describe as having been imbued with human values and significances" (Brandom 2005, 214). Hence the presence at hand is constituted by properties in themselves and not in relation to uses (occurrentness), while the readiness to hand is constituted in the use of things within a totality of relations. The classic distinction is exemplified in the hammer. We may derive a series of categories from it such as weight, size, and molecular composition, but this simply informs us of a mere presence at hand; the ready to hand of the hammer only comes through its use, through an involvement of it in the world where it functions as a tool to transform other things of the world. Thus, when it is in perfect shape, we use it as a ready to hand (and doing so lights up the world!), but when it is broken, it is just a useless thing laying there, a simple presence at hand, a heap of uncommunicable parts. Being is "within the world" (the first preparatory stage of *Dasein*) only to the extent that it recognizes itself in the use of things (tools). The fundamental point to grasp is that readiness to hand is the condition of the potentiality of being, what holds in its womb the deployment of *Dasein*. Thus, we discover the world as we discover ourselves in the use of the ready to hand. Hence, it is what lets us see, without a shadow of doubt, that *Dasein* is not the thing in itself or the being in itself but that only *Dasein* can reveal the meaning of being to herself.

The analytic of *Dasein* only gets constituted after it goes through a series of concatenated experiences (*existentialles*) where it gains, at every step, a more robust and finalized form aiming at constituting itself as the possibility of the meaning of the world. The concatenation between one state and the next is logically necessary; the failure in a previous state means the failure (impossibility) of the whole analytic. For example, there is no way to pass from "being within the world" (ready to hand) to "being with" (others-they) if "being within the world" has failed or is inauthentic. Care (*Sorge*), which is the final existential state of the authenticity of *Dasein* can only come to fruition if "solicitude," which is a previous existential state, is constituted correctly. The fundamental point is that readiness to hand is the axiomatic condition of the potentiality of being; hence, if the ready to hand goes astray, so will all of the analytic of *Dasein* and with it any possibility of accruing any meaning "in" and "of" the world.

The premise of this book is simple: without applying the theory of decryption of power, we could not know the difference between *Dasein-the ready to hand and the present at hand*. But, furthermore, when this relation is decrypted, what will be proved is the impossibility of anything to resemble a kind of thing as *Dasein* that is not a collective becoming of difference. Heidegger's constitution of the ready to hand is the hindrance of being and becoming, of meaning and existentiality. Our effort is thus concentrated in reinstituting any meaning in and of the world with contingency and thus in unveiling how the becoming of being can only be accomplished by a collectivity expressing its infinite and intensive difference.

One of the mainstays of our decrypting enterprise is to realize that the idea is the reason within an object that is actualized in a concept. Consequently, decryption must traverse all the dimensions, that is, the idea, reason, the object, and finally the concept.

OBTRUSIVENESS (AUFDRINGLICHKEIT)—
OBSTINACY (AUFSÄSSIGKEIT)—
CONSPICUOUSNESS (AUFFÄLLIGKEIT)

The red traffic light. The lid that won't open. The cork that won't pop. The song that will not play. The keys that seemed to have eloped. The woodchip that won't fit. The queue that does not move. Our airplane seventeenth in line for takeoff. Confessions of the flesh. The air that stops circulating. That rusty feeling in our eyes proper to every waiting room in the world. The voice at the other end of the line, saying in a robotic drained down voice, "we are sorry our system is still down." The lid still does not open. The broken jar. The bloated steel. The s,scr,Scra,Scrathed, record. The guns that don't stop firing. The chainsaw that cuts through tissue, reaching bone like if it was hot butter.

As Heidegger explains

> In conspicuousness, obtrusiveness, and obstinacy, that which is ready to hand loses its readiness to hand in a certain way. But in our dealings with what is ready to hand, this readiness to hand is itself understood, though not thematically. It does not vanish simply, but takes its farewell, as it were, in the conspicuousness of the unusable. Readiness to hand still shows itself, and it is precisely here that the worldly character of the ready to hand shows itself too. (Heidegger 2001, 104/74)

When the equipment is disturbed, malfunctioning, broken, useless, we are not only impaired in the world that the tool may open up, but, at that very same instant, we also realize there is a world, and we grasp its possibilities. When the ready to hand is affected in this manner, things lose their phenomenological transparency, but at the same time a structure and a vision of the world are revealed, though not in its utility. Through the ready to hand, we do not

Definition of the Ready to Hand 31

reveal the world speculatively or theoretically, but through practice and use. Through the thing that we use, we open new dimensions of the world. It is simple; there is no world without tools.

In the constitution of the ready to hand as being within the world, Heidegger recognizes that in our dealings with equipment, the forcefields that traverse it are opaque and difficult but, nonetheless, constitutive. Consequently, he states, first that "When equipment cannot be used, this implies that the constitutive assignment of the 'in-order-to' to a 'towards-this' has been disturbed" (Heidegger 2001, 105/75). The "towards this" is defined out of the (and as the) ontic structure of the equipment, that which gives it a directionality within a totality of relations in the world. Every piece of equipment belongs to a totality of involvements (*Bewenden*).

Nevertheless, the fundamental question, not formulated by the Heideggerian scheme, is what real access we have to the ready to hand and who determines its utility (instrumentality) and for what purposes. Here it is key to begin to define the outline of positive and negative affections and of living and dead labor. With encryption, the access to equipment is blocked and redistributed, not on the base of a universal utility but on the base of further constrictions and prohibitions of instruments of inclusion and exclusion. Henceforth, obtrusiveness, obstinacy, and conspicuousness are not only a matter of descrambling the lines of communication between supposed totalities of relations among things, but primordially a question of power relations in the naming and using of the tool and in the supposed totality (where the thing belongs to). As Heidegger continues his description, "The modes of conspicuousness, obtrusiveness, and obstinacy all have the function of bringing to the fore the characteristic of presence-at-hand in what is ready-to-hand" (Heidegger 2001, 104/74). Our wager is that it is encryption that makes language present at the hand of the ready to hand. In other words, the equipmentality of things (*Zeughaftigkeit*) is not only arrested by the three modes of limiting it in a striated line of events where things possess those limitations, as it were by either their own nature or the nature of their "equal" surroundings and the relations in which they enter. Or, put another way in which Heidegger is blind to, things are not only obtrusive by their own inner nature (if such a thing exists) but by destination; they are not obstinate only as they deploy themselves in a transparent life but also because they have been designed and previously related in order to be so within a relation of power; and, finally, they are not only conspicuous because they are in a penumbra of a color palette but because they have been placed out of reach, they have been concealed in a power play. Imagine pinching a white shell out of a dark background. How many things and actions are involved in it?

Equipment is always open to circumspection (*Umsicht*); it is what picks up equipment out of a totality of involvements not only to give it directionality but to conceive the said totality as an ordered field. In Heidegger's words, "The context of equipment is lit up, not as something never seen before, but as a totality constantly sighted beforehand in circumspection. With this totality, however, the world announces itself" (Heidegger 2001, 105/75). What the German philosopher does not conceive is the possibility that circumspection is tinkered with and reduced creating a false totality (in encryption). A valley of mere shadows, of projections (the cave) where the world announces itself in falsehood, in power plays that have already "staged" the relations among things and among things and people. That the light that illuminates a field of involvements may very well be flooding lights that dazzle us into blindness. What if circumspection is defined and altered beforehand by a previous decision that makes the availability of equipment scarce. And what if, before regarding opaqueness, and hiddenness, "scarcity" should be deemed the main problem of the worldliness of the ready for hand. Against Heidegger, we are to prove that what announces itself before there is a relationality, before there is even a regime of visibility, is not transparent and original but already the work of encryption, already an order designed to conceal meanings and make any possible intermingling of things and a totality utterly scarce.

But, let us not stop cold at the threshold of things. Let us steamroll ahead and investigate if with the introduction of a power play the lines between the ready to hand and present at hand are not blurred and upset, and if their convertibility (crossing the lines) from one to the other is not also a matter of power. We do not free things (flat ontology) simply by declaring unilaterally that they are free. We must dig out the power plays that have defined the tools and their supposed totality of involvements. First it is a question of crossing lines (between the ready to hand and the present at hand) and asking if what is at play there is not first and utmost hidden (retracted and transcendental) acts of power. And, second, it is a question of determining if the totality of involvements or whatever is the structure that contains the relations of tools and users is truly a simple question of a singular *Dasein* or is it rather a question that may only be answered by a collective multiplicity.

Our quarrel with Heidegger is simple, but the consequence is complex. It is a matter of his erroneous constitution of power, or better yet, his neglect to see how the ready to hand is constituted by forms of power. Without the decryption—and this is the key—of the ready to hand, we could not know the difference between *Dasein-the ready to hand and the present at hand*.

It is curious to see how Heidegger sees something like the encryption of the das Man (of the they) but not of the ready to hand; this is a phenomenological failure. Our theory is that the encryption of the ready to hand frustrates the possibility of the analytic of *Dasein in toto*. Hence, it is not an aspect of authenticity or inauthenticity of *Dasein* but of the world itself that is expunged from the world. Going back to the example of the hammer, what is not accounted for by Heidegger's ready to hand are the relations of power that reserve the use of the thing for a certain model of human being and for the creation of such and such things that some are deprived of, not because of the universal use of the tool, but by a disposition of power. In short, a power play that determines not only the availability of the tool but its disposition of uses and the world it creates thereof.

The problem is not that Heidegger introduces a supposition but that he neglects to see the presupposition of power as *potestas*. One of the key lines of enquiries we must follow in order to penetrate the question is to figure out the role that the configuration of space possesses within these elements of the ready to hand. Let us try to take the first steps toward a consideration of space (or rather, things in space), opening up a whole universe of questioning and weighing power through extensivity, intensitivity, reality and virtuality, naming and difference.[2]

Picture a symbol I cannot recognize as anything:

勺

At any rate, if I do get close enough to recognize the thing with my eyes and touch it with my hands and tongue, I can no less use it perfectly independently of the obtrusive name it has "there" or the name I use "here." Nevertheless I do not find the thing detached from the world, I find it within a role, and this role was somehow assigned linguistically (order-word), which includes the decision to make the thing, to make it out of these (porcelain) and not those materials (metal or wood), and to ship it to this and not that part of the city and to these and not those venues. Furthermore, according to conventions to use it in these and not those types of other things. When all meaningful graphs disappear, we will still be able to use it, even if we cannot recognize its graph.

For Heidegger, being is thrown onto an already-defined, given reality. However, this reality has to be inscribed into being all over again; it has to materialize within being where it is not an instantaneous flash but a long process of becoming through the things of the world. The fallacy? Heidegger thinks the ready to hand as a grand structure of homogeneity, reflected in the sameness of relations and things to themselves and to being. Heidegger supposes a closed frame and stability and linearity of systems of significations for the ready to hand. The latter not only misses the heterogeneity of things but the inevitable presence of orders and organizations coming from outside the realm of things and thus out of reach of *Dasein*. Accordingly, it is not only a political problem, but a political problem that is instantaneously ontological as well as existential.

Though it is true that Heidegger acknowledges that ready to hand only gets constituted through work (Heidegger 2001, 99/70), work must be decrypted. A division between living and dead labor must be established as the blade that cuts through the ready to hand and the present at hand.

NOTES

1. The double number indicates the page number, the English translation page first and second the original German edition.

2. We will use the concepts of virtuality and intensity regularly throughout the book as they are vital for flat ontologies. For a definition of the terms refer to Bergson (2002). A very good explanatory synthesis of the meaning of Bergson's "duration," where the concepts of the virtual and extensive are built is given in Winkler (2006).

Chapter 3

That "Thing" with the They and the Hinges of Signification

For Heidegger, being with (others) is the essential existential structure of *Dasein*. It does not mean being spatially alongside others (in terms of measurable distance) or a pregiven "I" that encounters the others through a preestablished knowledge of them as present at hand. It means that being "I" is always being with others as constitutive of being in the world. In Heidegger's words:

> Dasein understands itself proximally and for the most part in terms of its world; and the Dasein-with of Others is often encountered in terms of what is ready-to-hand within-the-world. But even if Others become themes for study, as it were, in their own Dasein, they are not encountered as person-Things present-at-hand: we meet them "at work," that is, primarily in their Being-in-the-world. (Heidegger 2001, 156/120)

These others constitute the "they," yet another obstacle-constitution of the foundation of the existentiality of *Dasein*. For Heidegger's the "they" constitutes inauthenticity and *Dasein* can only bear beingness or ask the question of being from its capacity to disclose entities overpowering the concealment of the world executed by "them." But then the question is begging: if *Dasein* can disclose a world without decrypting "being within" (ready to hand) what would "being with" (being with "them") amount to? The question is equivalent to asking how things as tools can exist without a human creator or user, things in the vacuum altogether. As we marked before, it seems Heidegger establishes two different contexts for the "they": first, a presupposition of a given relationality of equality among beings (the "they" is composed of equal parts) that results in the full transparency of tools; second an "I" standing in quivering solitude before an abstract "them" that shape its world as inauthentic. One context is transparent and the other inauthentic. Nevertheless, and this is the sleight of hand, the transparent context is created through inauthenticity. Inauthenticity, as the fascination with the "they," remains on the shores of das Man and does not cross to taint the ready to hand. The crystalline essence of tools is created by soiled hands; this cannot logically stand. The fallacy is that this supposed equality breaks up into pieces once we enter the realm of the "they," but the tools remain, unbelievably, transparent! As we warned, Heidegger sees something very close to the encryption of the d but not of the ready to hand; this is not only an ontological hindrance (flat ontologies) but a phenomenological fallacy (where otherness and the access to things of the world, as well as the meaning of science, all get maimed from beingness).

Regarding the first context, on one side an immaculate totality of relations of things that are ready to hand as their use is absolutely transparent, the tool is there present to itself with no previous commitment to the world. On the other side, a septic tank that reflects that being with others is inauthenticity, the impossibility of gathering the world and bringing it into meaning, the image of a being dumbfounded by the noise "they" produce, unable to find its way through the maze of life. Full transparency and ductility of the tool, total opaqueness and stubbornness of the "they." Nevertheless, we must ask, if the latter is thus polluted and impairing the path of *Dasein*, until a further operation is performed, would it not render the former polluted and impairing the path of *Dasein* as well? As put by Heidegger, "The Others who are thus 'encountered' in a ready-to-hand, environmental context of equipment, are not somehow added on in thought to some Thing which is proximally just present at hand; such 'Things' are encountered from out of the world in which they are ready-to-hand for Others-a world which is always mine too in advance" (Heidegger 2001, 154/118). Heidegger sees the effects of the they as dead labor, for example, but cannot fathom dead labor as constitutive of the ready at hand. What he forsakes is that the "they" and the ready to hand are joined by a logical hip. We cannot reveal the ready to hand in its use if we cannot account for its constitution in the they. Or else, where is the factory of the tools to which ready to hand refers to?

We have then an intricate landscape in trying to sense the difference between the others (they), the present at hand (nature), and the ready to hand (equipment). Heidegger cannot reach what he set up to do. The impossible "I" in Western metaphysics pours over to the fact that since everything is becoming, then the "I" would always be de-centered eccentric, out of joint, movable, and highly volatile; hence, this would also be the case for the they and thus the ready to hand would find this logical link inescapable.

If this was not the case, we would have to think of the possibility that there would be a fourth metaphysical category not accounted for as such by Heidegger's phenomenology, narrowed down to the uncanny link between equipment (ready to hand), the "they," and Nature. This unaccounted-for entity would perform a separation between the ready to hand and the present at hand before the "they" have entered the phenomenological landscape. A fourth entity that has made the ready to hand translucent and separate from nature. Again, the footsteps of the unimagined transcendent model (of god?) are heard, stumping at the threshold of metaphysics.

Further proof is given by the man himself when describing the "they": "These entities are neither present at hand nor ready to hand; on the contrary, they are like the very Dasein which *frees* them in that they are there too, and there with it. . . . So, if one should want to identify the world in general with entities within-the-world, one would have to say that Dasein too is world" (Heidegger 2001, 154/118 our italics). Here the term "free," which is an articulating point of the phenomenology of being is used in a very ambiguous way. Hence, encrypting or restricting the use of some ready to hand is also a way of freeing in the sense of fating a thing for a certain use. To be sure, said use is not under the magnifying glass of democracy, such as in the phrase "that orange human blob has 'freed' the building of a wall." Freeing a totality of involvements is logically in line with maintaining the façade that what is "there" accounts for a totality of involvements. There is no logical difference at all between both statements, no way of telling them apart within Heidegger's construction. Freeing as purporting does not mean freeing as sharing in difference.

But also the pretense is that other potential *Dasein's* are equal and equivalent to 'the' *Dasein*. The latter would be the case, if and only if, the human reaches (or has the potentiality to reach) *Dasein*, but this would be a final degree of existential evolution that has first constituted itself in the use of the ready to hand as an initial and insurmountable logical condition. The circle is thus vicious. Our issue, and a primordial issue it is indeed, is that the chaotic meeting of beings and the significance in which they are imbued, the rigmarole of life, already supposes the coming forth through the ready to hand. Thence, there cannot be a passing from one to the other in time or in language since they are both simultaneous and presuppose each other. "Being within" and "being with" one another are not consecutive or alternate moments but are simultaneous to another. Consequently, what happens in one resonates in the other. If there is a failure or a lack on one dimension, it immediately affects the other as well; not as a consequence that would entail mediation, but as immediacy. They are one and the same thing, pure (Bergsonian) intensity.[1] Hence, the variation in one (if there is one) amounts to a change in the nature of the other. It is a symbiosis and not a state. If this is so, then the same language not only applies to it, as a description, but the same language is used and disclosed; furthermore, the becoming of both things "is" language, as "is" is equality. It is not a species of a Channel tunnel, each thing carving up the stuff of reality from one side until there is a middle meeting point. They happen in the very same space-time called language. They both express a multiplicity. If there are two of anything, it is rather an encrypted language on one side and the hidden multiplicity on the other. The bridge is already there. *Dasein* does not discover itself in others nor the others in self; *Dasein* is already being with as the existential structure of being.

We have taken the first step to disentangle the problem. We cannot talk of a transparent ready to hand if the "they" that constitutes the ready to hand is not transparent as well (the bare festering hands of the baker cannot make clean bread). A further step must be taken in the clarification of the "they." Heidegger establishes that by "'Others' we do not mean everyone else but me-those over against whom the 'I' stands out" (Heidegger 2001, 154/118) But what about the "virtual" others? What about all others and the systems of positions in which they are instilled? And the subterranean connections between all beings that we do not perceive but its thinnest surface?

We have to restore a little air to the picture here, open the windows into the wilderness of being. There is, in the fetching of the being into beings, something like an environment to which we all belong to—we belong not passively, but determining its potentiality and actuality at every instant. The infinite perceptions of the world do not separate us but connect us more intimately because it spreads our beingness in alternate virtual universes where everything is connected as the premise of all existence, and all difference is dependent on its very design, as the design is simply the result of every intensitivity of difference. Nevertheless, connectedness is not an aspiration but the constitutional lack. Why constitution? Because there is no life that is not connected. Why lack? Precisely because this connectedness passes through definitions of structures of power, of encryption of the relations, but as such this is the relationality in which we are enmeshed. We cannot pinch essence out of reality. The power play of encryption consists precisely in turning diffuse lateral communications into vertical centralized transportation. The crack in between is the becoming of politics.

Until this point, Heidegger has established a hierarchy between forms of beings (between transparent ready to hand and inauthentic "them"); while not observing that the political inequalities among beings in the configuration of the "they" that necessarily constitutes the ready to hand will bestow its inequality upon it as well and with equal intensity. This affects every chain leading back and forth to "concern" (*Besorgen*) as the circumspective dealings with the ready at hand.

Dasein is wrong about one disguise: ready to hand is encrypted not in its totality of involvements but in the path toward authenticity as the creation of a sign. Decryption does not mean breaking free into an open country where everything preserves some original meaning but to establish how things that seem free for use established their limiting meaning got blocked and made impenetrable. That is, in what language-game-of-power (power play) they were established.

Regarding the existential *Dasein*, Heidegger states, "Not only is being towards others an autonomous, irreducible relationship of being: this relationship, as being-with, is one which, with Dasein's being, already is" (Heidegger 2001, 162/125). In line with the previous quote, someone may retort that since "being with" does not have an ethical bearing, it is pure existential meaning, then the perversion of the chains we are showing miss the target. Being with others is not dependent on being "decrypted" with others, there is no ethical claim as to this (it just facticity), or the retort goes. Nevertheless, can this objection hold for the link between being with and being within? Must the world be decrypted in order to even think *Dasein*? The answer is yes, it presupposes it. Because there is no objective (more than objective, implicit) way to tell apart the ready to hand from the others without bringing their logical link into the picture of "usability" or "utility." While Heidegger's answer is that the "they" constitute inauthenticity and *Dasein* can only bear beingness or ask the question of being from the disclosedness of being, we must push the envelope as follows: Can Dasein disclose a world without decrypting being within and being with (even if it recognizes the "they") or even more, notwithstanding, the recognition of the they? The answer is a clear no. The passage is no more obstructed than that it is inexistent.

We get a sharper picture of the problem when we move on to reveal the stuff that the "they" are made of, "the others." "These Others, moreover, are not definite Others. On the contrary, any Other can represent them" (Heidegger 2001, 164/126). The key word, of course, is representation (*Vorstellungen*). The others are fungible goods, interchangeable; they all carry the burden of inauthenticity when they represent the whole of it. Spectacle, the law, the market are all good examples of this figurative and stern displacement, of the structure of representation that embodies the "they" at every step. These others are not definite; they are institutions, abstractions, and individualities that crush other institution abstractions and individualities. Nevertheless, our encounter, as Buber (1996), Levinas (1979), and Nancy (2000) have shown us, is always with a particular other. With the interpellation in the face of others that breathes life into us, that asks us for something specific. There is then the division between the neuter they as a totality, an abstraction that conjures the extent of the fabric of life. Those "they" never remain in abstraction; they are flailed of in a reality that tears the fabric of quantities bringing clusters and singulars into the storm of life. We have then the abstraction of our all-too-familiar "hidden people," the excess of our "people as totality"; this is not only the site of alienation, but the melting pot, the site of the encounter that is always a specific other. The face that carries all this life through and that respires all frustration and all possibility of it through every pore and communicates it in its everyday language. Opposed to the neuter and abstract "they" of alienation is the specific they of the interpellation of alterity, of being with the life of others.

The "they" is no universal subject, no genus or species; when it acts, it is always through a singular that is plural, and it is plural because it speaks of an intensity without hierarchies, of a becoming with no totality. Heidegger has taken difference, and for the sake of an ideal and modelic difference, *Dasein's* difference eradicates difference from everyday life. He forsakes the dismembered body and the eyes that carry all human suffering within them and reflect all possibilities through them.

The glitch, the disparity of seeing one thing and not another (open and unrestricted ready to hand within the world but restricted with the world), is what demonstrates the impossibility of "being" as the only question of metaphysics. The other can be without me, but I cannot be without others and without the tools through which I meet the others and the world, and through which I understand my self and give meaning to all. The true question we must be asking is how can difference overpower identity. It involves a question of how we recognize or tell the "other" apart from *Dasein*, not as an ethical but ontological question, keeping in sight how the other is already imbued and entrenched in and with the ready to hand.

Take, for example, Heidegger's affirmation that "Dasein is for the sake of the 'they in an everyday manner, and the 'they'" itself articulates the referential context of significance" (Heidegger 2001, 167/129) A simple Wittgensteinian way to say this is that language predates singular beings of language. And this is crucial for encryption. We cannot grasp a language without its uses, and we cannot begin to imagine a world of significance that does not cross over to the ready to hand. Language without uses and uses of the ready to hand without language is an impossibility. According to this picture we could encounter an extensive thing called lever, but we would not know what it is for. Can we think of a lever without involvements? Well, the unmoved lever, a Thomist picture of God . . . but then again, in this instance the involvements are attached like tissue to bone to a supreme organization. The consequence is not only that we are impaired to think movement; what we cannot think of is a lever without context and therefore a use. Not only do we need a name that distributes its affections upon a world called "the ready to hand" but its function within the assignations of its capacities that are the capacities of she who uses it.

The existential structure of "being with" is the pre-ontological condition of interpreting being. The "they" covers *Dasein* because of the everydayness of *Dasein* in the they. The covering is the constitution! But this covering, which oscillates between it and unconcealment (*Aletheia*), as we will prove, is not, and it cannot be an exclusive trademark of the "they" but is extensive to the ready to hand. To the extent that every piece of equipment is within a relationality, if the "they" are retracted from Dasein in their inauthenticity, the ready to hand is thus covered from sight, set out in regions beyond a simple calling or any definition that plucks the singularity out of context. The principle is simple; anything that is a predicate of the " they" must apply to ready to hand and with the same intensity.

In Heidegger's words, "Being alongside the ready-to-hand, belongs just as primordially to Being-in-the-world as does Being-with Others; and Being-in-the-world is in each case for the sake (um-willen) of itself" (Heidegger 2001, 225/181). Henceforth, the existential analytic of *Dasein* is where the entities' basic state is being in the world. Being within, being with, and now being in-as-such or being there (the existential constitution of the "there" the everyday being of the "there," and the Falling of *Dasein*) are all interconnected logically as they share the same existential makeup. Our point is that there is a constitutive deviation for reaching this third constitution or *existentiale* of being if the first one is not decrypted. This deviation is the state of things that are proper to the "being in potestas"; hence the structure of potestas is existential, pure facticity that cannot be circumvented, that extends as the monumental obstacle-constitution of every form of facticity and existentiality. Potestas is not an accident or a potentiality; it is the form of power that determines life on this planet. How then is significance possible beyond the ready to hand and the they? How can it be so if one of them is encrypted and the potestas tainting and defining it goes unrecognized? The idea of unleashing pure difference to generate immanence ignores the strato-world of potestas, made up of layers of hierarchies, of occluded principles and concealed order-words. But, basically, the permanent operation of potestas over things separates them, stratifies them, reserves them, and ultimately impairs its free use. Even the act of naming is withheld close to the chest of those who enjoy potestas. The closest Heidegger comes to encryption is the "idle talk" (*Gerede*) of the they; nevertheless, it is still beyond the radar for the ready to hand, since idle talk has to do with being with and not within the world.

When and if *Dasein* comes out of the tunnel of being and meaning, it will still be wrong about one simulacrum: the ready to hand that it cannot muster outside the decryption of potestas. Within this picture empathy is not first, being with is. The rest of the question that is central is how does Heidegger's theses recognize the other implicitly?

Our argument is that the logical passage from being in the world to the rest is sealed upon the impossibility of the ready to hand that is encrypted. For example, anxiety as the ontological structure that binds *Dasein* with the world as the fleeing from self-fear and the involvement with entities in the world would lack a specificity through the incomplete constitution of the ready to hand. It would backfire. As we know, anxiety "does not know" what that in the face of which it is anxious. For Heidegger this is the region where it all lies, and therefore where any possibility of disclosing the world, "for essentially spatial being-in" (Heidegger 2001, 231/186) depends on. Anxiety is nowhere to be found, nowhere however, does not signify anything. Anxiety has its reflection in a system that toils incessantly with self-image that creates the impossibility of self. Anxiety bites down in the self or in the presence of the others but also within the things that are impenetrable or squeamish, not in their nature but in their constitution of power.

The closed passage we are speaking of is ontological. *Dasein* could not pass from one state to the other, for example, falling to "understanding" "being within" to "being with." Any passage becomes an impossibility. What would the impossibility of falling become? If falling would lack any point of friction, it is but falling in the vacuum, that by its own token could not be falling. The nucleus of the critique is to the futility of the individuality of the endeavor of *Dasein* in the face of anxiety. Anxiety, as the fleeing from self in the face of the "they" is the indefinite fear of being in the world as such "that which anxiety is anxious about is being-in-the world itself" (Heidegger 2001, 232/187). In anxiety *Dasein* can decrypt itself with the world (they) but is not able to decrypt (impossible) what the world of ready to hand is truly made out of and its place within it. Why? Because it is an individual effort and a state that forbids work, that forbids commonality in the work of the ready to hand, that blinds and pins movement down to a stressed-out knot. The idea of anxiety thus takes away from Dasein, the possibility of understanding itself, as it falls, in terms of the "world" and the way things have been publicly interpreted. As always, leveraging encryption in the they and ignoring the ready to hand leaves us without a world and thus without the commonality of and with the other.

CONTEXT AND ORDER WORD ("MOT D'ORDRE"): TOTALITY OF INVOLVEMENTS AGAINST THE INFINITY OF INVOLVEMENTS

A ready to hand is never alone; it is always within a totality of involvements that assigns its function and meaning. To the Being of any equipment, there always belongs a totality of equipment in which the equipment is fitting. For Heidegger, anything ready to hand is so only in virtue of the role it plays in a referential totality of significance of involvements. "As the Being of something ready-to-hand, an involvement is itself discovered" (Heidegger 2001, 118/85). We are before a thick constellation of meanings here. There is the supposition of a totality of involvements as a finalized form where a thing called tool enters into a relation with a whole. But as we use the tool we are not and cannot be aware of the totality of involvements, so there must be a rule that oversees such a supposition. The consequence is that every discovery of the world the tool opens up entails a chain on the basis of a prior discovery of a multiplicity of involvements, where lastly a totality must be simply supposed.

To be certain, for Heidegger, "this primary 'towards-which' is not just another 'towards-this' as something in which an involvement is possible. The primary 'towards-which' is a 'for-the sake-of-which' But the 'for-the-sake-of' always pertains to the Being of Dasein, for which, in its Being, that very Being is essentially an issue" (Heidegger 2001, 117/84). Totality is the quilting point where being is defined as being in the world in the totality of involvements of the ready to hand—(better yet) the being of entities is the totality of involvement in the toward which. It is here where we break the chain. For Heidegger the link is as follows, "this 'a priori' letting-something-be-involved is the condition for the possibility of encountering anything ready-to-hand, so that Dasein, in its ontical dealings with the entity thus encountered, can thereby let it be involved in the ontical sense" (Heidegger 2001, 113/85). The question we most pose is, is it a decision? It seems Heidegger is saying that the need for an opening depends on letting something be involved, but, is this a possibility of will? A precondition of being? Where does the relation circulate? In what sense? In the opening of a plane between object-subject? In the disposition of being toward things? As we anticipated, totality is the quilting point where being is defined as "being in the world" through the totality of involvements of the ready to hand.

A totality of involvements is nothing but the massive vascular system of power. We encounter things in space; we trip over them, touch them, now use them, now lose them; there is no form that is not through them. Here is where a totality of involvements begins. However, it would be counterfactual to know this at the beginning and simply stumble onto things or use them in an inconsequential form, you see? There would be the need for a previous definition of what is ready to hand and present at hand before any involvement may take place. Before the clock is clock and it relates to time, there must be a predefinition of the singular clock and its relation to time. The problem is that such a definition would anticipate the work to create, name, and destine the clock and its relation to time. Hence, a power play would be necessarily involved, and as such it would make itself present from a place we cannot locate within the relation, a place external to its composition, that is, transcendent. In every and any relation, a divinity (external to the relation and thus forming the relation) would have to be presupposed. This uncanny place would also have to be complete (perfect in time and space and thus immovable) and at the same time external to the relation. This is the very definition of presupposition. A transcendent world from where our world is defined and ordered. It is thus the barring of time and change, of any potentiality and becoming. The world and all that it holds inside it would be separable as all is actual and petrified in a single extension of space where time is senseless. As we have stated before, "If time is a totality, language faced with the universe must duplicate it, and it must destroy its own representation to mimic itself as totality" (Sanín-Restrepo 2018, 199). If yet we are not clear of the magnitude of what we are saying, we may ask: what does it mean to "presuppose"? Well, it is simply to understand something as the ground for the Being of some other entity, it is Heidegger's ready to hand.

The ready to hand is not a secondary condition of being—it is fundamental; without it there is simply no world. Hence, any presupposition is essentially contradictory. Entities are set up beforehand in a totality of involvements where not only the entity may be made inaccessible (obstinate, obtrusive, and impenetrable), but the totality of involvements is maintained hidden. The fundamental point to mark out is that the individual ready to hand can be transparent (the hammer, the book, and the gun), but it is the totality of involvements that is obscure and encrypted. Hence, we may disclose one thing but not the networks and its organization as a world. Consequently, what is inhibited is the possibility to discover things and to dislodge the singular from the composite, to use things against their design and to design new relations as revolutionary political acts.

Heidegger supposes a closed frame as well as stern stability and linearity of systems of significations for the ready to hand. This not only misses the heterogeneity of things but the inevitable presence of orders and organizations coming from outside the realm of things and thus out of reach of *Dasein*. Here we take the hand of Actor Network Theory (ANT from now on) to flatten what has become transcendent, to eliminate the passage Heidegger has opened into a totality as an end and finality. Manuel DeLanda entices us to think of a meshwork instead of totalities, as he proposes, "Perhaps the most novel type of stability is that represented by 'deterministic chaos', in which a given population can be pinned down to a stable, yet inherently variable, dynamical state. These new forms of stability have received the name of 'attractors,' and the transitions which transform one type of attractor into another have been named 'bifurcations'" (DeLanda 2008, 4). We are set beside "nonlinear dynamics," we can see a whole, but no sight is privileged to inform of its composition. No form of counting the elements of the whole may exhaust it, even more so, every singularity is potentially another and a multiplicity of its own at every time. As DeLanda continues, "One of the most striking consequences of nonlinear dynamics is that any population (of atoms, molecules, cells, animals, humans) which is stabilized via attractors, will exhibit 'emergent properties,' that is, properties of the population as a whole not displayed by its individual members in isolation" (DeLanda 2008, 4). Delanda here follows the groundbreaking work of Ilya Prigogine (1980) regarding dissipative systems in thermodynamics. Hence, while traditional thermodynamics systems are closed off to their environment and entail static conception of stability under the elegant disguise of autopoiesis (e.g. conventional history, constitutionalism, economics,biology); dissipative systems are subject to a constant flow of matter and energy from the outside that transforms the principle of stability. We would like to call emergent properties "synergistic properties," where no outcome, either political or aesthetical can be anticipated by a previous final form, where everything is to come in an incessant crossing of potentialities of differences. What is characteristic of Heidegger's thought is the necessary presence of a crew of engineers organizing parts that fit into wholes guided by a planned and hierarchical, finality. The ready to hand that is not decrypted, not only slides into a political pit of transcendence, but one that is instantaneously ontological.

For ANT the question is not one of distance or scale but of connectability. For synergistic properties there is no outside/inside conundrum, everything is becoming through difference. Outside/inside are just momentary settlements that orient flows and encounters. The only question one may ask is if a connection has been established between two elements and if these two elements can transform their energy onto three and from there onto infinity. Regarding the relation of the distance between the ready to hand and the present at hand Heidegger establishes, "The Objective distances of Things present-at-hand do not coincide with the remoteness and closeness of what is ready-to-hand within-the-world" (Heidegger 2001, 141/106). As ANT (Latour 2016b) has taught us, present at hand always involves a measure of space that is objective. Stockholm is X miles away from Rio de Janeiro, but ready to hand is relative to certain type of distribution of space, a certain type of order. Thus, the best beaches in Rio de Janeiro are more accessible to someone living in Stockholm than to some natives living a few kilometers away from it.

It is in the struggle for language and the formulation of its rules of transmission where potestas shows us its bitterest face. The key to encryption lies in showing what is at heart an un-centralized network of creation, an infinite interlocking of flat language games that flow ever horizontally within a virtual spiral rotating on infinite axes as if it were a system of reception, ordering, and hierarchization. We can begin to deem it at first as the opposition between rhizomes and arborescent systems proposed by Deleuze and Guattari. Arborescent systems "are hierarchical systems with centers of significance and subjectification, central automata like organized memories. In the corresponding models, an element only receives information from a higher unit, and only receives a subjective affection along preestablished paths" (Deleuze and Guattari 1987, 16). Tis the world of organized power in ascending forms of communication that trap the internal as well as the external energies of humanity within an impenetrable vault (*arch* in it most primordial meaning). The release of language and human energies is up for ransom. Not only is the use of the correct forms of language necessary, but most importantly that we buy into the very forms of systems of reception, ordering, and hierarchization. It would make no sense if the circle did not come full round. We have to buy back the language we create as slender forms of life, massive forms of the law, and impossible images of desire.

The transmission of information is horizontal; the absorption of power-information is vertical. The upward organization cannot predict the transitions and absorptions, or preestablished paths of desire, and the subjective affections it therefore creates. The solution of the encryptor? To invent the forms and protocols, the empty formal carcasses where the transitions and absorptions may validly occur. To carve out the paths where subjective affections may flow, to direct the traffic of desire and to control its outcome. The question is how the central organ absorbs energy from the bottom and translates it to ideology while homogenizing the contexts of the transmission of the relevant information from top-to-bottom, while also preserving the site of enunciation as a hidden and stratified palace beyond the skies.

Information is all about transportation or better yet transmission. When language is communicated in a hierarchical form, it is transported; when it is communicated in an immanent form, it is transmitted. Deleuze and Guattari stand in the concept of "transduction of intensive states" that "replaces topology, and the graph regulating the circulation of information is in a way the opposite of the hierarchical graph" (Deleuze and Guattari 1987, 17). Transducing turns energy or a message into another form. Lefebvre helps us see it more clearly, "Transduction elaborates and constructs a theoretical object, a possible object from information related to reality and a problematic posed by this reality" (Lefebvre 2000, 151).

The beautiful thing about transducing comes around in contemporary studies of DNA communication chains of virus (Griffiths et al., 2000). In transduction, a foreign DNA is passed (transduced) from one cell to another, and here is the magic—there is no physical contact between them. Energy is its own becoming, as physical energy is transformed into a nervous signal. Encryption slices at the heart of this virtuality where communication requires no physical contact. What encryption wants to create is a mediator that does away with transduction so that every time we communicate anything, a mediator is needed to stand in the place of a transducer that in its own becoming is immanent. Thus, while transducing is the quintessential refusal of any mediator, encryption imposes it as the condition of the occurrence of communication.

Henceforth, the mediator does not enter the relation in order to extend it in difference but to halt it and bring it back to unity, to stop the spread, and to insert itself as the ordering order that flows power back to the concealed model.

The problem does not necessarily reside in the false dichotomy between hierarchies and orders, or hierarchies and despots. It is all down to the horizontality of communication and its potentiality toward infinite difference. Let us think of a picture, the conductor of a philharmonic or the bass player in a jazz band that carries the rhythm. Are we before transduction? Are all hierarchies despotic? It is less about a physical representation and more about the potentiality to spread and transform energy into messages or turn work into life. Is the hierarchy only apparent? But then, we would have to revise what hierarchy means and sustain there is no hierarchy between the king, the rook, and the pawn but only different functions. Forthwith, we may examine hierarchies within transportations and transmissions as transduction and the hierarchy of a thing traversed by a medium of light and its nature. What is central to a hierarchy? Obedience? Synchronicity of actions under an order? Following rules? Is it a moral bearing? An ontological one? The maxim that we must bring to its saturating point is that there are no hierarchies in politics as the order of difference, but what happens beyond politics? Or rather once politics is placed as the order of difference? Can we speak of such a thing as a functional hierarchy? A *synergic* hierarchy? A hierarchy without eminence, hierarchy without potestas? Hierarchy comes from the "sacred order"; a profaned order would wash away any hierarchies as the imperious model of orders and would introduce difference and infinite production of contingency. As a hypothesis then, in a decrypted world and in decrypting actions, let us speak not of hierarchies but of horizontal functionalities. We must remain tuned to the fact that any functionality that dares to describe synergy only in its own centralizing terms, or that justifies the operation of the whole on its sole behalf, steps back to hierarchies.

For Heidegger, "the totality of involvements itself goes back ultimately to a 'towards-which' in which there is no further involvement" (Heidegger 2001, 116/84). The latter is a clear-cut proof that the totality of involvements supposes a structure, and said structure is of an origin-base-transcendence design. Without decryption, *Dasein* as origin becomes blank transcendence. Totality ends the regress of involvements and "toward which" is a finalized form that either awaits its completion at the end of a given time or presupposes an outline already existing as a model in space. To the extent that toward which defines the totality of involvements, the world-hood will always be a world-hood that can only be ultra-mundane.

Such a metaphysical obfuscation is not even dealt with when Heidegger jumps into the concept of context, describing that "the function of a world is to enworld things, the essence of a context is to contextualize things, i.e. to constitute the meaning of the things found within it, by providing the medium whereby they make sense" (Dreyfus and Wrathall 2005, 197). It is not only the redundancy of saying something like there is no context that is not contextual, but also that the context is the medium of meaning. The metaphysical wheels keep rabidly spinning in the mud of self-reference.

The problem we are announcing is thus deeper. That all meaning is given upon an already contextual totality of involvements neglects to consider intensities of power, the overlapping of human and nonhuman agencies. In short, it neglects a phenomenology of power. A context drawn out in lack of a power play, of a phenomenology of power, makes for a completely visible totality with no bumps and obscurities, but it also makes the context an utter and inexorable actuality. Therefore, movement and becoming cannot truly exist as they already belong to the picture as an entirety. Nevertheless, the most relevant thing to grasp here is that when we do away with the circularity of the context that is contextual and inject it with power plays and decryption what is revealed is the very place of the constituent power as the context setting power, or as "the" power of re-contextualization. Heidegger, as the philosopher that breaks all continuity of the presuppositions, carries on the heritage of the blindness of Western philosophy to power and the relations it creates as simulated meaningfulness. With it, he has reconducted power to solid structures, denying power as a reserve of unlimited energy.

Here we can turn to Wittgenstein's critique of ostensive definitions of words.[2] In ostensive definitions,[3] the learner encloses the idea of a totality of involvements.

> Now one can ostensively define a proper name, the name of a colour, the name of a material, a numeral, the name of a point of the compass and so on. The definition of the number two, "That is called two"—pointing to two nuts—is perfectly exact.—But how can two be defined like that? . . . The person one gives the definition to doesn't know what one wants to call "two"; he will suppose that "two" is the name given to *this* group of nuts!—He *may* suppose this; but perhaps he does not. (Wittgenstein 1986, 28)

We can only grasp a totality of involvements if we are conscient we are involved in a particular language game, which means an ampler context where things are already involved in a certain way between themselves. That is to say: an ostensive definition can be variously interpreted in *every* case. There is no one singular context that lifts the truth of all contexts. It is evident that in Wittgenstein the context does not exhaust the concept of totality, there is no such overbearing thing that would inform every element. What we have is a series of indefinite definable contexts that interlock and pass away leaving traces and conjuring voices as they go, every element announcing its truth but never the truth of all truths. There is no context of or for contexts.

As there is a grammar of things (an organization with internal workings and forms of tracing its logic), there is also a grammar over things. When the question for the totality of involvements overrules the questioning for simple things (or individualities), we throw our questioning before the tribunal of totality where creation is smothered, and individualities lose all possibility of immanent communication among themselves.

We can only define words by means of other words. As Wittgenstein asks:

> Is there only *one* way of taking the word "colour" or "length"?—Well, they just need defining.—Defining, then, by means of other words! And what about the last definition in this chain? (Do not say: "There isn't a 'last' definition.") That is just as if you chose to say: There isn't a last house in this road; one can always build an additional one. (Wittgenstein 1986, 29)

When language games interlock and words are defined by means of other words, the final word (the final definition) remains always open. It is thus not a point of closure and the end of discussion; it is always *ad-hoc*, temporal, and open for new interpretations. Totality entails finality and closure. It makes any relation dependent on a hand that draws the outlines of the limiting form of forms. It is enclosed so every time we ask of the world, the answer is already anticipated. It entails a formula, a recipe to bring things together in the sense of always maintaining the impossible model intact and out of reach of difference. Context is the immanent presupposition of meaning. Immersed in context, we cannot go amiss; the question is for the fixation of "this" certain context and the rules attached to it. The contexts we are looking for are plastic, transient, and passing; they serve to open up evermore difference and not to bring all meaning to a halt.

As Wittgenstein has noted, "So one might say: the ostensive definition explains the use—the meaning—of the word when the overall role of the word in language is clear" (Wittgenstein 1986, 30). In this comparative-parallel reading between Heidegger's function of understanding with ostensive definitions, it becomes obvious that in the function of *Dasein's* understanding the ready to hand cannot cross the threshold of Augustinian ostensive definitions. Why? (a) Understanding is one sided (a one-sided phenomenology), the being that knows only what "they" have defined as use. (b) It suffers from an unprecedented dualism, there is understanding on one side of the spectrum and use on the other, and nevertheless they are constituted in different schemes. A clean transparent tool is produced by a "them" that are opaque and unauthentic. One has already to know (or be able to do) something in order to be capable of asking a thing's name. But what does one have to know? As Wittgenstein answers, "You must already be master of a language in order to understand an ostensive definition" (Wittgenstein 1986,

33). For example, you cannot deduce the rules of chess simply by observing the knight move within the board (simple ordinate, a still picture, a one) against the backdrop of a complex context that moves in time and defines shape and space.

ORDER WORD

Let us descend from the realm of context to the plane of rules, rule following, or what Deleuze and Guattari have termed the "order word" to see how the game of power is played out in language. In a "Thousand Plateaus," the French theoreticians specify the meaning of "order words," "Rather than common sense, a faculty for the centralization of information, we must define an abominable faculty consisting in emitting, receiving, and transmitting order-words. Language is made not to be believed but to be obeyed, and to compel obedience" (Deleuze and Guattari 1987, 179).

Beyond the dizzying abysses of suppositions, of a point zero of how the world is constituted in language, let us regard the clockwork of language by a simple transduction of energy. Wittgenstein's "now I can go on" is the primordial unwinding of knots pressed upon knots upon knots of the problem of rule following. Let us disembroil the mystery that has made philosophy a discipline of bedazzlement. For Wittgenstein, in rule following, practice alone can solve the mystery, which means that even the most precise instruction is up for grabs. But more importantly, it means that the initial instruction cannot capture (anticipate) in itself the very outcome, because there is no way of deciding its fulfillment beforehand. Only practice (that is public) may decide any outcome. As Wittgenstein reinforces, "Have I reasons? the answer is: my reasons will soon give out. And then I shall act, without reasons" (Wittgenstein 1986, 211).

Rule following is above all an agreement in forms of life (Wittgenstein 1986, 226). It is an agreement of what is true and false, the relevance of true and false, the sturdiness of the rules, and the consequences of their obedience. We separate "natural laws" from this realm; we are reflecting on grammar and its connection with logic. What is logic? Within this realm, would it be recognized in the connection with communicability? In Wittgenstein's words:

> If language is to be a means of communication there must be agreement not only in definitions but also (queer as this may sound) in judgments. This seems to abolish logic but does not do so—It is one thing to describe methods of measurement, and another to obtain and state results of measurement. But what we call "measuring" is partly determined by a certain constancy in results of measurement. (Wittgenstein 1986, 242)

Logic is the bone. It is in logic that such and such is the case, but only after we have agreed to call this "meter" and divide in such a manner and award it a certain consistency (repetition, frequency) within an abundant state of things.

Nonetheless, hereinafter we must engage critically with Wittgenstein. Any form of rule following is also a question of mixtures of freedom and hierarchies that are far beyond the simple practices between already horizontally equal subjects that function with equal standards within language. It is precisely this that makes potestas functional but incomplete. It is its Achilles' heel. The uncontrollable nature of language means there is no possible anticipation of its outcome. The ready to hand is thus forever changing in its own nature while its use is also made out of emergent properties and a wide range of orders that bombard language from every flank. It ultimately depends on many forms to capture the orders, where there is no single set of the ready to hand at one given moment, no one form of dealing or using it that stalls it. This is the ruse and the liberation of, and within, language. No single overarching moment where we can say, "here it is, this is the complete world of total tools."

As Wittgenstein beautifully puts it, "Every sign *by itself* seems dead. *What* gives it life?—In use it is *alive*. Is life breathed into it there?—Or is the *use* its life?" (Wittgenstein 1986, 432). If use is life, no one may hold the strings of the consequences of truth. No one can anticipate what language may do and create, and how it may reckon with veracity. Nevertheless, we must be aware, over and beyond Wittgenstein, and in order to have a sharp picture of the phenomena at hand, that potestas is always a movement to conquer the organization of language. Thus, the first thing to confront is always the simulacra it creates. Potestas moves to rule over the nervous system of language, to direct its flows and overshadow difference. The ultimate aim of potestas is to turn transduction into hierarchical transportation, and in doing so, to cut off the nervous terminals of difference producing difference through language. It is not that language is everything but that everything in language is passed through the sword of potestas.

It is not an oversimplification of Deleuze and Guattari's order word. Orders always produce a gap with execution. There is always something that is not present in the relationship. Something else has to be added to it, presupposed in the sense of an absence that operates a cut within it. Every order is just a conjecture of the rest of the world. As such, a third term, a third action as a reaction and the reaction as the spark of a new independent action always comes into the game. This new action-reaction is independent in the sense of immanence and not in the sense that everything hangs together in one bulwark of things that represent the world. Peirce, although not bothered by relations of domination, has a very intimate rapport here. For Peirce, the sign never stands alone and when it is interpreted it never enters the individual realm directly and undisturbed. When someone interprets (interpretant) a sign, another sign is always created that is different from the first sign (Peirce 1940, 99). Mediation is always multilateral; it cannot be exhausted in a relation of ordering and following, no matter how hierarchical the subjective relation may be.

The gulf between order and completion is also a gulf in the need for time and action, of space and repetition, and specifically of renewal. Disobedience is then germane to any order. And any order is simply a prophesy, a wish bankrolled in pomp and circumstance whose completion depends on the threat of punishment. It foreshadows action yes, as we may expect that a car going into a tunnel will come out the other way, but that is only an expectation. As Wittgenstein reminds us, "As if the mere prophecy, no matter whether true or false, foreshadowed the future; whereas it knows nothing of the future and cannot know less than nothing" (Wittgenstein 1986, 461). One thing we can say about potestas is that it feeds on dressing up in necessity what it knows is contingent through and through.

An expectation hangs loose in itself; I expect x and non-x. Contingency belongs as much to the (ideal) formulation of language than it does to the completion of the order. Its extension and probabilities, in time, to accord with the original order are contingent to the bone. This is why the world that can be accounted for is the facts in it and not the ideas of it. This is why novelty is in anticipation of the present as future as contravening an order as far as accomplishing its intention for itself (out of the rotation of the order). For pragmatists, objects come about only when we "Consider what effects, that might conceivably have practical bearings, we conceive the object of our conception to have. Then, our conception of these effects is the whole of our conception of the object" (Peirce 1878, 293). Against this creed, we see it flatter and we believe that the expectation is no more than the programming of the facts in advance in ideal self-referential language games. Of the facts, therefore, it cannot control its display or concretion in time.

Rule following intimates the what, the how, and the where only as a representation. A rule does not draw the road you must follow; it does not outline every single step. A rule as such would be closer to a map (of signs of course), that to a sign itself. Freedom is not walking away from the sign you need to follow (or the direction you have asked for) and then immediately turning to yourself saying "finally I am free" . . . at least not necessarily.

Probability is not certainty, nor prophecy necessity. This does not mean that we are building airplanes that are not aerodynamic. We do better if we take a look at how the concept of aerodynamics has changed and brought about new forms of knowledge and ethical relations and new ways of creating things in the world. For example, compare airplane wings in the 1960s to today's Dreamliner (or its counterpart in a decade or in nine hundred years).

Nevertheless, the problem of who uses airplanes, for what purpose, with what environment mentality is still a thing we have yet to unearth from how orders and their completion are stretched apart, how contexts are imposed, and how to fill in the cracks in between the "them" and the ready to hand. The point is not that the one (potestas) that gives the order cannot determine after the fact if the order was or not accomplished (and to award the due punishment). The fundamental point for our argument of contingency is that the order cannot, at the time it is given, authorize the diverse forms of completion and its bifurcations. Or, in one word, it cannot anticipate the new.

Certainly, there is a thing as the arch-factuality of experience of facts based on a manifold experience (time as past) as the ground of action. It is the same experience that Wittgenstein refers to when he says nothing could convince him to put his hand on a hot stove. Our point is that neither that said experience nor anything that purports to convert itself on the ground (foundation and origin) of things may satisfy the undecidability of language. There are no grounds for a ground of grounds, and nothing at all can establish a standard of grounds. To each case its own, to each attribution its own difference. It all lies in the limits of justification. The simple fact that a justification can be more or less universal (the hand on the hot stove) does not mean it can be elevated to a transcendent form of forms.

Let us imagine for a brief instant the mad scientists' dream of inventing a brand-new language, one that speaks of and through nature in one public, neutral voice. And how could that language, consistent with the laws of nature, arise outside or beyond "these" games in which we invent games of language. Where would they get the notion of "distance," "weight" "number," that is not used also to poke fun at the mad scientist? And are not all words, feelings, and intensities embroiled in meaning forms that cannot be hierarchized?

What is the use of the alphabet? Are letters in natural order? And, does the alphabet program all the possible combinations within it? If the answer is no, then we have understood how letters go into words within a language game and we can now understand the formation of sentences as forms of communication. But more importantly, we have begun to give conceptual flesh to our intuition of power. For example, to misspell the word "orthography" does not mean that I cannot find footing in language, that I must be deprived of the letters. Encryption is meant to have an effect (and affect power) but not always sense—it sometimes is destined to create a reaction of confusion, as the encryptor holds on to the intended meaning until the subject of encryption is driven straight out of language. The grammar in encryption usurps the construction of languages; it takes charge of the sign prefiguring every outcome of it, not because it can factually anticipate it, but because it holds on to the power of describing its operation preeminently in an *ex-post facto* manner. As we have explained before, encryption intends a reaction of the sort: "I know what it says, but what does it mean?"

This is the primordial form of encryption, to replace a public sign for a private one, to withhold the table of correspondence and to make it practical only among a private group (philosophy sometimes thinks this is the only way it can operate correctly). Making sense is controlled by each language game. The making of sense is the creation of a language game (at least the potentiality), insofar, senselessness is also the result of the rules of the language game.

From Aristotle to Hume to Meillassoux, logic is whatever until now has happened. Is it possible? We do not know until it happens. Possible is everything we can say it can happen according to our experience. In terms of language, logic is whatever is possible according to the language game. What we cannot do is abduct this particular language game and make it rule over every other.

The most relevant question we can pose here is Wittgenstein's "has 'understanding' two different meanings here?" (Wittgenstein 1986, 532). Against Heidegger, the concept of understanding is not univocal. Understanding is a thick close-grained fishing net. It is a hook and an arrow, but also an oven and a potter's wheel, an indentation in paper and rocket fuel. The operability of a word is within a world. A sentence is a patch of the world; hence the operability is not exhausted in it as the whole of the mechanism. There is always something out of the mechanism. The operation with the word is multiple; we cannot make it run out within a function of a mechanism because neither is the word the whole of its function, nor the sentence the totality of the mechanism. There is always an exteriority—not a totality—of involvements, something that stretches into the word from outside of the world, and something that stretches from the word into the world. Henceforth, a sentence cannot exhaust a language game but simply reflects it; it expresses it.

The question is, what makes up a context? What patch conforms a context? Or better yet, how can we tell what a context is? And this is fundamental for encryption. For example, Giorgio Agamben denounces that the "Declaration of the Rights of Man and Citizen" truly covers a performative fallacy (Agamben 1998, 75–76).

As the Declaration goes:

1. Men are born and remain free and equal in rights. Social distinctions may be founded only upon the general good.
2. The aim of all political association is the preservation of the natural and imprescriptible rights of man. These rights are liberty, property, security, and resistance to oppression.

3. The principle of all sovereignty resides essentially in the nation. No body nor individual may exercise any authority which does not proceed directly from the nation.

In the performative transition from the first to the third article, man is devoured by a performative act, spat out, and shrunk to a determinate particularity outside of which there is nothing, not even man. In article 1, Man is a universal concept of equality of rights. Then, in the second article, man has to be part of a political association; hence the concept of man cannot be a universal outside of it. Then, in the third and final lash, the only political association is the nation(-state); thus no man exists outside of it. Man is a citizen; citizen is a national; thus man is a particular universal, and no universal man can breathe out of the stringiness of the national state. Man is a chimera or an addendum of the nation-state that by the performative act has become the center of all significance, making any idea of man disappear under its wheels. A sign of equality cannot exhaust the substance of a thing; hence "is" as equality is a malleable patch of identity (this is another problem) that forms transient contextual connections that are held together during their application to a context.

Think of the function that "is" as equality has in the coin toss. Is the coin toss part of football? How is it decided who calls the coin toss? Is there a rule determining that the home team call it? But then, is this rule part of each game? This would be endless regress. There has to be a decision as to where it is that the game begins (relevant context). Nevertheless, and in line of our previous distinction between *Entelecheia* and *Energeia* (Sanín-Restrepo 2016), a relevant context does not constitute origin nor finality beyond itself. It is immanent; its only rule of actuality is *Energeia*, and its only finality is to communicate.

There are no identities (as logical necessity) outside the game. Identity is also in the use of an element within a context, and the said context is always interlaced with others that make the identity functional. Identity is a purpose assigned within a game; as such there are no prefixed identities that carry their weight and impose themselves within every set of games and that are valid at all times. But we cannot employ just any concept (not always, not as a rule). As Wittgenstein would have it, "Concepts lead us to make investigations; are the expression of our interest, and direct our interest" (Wittgenstein 1986, 570). Words refer to things in the world and only of the world. Concepts guide, and every know-how is, first of all, conceptual. The vitality of meaning of the surroundings of symbols is not there in an instant; in the words of Latour, "the literal meaning of a concept is nothing but the excision of one of the many figurative meanings still active in the background" (Latour 2016a, 3). Hence, we must ask of concepts and identities if they are always sitting still in time, making present as having been projected into the future. Does the astronomer not look into the past when observing the light of the star extinguished long ago? Is the same not true of the geneticist and a linguist?

As stated in a "Thousand Plateaus," "In both psychoanalysis and its object, there is always a general, always a leader (General Freud). Schizoanalysis, on the other hand, treats the unconscious as an a-centered system, in other words, as a machinic network of finite automata (a rhizome), and thus arrives at an entirely different state of the unconscious" (Deleuze and Guattari 1987, 18). The problem word here is "finite." If numbering is a function of the totality, how could we be before finitude that refuses to count itself? We can overturn the problem as follows; the finitude can count itself, the problem is not the numbering, the problem is when the numbering becomes constitutive of a totality and then pincers it off the medium in which it lives and feeds (retro-feeds). The problem is constituting that number as finalized and ready-to-hand form that is in a state of solitude and paralysis and at the same time orders every element as a tributary of itself.

The problem that arises is the redundancy of ordering. The involvement of all things in a totality of involvements through ordering supposes at least a chain of command. But the chain of command is just one form in which orders get around, the dispersion of language has many forms (imitation, repetition, reports, conversations, poetry, dancing, rumors, gossips, etc.).

Language is transmission; Deleuze's and Guattari's order-words are a still photograph of language. They do not capture the struggle; every small vacillation and inflammation of speech that suppose a mutation in structures of communication that become structures of power. For them, "language is neither informational nor communicational. It is not the communication of information but something quite different: the transmission of order-words, either from one statement to another or within each statement, insofar as each statement accomplishes an act and the act is accomplished in the statement" (Deleuze and Guattari 1987, 79). This appears to me that misses the multidimensionality of language and its place as a site of struggle. Encryptors are desperately trying to convert it in order-word, but there is always friction, resistance, deflections, maneuvers of distraction, and evasions where the language is a battlefield; nevertheless, the battlefield is always laden by potestas. As Bakhtin sees it clearly,

> Alongside the centripetal forces, the centrifugal forces of language carry on their uninterrupted work; alongside verbal-ideological centralization and unification, the uninterrupted processes of decentralization and disunification go forward. This interplay is where the production of text messages can emerge. (Bakhtin 1981, 272)

Deleuze and Guattari argue that

> language seems to be defined by the syntactical, semantic, phonological constants in its statements; the collective assemblage, on the contrary, concerns the usage of these constants in relation to variables internal to enunciation itself (variables of expression, immanent acts, or incorporeal transformations). Different constants, different languages, may have the same usage; the same constants in a given language may have different usages, successively or even simultaneously. (Deleuze and Guattari 1987, 85)

The function of language is then not decided by representation or by conveying information, but by repetition and redundancy. It seems that for the sake of difference the French thinkers dauntedly raise the iron curtain of dualism and binarism infecting their own construction of machinic assemblages and thus missing the mark of the ready to hand. The stark division between collective assemblages and language is fortuitous, as if one would not circulate and determine the other, as if one could be lived without the other. It is not the case that there is indistinction in this multiplicity, but worse, the multiplicity is distinctive from a framework that anticipates any use, even language. Through the order word, we are back to square one, the need to speak of parts that make a whole, a collective carved out from the flesh of order-words. If it is true that "assemblages, or regimes of signs cannot be equated with language" (Deleuze and Guattari 1987, 85), it will amount to Wittgenstein raising the tautological question, "to whom does the use of language belong to?"

There seems to be a proximity between the place allotted to the order-word and to potestas in the sense that they both are primary ways to conjugate the world. They are forces that thrive on begetting the primordial face of the origin. As we have been hammering for long, there is no way to circumvent the place of potestas as the realization of the confines of the world. Any project aiming toward liberation must confront it head-on. It would seem the order-word is also brewing in that message. As Deleuze and Guattari remark, "The redundancy of the order-word is instead primary and that information is only the minimal condition for the transmission of order-words, which is why the opposition to be made is not between noise and information but between all the indisciplines at work in language, and the order-word as discipline or 'grammaticality'" (Deleuze and Guattari 1987, 79). Nevertheless, potestas is not merely linguistic or an apparatus that can be analyzed simply as such; it is rather the hidden operation behind language, what lies in obscurity and extends its hands sculpting the measure of reality within the language. To engage with it is not to engage with a linguistic trope that is already ordered as something visible and thus definable. Order-word would be but one (main or not is to be decided) representation of potestas. Through order-word, we may make our way to unearthing potestas, but it is not the only way of doing so. order-word and indirect discourse still seem to be ruling over a dichotomy or a binary system. Let us see, rather, how both are impregnated with the other and how they cannot carry their own descriptive way through the end without resorting to the other or climbing back into potestas. To be sure, the minimal condition of the operability of the order-word and its dependence of potestas in any analytic of power is the opening of contingency. The "now I can go on" throws information out of any predictable finality. It steals the order-word of any possibility of construing the primordial form of language and any order that can be secured in it as belonging to the relation of power and potestas.

Order-words sit in a close guard of Austin's illocutionary acts (Austin 1975). The magic of speech that turns bread into the body of the Christ, people into hostages, and accused into the criminal. But here we must ask if the names James or London are noncorporeal; we are twirling with substances and names. The use of the order-word by Deleuze and Guattari seems to me is not only trite but implausible. They are falling back through their own trap door to Kelsen's imputation that makes language depend on authority (in this case a context of authority) and authority as the creation of situations that "are the case" as in the first Wittgenstein and Russel's objective language.

Language is a complex thing to define that no-less we use with extreme simplicity and ease. The difference of the "power play" to order-word is that the former happens in porous languages, everyday languages (come first) and then are hijacked into formal languages (through) power plays. Thence, order-word is still considering power as a solid state, as it plays with power as molar structures, with obedience as direct causality and a totality of involvements as its final result. The steepness of this vision is not grasping that order-words are functional make-ups of quantic elements that never cease to interact with each other in molecular structures of becoming. Taking aim only at order-words is aiming at structure instead of difference, of extension instead of intensity and at finality instead of potentiality.

As Verena Conley instructs us, "The 'order-word' is a function immanent to language that compels obedience. The fundamental form of speech is not the statement (énoncé) of a judgement or the expression (énonciation) of a feeling, but the command" (Conley 2010, 198). The effect would be that obedience in itself would always be metalinguistic, an irrepresentable excess. But here there is no clarity: is the order word a metalanguage or a simple function of language? Deleuze and Guattari need it both ways. Therefore, we must explore its next cave. Is the function metalinguistic? At least its essence "obedience" is. But here is a contradiction, at least an incongruity. First, they hold that the "order-word" is a function immanent to language that compels obedience. Then, "The order-word is the variable of enunciation that effectuates the condition of possibility of language and defines the usage of its elements according to one of the two treatments; we must therefore return to it as the only 'metalanguage'" (Deleuze and Guattari 1987, 106). The question that spikes the thin air of difference is how could something immanent be "meta"? The order-word in this duplicity evades the multiplicity of the unity of ordering and obeying. Not only the nuances of orders (potestas) and the simulacrum (how it is able to mimetisize difference) but also the many dispositives of ordering-obeying and the subtleties of resisting are lost within a solid and impenetrable unity. There is an uncanniness in becoming that slices through the walls of the order word, it is the impossibility of writing it down, of decomposing it (analyzing it) into categories and fixing its limits as essence. The eventfulness of the new, to become, is not to fill in the image, of what it seems. It is not covering the shadow or fulfilling the blank space. Becoming is not a correspondence between relations, but neither is it a resemblance, an imitation, or, at the limit an identification. For example, for Rorty (1979), no sentence can hold its own analytical truth outside a context of practices of language. There is no order of orders of language that may bring truth to all language.

What is missing in the post-structuralists account is the fact that what is encrypted is this territory from where words accrue a certain meaning and from where they can be re-interpreted over and over again. The word does not come first, first is a (mythological) relation then the word as name tries to stabilize any given relation. The mythical circle of the sign guarantees that there is no freedom from the sign, thus the sign is lock and key.

SIGNIFICATION

Regarding signification of the ready to hand, and this is the heart of the matter, for Heidegger, "A sign is not a Thing which stands to another Thing in the relationship of indicating; *it is rather an item of equipment which explicitly raises a totality of equipment into our circumspection so that together with it the worldly character of the ready-to-hand announces itself*" (Heidegger 2001, 110/80). A sign lets the totality come forth and show itself; it lifts the context. The sign is a special case of the ready to hand, but even the use of the sign comes not spontaneously but enmeshed within a relation of economies, of systems of communication engaged by power. The sign, as referring to equipment as ready to hand, does not necessarily liberate them; rather well it organizes, codifies it, and hides its strata.

So although Heidegger realizes that the ready to hand has been previously assigned, he dares not the question of how and within what logics of distribution of power. Consequently, the ready to hand becomes present at hand

and reference to it becomes the "given" of the world, pure transcendence. To assign meaning is to reserve the equipment for some, and in a certain way; and to deprive its use for others and in a certain way. But it also means, at root, to define what is epistemology, what is morality, aesthetics, etc. The distribution of meaning in language defines not only the things of the world but also the mechanisms, the clusters of narratives, the disciplines through which they can be named and consequently the right formula, and the correct subjectivity to do so.

Heidegger sustains that "in a workshop, for example, the totality of involvements which is constitutive for the ready-to-hand in its readiness-to-hand, is 'earlier' than any single item of equipment" (Heidegger 2001, 116). The workshop may be a free space of creativity, but it may also be an oligarchic organization of sweat labor where only a few determine the utility of the space and the things that are created within it. Thence, if we apply encryption, it becomes evident that the assignment of references (encryption) is the condition for serviceability and usability, and thus we are within the dominance of the past over the present, of actuality over *potentia*—a time overbearing becoming and the rule of the actual (extensa) over the virtual (intensive).

Accordingly, for Heidegger, everything is embedded in a meaningful context, and that context *is what gives it meaning*. What is crucial here is the activity of giving meaning and the relation to the ready to hand as the first possibility of the authenticity of meaning. Furthermore, what is at play is the possibility of disclosedness (*erschliessen*) of said meaning. Hence, what is "at hand" is the very possibility of the potentiality for being through the potentiality for meaning and meaningfulness.

Here we must confront two diverse, but adjacent, constructions of what signification means. Heidegger's and Wittgenstein's definitions that have marked the philosophical landscape of our times. We will do so to find the cracks in between them and to round up what we mean by power plays and encryption of power. Let us return to ostensive "definitions" of words. In the latter, the learner must already dominate the "what's and 'how's" of language. It must be ready to ask specifying questions: are you pointing to color? To a function? To a shape? But also the act of pointing must be within a language-game; it must be differentiated; it cannot be a "constitutive" pointing that inaugurates the world. Why is it important here to think of ostensive definitions? The ready to hand is already imbued in a language game rather than an ostensive definition; it consists of complex parts of learning through use, insofar meaning can only be attributed partially, within a given function, and never within a finality.

Following the second Wittgenstein, "the red which you imagine is surely not the same (not the same thing) as the red which you see in front of you; so how can you say that it is what you imagined?" (Wittgenstein 1986, 443).

The answer to the conundrum of ostensive definitions is simple. I have been taught what color is and have been pointed out to red many times; I have dealt with red on countless occasions; I have experienced red before; I know how ambiguous red can be; I have discussed red. Let us follow the question further, "Suppose I give someone the order 'Imagine a red circle here'—and now I say: understanding the order means knowing what it is like for it to have been carried out—or even: being able to imagine what it is like?" (Wittgenstein 1986, 451). What do you imagine first, the circle or the color red? Do you first think of an empty outline and then color it with the brush in your mind or does the image come as a compact unity? The ready to hand does not show itself as whole in every use; it carries a strain of past decisions, it projects a function that has been assigned to it outside the materiality that brought it fore. The hammer is never the hammer; we do not solely disclose it and a world in its use. Its use is at a crossing of saturated meanings that flow to and from it in order to represent it, deny it, and make it completely useful when it is in these hands and to impair it when it is in different ones. A hammer's clank never repeats the same sound even though the hammer always reveals a finality.

And here, in finality, we have to think its two main aspects: (a) finality as the final closure of the thing, a collapse of a thing in time and space, the final word that constitutes its totally ("the game is over"); and (b) finality as *telos*, as a pregiven directionality that purports an end not imbedded immanently in its use. Think of a piece in chess; two master chess players are discussing the king, at the same time two master chess piece makers are discussing another piece while two children that have never seen the materials with which the game of chess is played are talking about the same things. Are the three parties talking about the same thing? Where is the prerogative? Where the hierarchy of these discourses? Who has a privileged access to the things, their relations and their properties, and most of all to their beingness?

Time is fundamental for any showing, for any definition, everything depends on a before and after the definition (circumstantial); it depends on aims and purpose in the traffic of language and meanings. For Wittgenstein's example 2 (a man pointing to a slab, instead of saying to his colleague "pass me the slab"), one must already know what a slab is and what it serves for. Henceforth, the ready to hand must also have gradients of orderings, degrees of intensity of its uses in order to work. To clarify this is our first task in order to move to the big game: to find out where, or at what point does it become encrypted. And here is where Wittgenstein jumps from ostensive definitions to the "language game": "We can also think of the whole process of using words in (2) as one of those games by means of which children learn their native language. I will call these games 'language-games' and will sometimes speak of a primitive language as a language-game" (Wittgenstein

1986, 7). And then he clarifies its use: "I shall also call the whole, consisting of language and the actions into which it is woven, the 'language-game'" (Wittgenstein 1986, 7).

Western thought has been a devilish contest of philosophers to do away with suppositions only to saddle the world up with new ones. Every time the process is more mystifying; every time the process is tainted by the promise of the end of presuppositions only to open the door to more stringent ones. Wittgenstein deals the first major blow to this ineffable beast. The lightning that strikes at the core of philosophy shattering its unidimensionality is Wittgenstein's understanding that signification is nothing more than meaning something by something. That we create signification using language, that the medium is the non-original origin of nature and finality, and that only through a use that is plain does the word signify.

> Now what do the words of this language *signify?*—What is supposed to shew what they signify, if not the kind of use they have? And we have already described that. So we are asking for the expression "This word signifies *this*" to be made a part of the description. In other words, the description ought to take the form: "The word signifies . . ." (Wittgenstein 1986, 10)

How do we know that an utterance is a word? Not because it signifies, a groan signifies too. Is it that it signifies within a given context? But the groan also has an impending context. It is that it can be used to describe itself within a given context? Is it that it denotes and hence belongs to a multiplicity? No final answer can be given. No definition can anticipate fully all the uses of an utterance; no description of "states of affairs" may alter the ramifications of the use of meanings. Therefore, the first step toward the dis-mythification of both names as original and transcendent, and the language corresponding to occult origins is accomplished through meaning attached simply by meaning something by something. In it, games interlock and no hierarchy can be attributed to them from any place whatsoever. What is clear is that if we give meaning to the groan, then we have included it in our language game.

Wittgenstein moved language from a "still picture" where a hidden origin commands its limbs and organs to a "moving picture" where everything affects everything within its own becoming and rules and where "rule following" is practical and not normative. The question we must push, because we are creatures of potestas, is if this is achieved through horizontal lines of difference or if there is a power play at the root.

Again, our creed is that we cannot think of the demise of potestas without locking horns with it. There is no way to circumvent its power. To define our life and where it begins is to ignite the question of signification. Take, for example, our affairs with computer applications as ready to hand, as John

Culkin brilliantly warned us, "We shape our tools and thereafter our tools shape us." It is us who are programmed to run the apps, we are its tributaries, and we have to learn how to ride them in order for them to represent a world that is fluid, regular, and always predictable. They are both poles; if we become literate then they are predictable and regular, and so does the world appear as such, but, if we are not literate, they are stubborn and inaccessible and thus the world seems to run awry. The other side is equally macabre. The apps fill in the gaps between mediocrity and desire. The intelligence and imagination crafted into the machine appear as personally ours. When we buy the machine, we do not only buy it, but its intelligence and flair come to pose as ours. We flamboyantly parade our machines as if they were our makings, as if their capacity was ours and as if their beauty is ours. Programmed obsolescence is aesthetic before it is machinic. When we (our machines) cannot execute the latest feat, we are thrown under the wheels of development, we must catch up, and we must buy the cutting-edge techno-wonder in order to put us back at the forefront of life. But the bottom line is that in order for the world to show any significance at all, we must encrypt ourselves into the machine.

Technology is predictable and uniform; it always seems to repeat the same patterns of use. Nevertheless, to obtain such traits, the user must concede everything—language, movement, and time—to the machine. We must become literate in the form that the machine teaches the subject for there not to be any unbalance. As long as we learn and replicate the language of the machine, it and the world appear transparent. The use of the machine itself appears decrypted, but this is only because its core (programming) is highly codified so that the use and the *telos* of any action remain encrypted. Hence, although the use is decrypted (flat) the world (outside) it relates to, it unveils, and to a great degree creates, is still made up of the fairy dust of ideology; pure encryption.

Machines, especially apps, regulate desire and determine the visual field of the world. In the sense they are partly automatons; they are objects that determine, in their use, the conditions of possibility of our understanding. We still have to study how Artificial Intelligence may decipher the Kantain a-priori conditions and to understand that the order of things is reversed completely.

It is not, as Heidegger would have it, that things turn into resources, but what does turn into a resource is the human energy, its language, and its industry. What the encryptor accomplishes, through very sophisticated uses of Artificial Intelligence and downright monopolization of information (for example, through the military-industrial-virtual-technology complex), is to create a funnel where all human intelligence is distilled, bottled, branded, and destined. All this process is conducted from within five or six corporations and an alliance of a handful of nation-states. "Resource," which is

Heidegger's funny little corporate name for the way in which objects will come to appear and be experienced, is inverted by this type of encryption. In our times of unleashed neoliberalism, human flesh is the dire fuel of the machine.

But an important thing is left for us to scrape from the bottom of the barrel of significance. Let us follow Heidegger's organization of the sign. Accordingly:

> The relation between sign and reference is threefold 1. Indicating, as a way whereby the "towards-which" of a serviceability can become concrete is founded upon the equipment-structure as such, upon the "in-order-to" (assignment). 2. The indicating which the sign does is an equipmental character of something ready-to-hand, and as such it belongs to a totality of equipment, to a context of assignments or references. 3. The sign is not only ready-to-hand with other equipment, but in its readiness-to-hand the environment becomes in each case explicitly accessible for circumspection. (Heidegger 2001, 113–114/82)

Here we follow in the footsteps of Charles Sanders Peirce and his revolutionary conception of the sign. Peirce washes away the Cartesianism dualism of mind and matter (Peirce 1905). Ideas are not seared internal processes with no material bearing; ideas are signs and signs are everywhere. The relation between ideas and signs is not a division of a lapse of time where ideas capture signs and devolve them back into a separate reality, but, rather, every idea is expressed in a sign and every sign is the product of ideas; they are indivisible. Signs steep the reality we live in. Peirce substitutes the Cartesian dualism for a semiotic monism where the units of analysis are not individual signs (something that does not really exist), but the process of signs relating to each other in a process that he calls "unlimited Semiosis" (Peirce 1905, 25). Humans are not isolated things that possess ideas and express signs; rather, the human itself is a sign, a node immersed in a vast network of other semiotic processes. As Gabriel Méndez-Hincapíe, an expert in the Peircean Synechism beautifully explains:

> People have a hard time understanding the continuity between man and sign in order to understand Peirce's brilliant discovery that "man is a sign." However, we can understand it by means of a simile. (homeomorphism): The relationship between a tornado and the air or atmosphere or between a river and a whirlpool in the river. The tornado is not a substance that can be removed from the air. It is a configuration of the air itself. The swirl of water is not a substance that you can remove and isolate from the river, it is a state of the river itself. (Méndez-Hincapíe[4])

Through Peirce we flank Heidegger's move toward a ready to hand that is existentially and factually separate both from the human creature and the sign. The separation in Heidegger supposes a triangulation where the sign has not been constituted, yet, nevertheless, amazingly, the ready to hand gets its full instruction from it. Hence, we must inquire Heidegger through Peirce's theory, as to how does the representation of a representation work? How do we represent signs if not by signs themselves? Is there a point in time when we can say that there cannot be any further representation? We exhaust representations for practical reasons and not because reaching a final point would be equivalent to reaching a ground (the essence of things or the substance). We exhaust representations because signs are brought on and defined by other signs where there is no hierarchy among them but simple down to earth alterity. Proof of this is that we can reach that point in an indefinite manner of ways, each one unique and with no central apparatus guiding (ruling over) every step as an axiom. As James Baldwin exquisitely put it, "How can one, however, dream of power in any other terms than in the symbols of power?" (Baldwin 1993, 80). To be sure, what is also lacking in the Peircian universe of the sign is that the constitution of any sign is a power play. But also that any employment of the sign within a language game also follows specific forms of moving power within hierarchies, and constructing and defending hierarchies through signs. Potestas as a sign creates the simulacra of exhaustion of signs by its own hand. Hence, although Peirce opens up a new consideration of the sign, we must also spike it through the works of power as potestas in order to see its full features and to capture the extent of its working upon the world of significations.

For Heidegger, a sign is constituted beforehand in the equipment; the signifying is the assigning of relations within a totality, where the latter belongs to *Dasein*, the former to tradition. Familiarity with significance is for Heidegger a type of disposition for discovering the entities encountered in the world; a kind of separating tool between the ready to hand and the present at hand where the former makes themselves known as they are in themselves. Everything is a sign, all of the language is a sign. Language is always involved in itself as pointing or signaling to other things A sign is never in itself; it can never be exhausted in an internal relation to itself. A sign is illimited *Energeia*. The sheer potentiality of being other and of coming from nothing, of signaling beyond any material prefiguration of the stuff it is made of. This is the stuff we are made of. A sign is a sign for a sign; it is the Peircean thirdness. To dissect essences is taking the flesh out of the sign; it is a delimitation of the function of language and things. There is no ready to hand at one side of the shore and a sign-giving-entity in the other and a river called life where they blissfully meet. As we have pointed, every word, sentence, and thing stretch (point) out of itself and into the world. Consequently, in the Heideggerian universe, assignation and reference become the given of the world, and every assignment of reference a split of meanings that may never correspond to *Energeia*. Signifying is assigning a relationship.

Looking through the glass of potestas somethings become clear. Someone must know or claim to know the final signification. Some people must organize the meanings of the ready to hand in order to preserve it actively. This preservation is not a looking out for every movement upon every single thing but the programming of simple mechanic rules and action as rules of encryption. These rules are reserved to an exclusive use (only some can execute them and the movements thereof). The latter also entails the configuration of *ex-post facto* rules that gives authorities the capacity to name the event after the fact. All of this amounts to "power plays" determining the rules of the game before it is played but in a form in which the programmers of the game (encryptors) can intervene in it at any time and with no major perturbance. What is severed and re-signified by encryption is mostly the "totality of involvements" as the pre-established relation of the ready at hand. A simple example is the microphone. It is ready to expand the acoustics and therefore the voice and discourse itself but the totality of involvements of who can use it for what purposes and within what contexts of dispersion is already controlled and predetermined by attributions of power or power plays. What is controlled is therefore the outcome of the involvements, the determination of what a voice can mean and how far it can reach.

DESEVERANCE (*ENT FERNUNG*) AND UNCONCEALMENT (*ALETHEIA*)

Another key concept of "Being and Time" is deseverance "what is ready-to-hand within-the-world is desevered and given directionality, depending upon the degree of transparency that is possible for concernful circumspection" (Heidegger 2001, 146/111). This is key for encryption. Transparency depends on how the entity called human is given within the world. Heidegger repeats the ever-assuming posture of thinking of a potentiality of a human that is unrestrained, an equal among equals, that shares the possibility of addressing the world from equivalent points of view. He does not see race, nationality, and gender as conditions for this transparency of being. He does not see the obstacles and hinderances, the utter impossibilities with which some beings are put into the world, their unequal footing. This blind side is not minor and surmountable. In any case, prior to the possibility of circumspection and the potentiality of being, power is constitutive and thus defines the alternate virtualities of being in the world. Ready to hand is the world of work, and thus we have living labor (Marx 1973) that has been deprived and encrypted and subtracted and re-signified (mystified and alienated). In order for circumspection to de-severe, it must be free to do so, but if the ready to hand of work is privatized and elitized, de-severance is already marked by an external fate, an external clockwork organization of things in the world that Heidegger simply duplicates in the vernacular "ideal man" of all philosophy.

What a thing is remains slippery in its essence. We are not interested in constituting anything like essence or substance; rather, it is what a thing as a symbol performs, the connections and networks it is enmeshed in, that is relevant for our discussion. Work is decisive to constitute the ready to hand and to award its referential contextuality. It is clear that work must be living labor freed from any imposition and directionality of dead labor. If the ready to hand is only encountered within a referential totality, and if this totality has been constituted by oppression, then all of its components, down to the most capillary description and utility of a ready to hand is pulverized forthwith. The trails found in power as use, production as limiting, the possibilities of things, mediation of transductions, the predominance of dead labor over living labor are equal intensities that bring the ready to hand not only to a halt but to a disparaging form of a simulacrum.

Unconcealment is perhaps the Heideggerian concept that best portrays his construction of a supposition-free ontology. Within our incursion it represents the bridge that turns ready to hand into a necessary condition for *Dasein*. As we will analyze more thoroughly further, to even tend to unconcealment of an entity, we must first make the world available for all entities to share in their difference. There is then a previous concealment that is not the self-concealment of things, which is the power-in-concealment of the possibility of the world through encryption. It is the concealment of the capacities to approximate, live, symbolize, and name the world in its own instances of difference. Thus, unconcealmeant never happens for the first time.

Heidegger affirms, "When something is understood but is still veiled, it becomes unveiled by an act of appropriation, and this is always done under the guidance of a point of view, which fixes that with regard to which what is understood is to be interpreted" (Heidegger 2001, 191/150). Nevertheless, when we unveil, we are not unveiling the thing but the totality of involvements that, if encrypted, would only unveil the sense it was given by the encryptor. Nothing but an arrangement of things in space as a command. Nothing but extensivity where all matter is dead matter eating away at virtuality. This forces us to rise the logical bar even further: every unveiling must be double; it must first unveil the circumstances that deployed and organized the totality of involvements; only then will the ready to hand be unveiled in itself. We have already anticipated that the answer to being, regardless of its centrality to our project, is a question of a collective and not of a singular *Dasein*. Nevertheless, we must first ask if the world must be decrypted if we are ever to think of *Dasein*? Or, is the question thus poised to be, can we only arrive at *Dasein* through decryption? Or else how can meaning be awarded if *Dasein* is not structured licitly? We agree with Heidegger that unconcealment occurs only when it is achieved through work. Nevertheless, as we will prove, work as political immanence only arrives in decryption. Even to aspire to a flat ontology, we must first decrypt our language from which we name it, so it may be autonomous. Even more so, we must decrypt ourselves so we may be disposed to any flatness of the order of things.

CO-STATES OF MIND (*MITBEFINDLICHKEIT*)

Let us penetrate an important passage in the coming forth of Dasein, the "co-states of mind." This, I believe, is where the arguments of the book begin to be laced together in a powerful potentiality. In Heidegger's words,

> Communication, in which one makes assertions-giving information, for instance-is a special case of that communication which is grasped in principle existentially. In this more general kind of communication, the Articulation of Being with one another understandingly is constituted. Through it a co-state-of-mind [Mitbefindlichkeit] gets "shared," and so does the understanding of Being-with. (Heidegger 2001, 205/162)

Through decryption, we can safely establish that communication and understanding are not co-states of mind, something that accompanies being in its becoming as something supplementary. There is not a general kind communication alongside a special kind; they are both the same case under the same rules. It also goes to say that even in encryption, communication and understanding happen. Furthermore, it is a condition of encryption (the political solidification of difference) that communication and understanding may go on "as if" nothing irregular is taking place. Words have a quotidian down-to-earth meaning and logics, and natural laws are respected by it (better yet, it is encryption where they are idolized). When we decrypt, we do not find another absconded language or a new form of language but new forms of communication. Decryption is, in a first approximation, "spiritual." In encryption we speak among the present, but there is always something or someone else absent (not the transcendent presupposition, but the immanent exclusion). As we know, making the un-sensed sensible is the function of spirituality.

The fundamental question thus posed is if we should talk of a state of mind or an interaction. States of mind are misty and muddled; they could mean many things and nothing. Wittgenstein, as far as I can see, has brought down the walls of states of mind as primordial and analyzable stable things. In his words,

> If one says that knowing the ABC is a state of the mind, one is thinking of a state of a mental apparatus (perhaps of the brain) by means of which we explain the *manifestations* of that knowledge. Such a state is called a disposition. But there are objections to speaking of a state of the mind here, inasmuch as there ought to be two different criteria for such a state: a knowledge of the construction of the apparatus, quite apart from what it does. Nothing would be more confusing here than to use the words "conscious" and "unconscious" for the contrast between states of consciousness and dispositions. (Wittgenstein 2001, 149)

If one thinks of a state of mind, one thinks ineradicably of divisions within an apparatus. One must then think of the construction of the apparatus and what it does, and how it is we use it the apparatus (or as many of them) without knowing how it is constructed. The use is not involved at all with its construction. Knowing how to use it is as far as the use can go. Use can outline the construction, but not even the one who knows the finesses of the construction can understand its final form, its coming together in the idea of apparatus. Now, thinking of an apparatus entails a designer, private parts, and an assembly of things coming together under a master plan. Therefore, it is problematic; it denies the difference and the network type of things. States of minds as apparatuses cover the pair of terms in a mist of grammatical indifference.

Now, let us contrast two possible forms of dealing with states of mind as apparatuses. For the first option we have seen, the design is final, and as such it outlines the limits of its use and the use itself. Here the relation of the apparatus and its uses are determined by the final design (totality and finality as *Entelecheia*) of the apparatus. It would thus be "use" as in the hamster in the wheel and use as a performance within a given rationality of things. In this first option it would appear the finality of the use is to uncover the secret formula of the design of the apparatus, that, notwithstanding, guides use as it hides itself. It is thus an impossible image to muster from use. But if the apparatus is not a division between materiality and ideality, or a separation between extensity and intensity, then the use, every use, is a form of altering the apparatus through use. Every form of use is directed to take it immanently to the limit where the very idea of apparatus is blurred in itself, and thus distorted and turned into another set of things. This form of use (*Energeia*) turns the very idea of apparatus into a network that has no pregiven reality but that in its use preforms any reality. It is intensity in its purest form. Hence the division of a supreme designer that anticipates every use, and the simple user, is struck down to the immanence of the use.

At least the machine (apparatus) called language has no (foundational) designer. Let us think of a singular machine, the mill, for example. There are infinite interactions between it and the designer, the user, and the beneficiary. (Are we not using the machine when we eat the bread?) Language becomes an apparatus, and the apparatus domains over that slippery thing called states of mind exactly because it is the product of a "power play." As Wittgenstein observes, "The grammar of the word 'knows' is evidently closely related to that of 'can,' 'is able to.' But also closely related to that of 'understands' ('Mastery' of a technique)" (Wittgenstein 1986, 150). In these forms of interactions of potestas and power, what does encryption do? Well, it favors one kind of doing, one kind of knowing. When we decrypt, we come around a basic understanding that there are kinds of interactions and not solitary states of mind.

Wittgenstein is not defining or describing knowledge but rather how words are used, how communication happens in the practice of its use. Knowledge certainly circulates, but it gives no answer as to what knowledge itself is, or how knowledge is instilled in the mind (consciousness). For Wittgenstein, the vitality is that there is no single reducible form of mind processes or states or consciousness; they all flow into the sea of language. Henceforth, "telling," "speaking," and "informing" are forms that come together, creating language without one of them taking preeminence over the others. As the black glue pot within the toolkit informs the use of what is broken outside the kit but can also mend any of the object-tools of the kit, when all those queer transcendent ghosts of metaphysics flow into the sea of language, they become a simple tool that informs the quantity and quality of a possible world.

NOTES

1. If we must speak of number, as a distinction of identities, it would only apply to dimensions (as if there were two in "sunlight," sun and light, as two separate things).

2. Wittgenstein refers to ostensive definitions as follows: "(I do not want to call this 'ostensive definition,' because the child cannot as yet *ask* what the name is. I will call it, 'ostensive teaching of words'.——I say that it will form an important part of the training, because it is so with human beings; not because it could not be imagined otherwise.)" (Wittgenstein 1986, 6).

3. "When a child learns this language, it has to learn the series, of 'numerals' a, b, c, . . . by heart. And it has to learn their use.—Will this training include ostensive teaching of the words? Are "there" and "this" also taught ostensively?—Imagine how one might perhaps teach their use. One will point to places and things—but in this case the pointing occurs in the *use* of the words too and not merely in learning the use" (Wittgenstein 1986, 9).

4. Personal correspondence.

Chapter 4

Naming and Difference
Multiple Worlds and the Power Play

PARTS, SIMPLES, COMPOSITES, AND FUNCTIONS

Philosophy always hits solid rock when it asks for names and their function within reality. We will strive for the demystification of names as a form of transcendent meaning. Let us begin with a too-familiar example, the meaning of Excalibur as employed by Wittgenstein and the depth it attains when we treat names as "meaning something by something." "It can be put like this: *a name ought really to signify a simple.* And for this one might perhaps give the following reasons: The word 'Excalibur,' say, is a proper name in the ordinary sense. The sword Excalibur consists of parts combined in a particular way. If they are combined differently Excalibur does not exist" (Wittgenstein 1986, 39). We are flirting with the ominous world of substances and essences. What makes Excalibur, Excalibur? Is it the name? The corroboration that the parts are installed one upon the other according to a previous model that defines these combinations? If it is the latter, then there must be a Platonic ideal of Excalibur, and the one drawn in paper (the blueprint) must be the real Excalibur (even if it was drawn after a sword that existed first), for what does it mean to say that "this" is Excalibur while pointing to the model? Or is it, at the end, a "power play" within the language game? One designed to impose a name and a unique feature to a sword and letting that gest define what are the components (form, matter, and the coming together of the two) of Excalibur. Could you combine the parts and then take away the name for good? Where is the mystical in Excalibur? Its function within a contextual history?

As Wittgenstein continues:

> It is clear that the sentence "Excalibur has a sharp blade" makes *sense* whether Excalibur is still whole or is broken up. But if "Excalibur" is the name of an

object, this object no longer exists when Excalibur is broken in pieces; and as no object would then correspond to the name it would have no meaning. . . . But then the sentence "Excalibur has a sharp blade" would contain a word that had no meaning, and hence the sentence would be nonsense. But it does make sense; so there must always be something corresponding to the words of which it consists here. (Wittgenstein 1986, 39)

We must tie this with a fundamental question for difference: the capacity to name oneself from within. This corresponds to the most difficult trait of power, the balance between identity and difference—phenomenology and its creed of "to the things themselves" covers some ground, but only goes part of the way. What is paramount is to dislodge naming from necessity and ride it back to contingency as well as to reveal, once and for all, the capacity of difference to thrive within the realm of names.

Let us pick up at the historical discussion harkening to Wittgenstein: "Let us first discuss this point of the argument: that a word has no meaning if nothing corresponds to it. It is important to note that the word 'meaning' is being used illicitly if it is used to signify the thing that 'corresponds' to the word" (Wittgenstein 1986, 40). Thus, we could not logically refer to Mr. NN or Excalibur if they were destroyed. There on lies the reason that we agree with the affirmation that meaning only comes about in its use. The word "this" as a kind of formal compass for names only ensues when there is a "that" and when there is a "here" and a "there." Although Wittgenstein warns us "not to call these words names at all," he also grants that "Yet, strange to say, the word 'this' has been called the only genuine name; so that anything else we call a name was one only in an inexact, approximate sense" (Wittgenstein 1986, 38). "This" and "that" implicate each other, and, as such, they define the fundamental reference points of placing, timing, and thus naming. But let us take it to an extreme. Is empty space contextual? Of course it is; even for Leibniz (1989) empty space opens up the possibility of using things in a medium. This allows Wittgenstein to question:

What lies behind the idea that names really signify simples?—Socrates says in the Theaetetus: "If I make no mistake, I have heard some people say this: there is no definition of the primary elements—so to speak—out of which we and everything else are composed; for everything that exists1 in its own right can only be *named*, no other determination is possible, neither that it *is* nor that it *is not*. . . . But what exists in its own right has to be . . . named without any other determination. In consequence it is impossible to give an account of any primary element; for it, nothing is possible but the bare name; its name is all it has. But just as what consists of these primary elements is itself complex, so the names of the elements become descriptive language by being compounded together. For the essence of speech is the composition of names." . . . Both Russell's "individuals" and my "objects" *[Tractatus Logico- Philosophicus]* were such primary elements. (Wittgenstein 1986, 46)

In assemblages, there are no individuals, nor groups that can take a preeminent place from where we could name all parts within a whole. The passage from individuals to genres and from there to kingdoms as forms of counting and of unifying are all arbitrary, they all behest a decision that is unfounded and un-original. There are only assemblages made up of transitory arrangements that guide things within language and language as a matter of things.[1]

In the Theaetetus, Socrates weaves "maieutically" in between Heraclitus and Protagoras as he states:

> But great philosophers tell us that we are not to allow either the word "something," or "belonging to something," or "to me," or "this," or "that," or any other detaining name to be used, in the language of nature all things are being created and destroyed, coming into being and passing into new forms; nor can any name fix or detain them; he who attempts to fix them is easily refuted. (Plato 1992, 156)

Regarding the correspondence of things and names, Deleuze and Guattari are keen to affirm that "it is not impossible to make a radical break between regimes of signs and their objects. Even when linguistics claims to confine itself to what is explicit and to make no presuppositions about language, it is still in the sphere of a discourse implying particular modes of assemblage and types of social power" (Deleuze and Guattari 1987, 7). As they continue, "There is no language in itself, nor are there any linguistic universals, only a throng of dialects, patois, slangs, and specialized languages. There is no ideal speaker-listener, any more than there is a homogeneous linguistic community" (Deleuze and Guattari 1987, 7). In other words, there are virtual contexts and partial language games. Sitting comfortably close to the French duo, Bjørn Ramberg highlights Rorty's work as the "complete lack of faith in the idea that there is an ideal vocabulary, one which contains all genuine discursive options" (Ramberg 2009). Let us use these insights to deepen our research.

"Manifold is the uncanny": this mounting phrase in Sophocles' Antigone is for Heidegger the spitfire that opens a vein in the relation between singulars and groups. Any grouping can be decomposed into many singularities (atoms, protons, etc.). And, if it can be decomposed, then it can be linguistically composed into bigger units (packs, groups, classes, and kingdoms). The problem is, as always, where to begin? (not as a practical question of time but as the problematic question of origins). And, even if we could determine a starting point, any starting point would be a composition of sorts, and therefore, the question that this situation begs is, which composition would take the upper hand in naming any other composition? How do we define a singularity that serves as unity for decomposition or composition? It seems the problem is easier to observe in decomposition (it seems natural) while composition seems artificial and arbitrary, but this is just a problem of optics, of believing that seeing things upside-down is the wrong way to see, or worse, not seeing at all. Are all singularities heterogeneous? Is every sheep in a herd singular? The answer is yes; names as herd are simply functional and not foundational; they are temporal and not definitive; they are contingent to a situation and do not decide the necessity of the situation. They do instantiate a type but only when it is within a relation of mobility, and thus the affirmation such as "the type is" only arises in passing. Hence, not only a sheep within a herd can be a singularity, but also the herd is a singularity in becoming.

Heidegger saw clearly in the Greek "inception" a thirst for unifying and creating ranks (Heidegger 2000). Who but Heidegger himself denounces the deviation of logos into thinking and thinking as the primordial force that conjoins the manifold? In this context, *Phusis* is a gathering that is unifying and whose thrive is to create rank among beings and things of the world. Since the Greek inception, logos becomes twisted into a machine of gathering, selecting, ordering, grouping, and classifying. The act of thinking is teleological. If *Phusis* is transformed into an idea, an archetype, then any *logos* as thinking must repeat the model. Who but Heidegger brought into modern sight the fact that being as logos and logos as the gathering is spearheaded to the permanent creation of rank and dominance? But, then again, who but Heidegger is daunted by the shadow projected by his own philosophy and renounces its spoils? Potestas is all too quick to replace the same by the identical (when it wants to draw a lot, a pack a class), and it imagines a family resemblance so as to throw everything in a pit of indistinction. There is nothing identical except for one thing to itself at a given moment of the past. The cunning of potestas is evidenced in its capacity to throw the blanket of the identical over the reverberating world of difference. But even in the flattest of ontologies, how do we know what a thing is? The answer is that everything depends on a function given inside a language game. But then, we are still left with the fundamental questions pounding their way through: How do we know what difference is in each instance? What is the relation of identity and difference?

Heidegger is still haunted by identity as a form of hierarchical logos. Here, we can employ Rorty as he calls out the idealist trick. For Kant the "paradoxical but unquestioned assumption which runs through the first Critique is the assumption that manifoldness is 'given,' and that unity is made" (Rorty 1979, 153). The Kantian machine, as every machine of unification, and Heidegger is still trapped here, is centered on bringing multiplicity to unity; this and only this is the meaning of synthesis. For Kantian synthesis there is no manifold unless we can grasp the universal within a concept. We are trapped in the dungeon of the mind. How do we know if what we see are multiplicities and not a mere representation of universals? In order for Cartesian and Kantian representation to work, we would have to have complete knowledge of the universals and how singularities simply coalesce within them. Heidegger is still trapped in the Kantian axiom that the multiplicity is the illness of the given and thus unifying is the therapeutic that heals life through reason.

Logic is what is possible in fact or in thought. If of the impossible it is said that it exists, then it is possible. If we can think of it, then it is possible. But logic truly applies to relations, to modes; it is formal only once it is given certain conditions. It necessitates a relation, an interaction, so, singulars are not singulars because there is no further discomposure; they are singular because no relation (interaction) is taking place at an x time (at any given time).

In any case, we must first know what it is that can be named in the sense that it lacks any name or that it is a primary element, so at least we must know how to recognize a primary element before we can attach the name to it. But then again, how can we know the primary element without a name, without a "this" and "that"? Without it having a function that can be traced within a relation. Here Aristotle's substance as the form of existence and *Thaten* as the point of transition between potentia and actuality may help us place a finger on top of the uncanny thing. To follow its stealth within an outline and to press some categories out of the flux of the relation. But the name itself remains in slippery silence. Thus, it is here where we must take a firmer stride toward difference as *Energeia* in order to begin to understand the dilemma of potentiality and actuality as proper to *Synergia*. Nevertheless, the stubborn problem that keeps barking back at us is what is a singular. Difference must be differentiated, but must there be some kind of unity? At any extent, it must bear some kind of identity, or everything is sunken on a swamp of sameness. Yes, we must follow the path of flat ontologies, but we need to accelerate its movement, turn it into a kinesis. That everything is the same cannot entail that everything must remain undifferentiated because there would simply be no change, no continuum, no mobility, and, finally, no contingency at all.

Wittgenstein makes it clear in the following passage:

> But what are the simple constituent parts of which reality is composed?—What are the simple constituent parts of a chair?—The bits of wood of which it is made? Or the molecules, or the atoms?—"Simple" means: not composite. And here the point is: in what sense "composite"? It makes no sense at all to speak absolutely of the simple parts of a chair. (Wittgenstein 1986, 47)

The question of simple and composite is again a question not only of language games (flowing in a flat surface) but of a "power play" that stratifies the flows and verticalizes the surface. What is then complexity? The multiple forms in which any things can be talked about, color, form function, relations, beauty, all within complex systems of awarding meaning. We do have to know what we are talking about when we talk about a tree, and if a tree can be isolated from the woods or a rhizomatic plane. We do have to know how to attain information of its affections and synergistic powers. We do have to know if we can cut it down for timber or, not according to what imposition of identities and which distribution of differences. We must never lose sight of the fact that we are still the creatures that name things and that decide the outcomes of their relations. Nothing in the world goes untouched by our mighty power of naming and deciding. Maybe a new ethics will land us in the impossibility of naming anything, or at least not deciding destructive outcomes. But we are still the parasite that is parasitic because it names things. Flat ontologies and speculative turns are valuable (decisive) movements within philosophy; they are ontologically sound and phenomenologically revealing. But the fact remains that we are the creatures that generate the conditions of possibility for life on the planet. For worse, undoubtedly, we have an enhanced power of destruction through naming. Henceforth, it is important to think of what things mean, when can we say that a name exist, when a singularity, when an identity. Surely, we must learn not only to recognize and cope better with difference, being open to it, but most importantly we must overturn the conditions (potestas) that have undermined it, including first of all the normative sanction of Western philosophy. As we have stated repeatedly, the only true world is the world composed of all differences that it takes to make a world.

As pronounced elegantly by Don Quixote (Cervantes 2010 L. 8949) "el primer escalón de las esencias, que es el de las lenguas" ("The steppingstone of essences is that of languages"). Flat ontologies and the speculative turn get us off the high horse of Anthropos but do not tell us how to interact with the world after the deed. We still have a language that is not innocent or neutral, and that compounds every sense of reality. A language that is us and that defines the destiny of cells and infrastructures and the aesthetic weight of the universe upon every pore of our racialized skins.

As Wittgenstein helps us clarify, "If I tell someone without any further explanation: 'What I see before me now is composite,' he will have the right to ask: 'What do you mean by composite'?" (Wittgenstein 1986, 47). There is no model of simplicity or compositeness. One important fact to grasp is that composite is not equivalent to complexity. Composite is not and cannot be a rigid identifier, a model of sorts that determines from an apex the interactions of parts or that programs wider relations. Composite can be simplified or made complex in its use. Great part of the answer is that a thing (individual-identity-difference) is what it does. A thing is its interactions and, as such, there are innumerable forms to enact reality within a context as there are innumerable ways to name it (and no form of identifying the thing and its actions and relations has priority over the others). Have a poet and a biologist establish the simple and composite components of a tree or of a colored square. Which would we say is richer? More precise? Or more valid than the other? The answer reverberates in the transitions and intersections between language games and its power plays.

SAMPLES, NOT MODELS. CONTINGENCY AND RIGID DESIGNATORS

If we extend our logic toward abstractions, we find that the function of abstractions, as a way to exemplify and illustrate certain possible relations, has been abducted by Western philosophy in order to create transcendent models that define order from the obscurity of potestas. Nevertheless, we now know, it makes no sense to say of the model that it exists, or that it does not exist. Being cannot be attributed to a model; a model within language can only be deemed as a sample. The sample (model) is a means of representation of singulars and passages to composites (either in creation or destruction). The only difference, logically speaking, between the sample of green in a haberdashery, the sample of macadamia nut brittle ice-cream, and the sample of humanity in a declaration of rights is that in the latter case something inexistent is elevated to serve as the only possibility of existence of what potestas may decide to apply to it and to every other sample, including the green fabric or the macadamia nut brittle ice-cream.

If the service of models as samples is to extract a piece of a wider reality in order to direct certain traffics of language and clarify positions within in it, we must now ask of rule following within and without samples. Thus, can there be any type of game (language included) without rules? What is the relation between game and rule? And, between language and rule? Can there be a language without rules? Then, is language simply a form?

We are now interweaving a wider spectrum of concepts, names, difference, samples, and rules. We follow through Wittgenstein:

> What the names in language signify must be indestructible; for it must be possible to describe the state of affairs in which everything destructible is destroyed. And this description will contain words; and what corresponds to these cannot then be destroyed, for otherwise the words would have no meaning. I must not saw off the branch on which I am sitting. (Wittgenstein 1986, 55)

It seems Wittgenstein is saying that names must come from, at least, a once existing thing. A thing that once, in the past, existed is a prerequisite for a name, is it not? But then, what about a unicorn or the apocalypse? If something existed in the past and has perished, the only way we can ever know this is by the name it was given and/or its record in history. Some register of someone naming it most persist in time as history. Let us think that there is something like an arch-factuality of red, of round, or of love. Hence, the unicorn may not exist and the apocalypse may never take place (or it may have already taken place), but they both sure have a meaning dependent on a type of relationality within an arch-factuality of language.

Think of years as proper names. The passing of time is counted by a subjective decision. "2020" is just a name, but it becomes proper in its worldwide use, and, to be sure, these facts do not come without bloodshed. Time counting is objective as long as you de-absolutize and contextualize what objective means; in any case it is contextual and dependent. We could try to abstract how numbers starting from the decimal point toward the left are more intense, and textual dependent. While, to the right they are more independent and thus it seems to us they hold their own ground as creators of their own context, a millimetric precision (the pun tells itself) accompanies them. Be the latter true, the dance of the decimal point and the fluctuation of numbers to the right or left still express proper names that require a more extended context in order to exist.

Is it possible to navigate the world without names? At least names that do not rise as a barrier to impede difference. Here we are taking our aim at the possibility of conciliating two terms that have torn apart the ranks of philosophy and power as formidable forceps: naming and difference. We are looking for names that may help us differentiate difference through immanence. Never forgetting that the world may only arrive once we have struck down potestas, but, that such striking down can only be the product of difference in itself. Again, this is the paradox-obstacle of the strangest beauty in political philosophy. We are thus standing against the name as substance. For Wittgenstein, "A *name* signifies only what is an *element* of reality. What cannot be destroyed; what remains the same in all changes" (Wittgenstein 1986, 59).

We must rewind and ask again: What do we gain with metaphysical substances? Nothing else is gained further than the uses that a word has and the fact that said use can circumvent any metaphysical grounding. Parts and wholes, pieces and finished things, are all within the function of language. Hence, language cannot anticipate change (movement and transformations). Within the same logic, language can program certain things (orders decrees), or it can foresee others (eclipse), but most interactions remain contingent (including constituent power and what an eclipse may mean in art or politics). Subscribing to the likes of Meillassoux (2008), foreseeing something (predicting in science) in no assurance for all the possible futures (where everything is contingent). In the relation of parts and wholes there is no movement (just a picture) of decomposing and composing, or rather of the dis-composed and the composed, but they are just separate reels of a continuum (Bergson's spool) brought apart by a decision to do so. Taking a piece of a reel out of a movie can be seen as composing or decomposing; this is fully up to an arbitrary declaration to do so and no final interpretation is possible. But when I say "this" is a decomposable part of x, am I not moving the thing apart, at least ideally? Instead, think of movement and in change, when the seed becomes a tree, a transition (a change) has taken place, and even if it is predictable, its meaning is fully contingent. Consequently, any putting apart (ideal or not) is also contingent. Sudden contingent change forces language out of its tracks. At the sight of contingency, potestas will try to domesticate the change calling it by an old name, harnessing back to actuality as *Entelecheia*. This is why the true power of potestas is the power to name retroactively. But the matter of the fact is that in naming (simples and composites) there resides also a great political power to find new unsuspected contingent relations and to wield new forces from within things and language. Thus, the other true power of potestas is to hierarchize discourses and impose types of disciplines, so things always comport the same way. Do things have a different performance according to the names and descriptions they are given? Yes, absolutely, think of the difference it makes to say that "the river is alive" to saying it is a resource. The essentiality or not of a thing depends always on a power play within language, where samples and rules are simply diverse forms of bringing meaning together, of amassing significance.

Is a name what remains the same in all changes? Think here of Virginia Woolf's *Orlando* (1965). How does the name operate over time and the radical changes of our heroine? According to Saul Kripke, a name, as a rigid designator denotes or refers to the same thing necessarily in all possible worlds in which that thing exists. In his words. "Let's call something a rigid designator if in every possible world it designates the same object, a nonrigid or accidental designator if that is not the case" (Kripke 1980, 48). How is the name Orlando necessary in Woolf's novel? Is Orlando the male writer of The Oak Tree? The desolate child of two empires in Constantinople? Orlando's transmutation, from man to woman, that slashes the entrails of the kingdoms of narratives, is *the* transmutation, or is it? It is still just *one* of the multiple transmutations that Orlando suffers and procreates in her lifetime. Would Orlando lose her essence if she captured the grey goose? To whom do the clay and diamonds of nature belong to? Who has loved so dearly and desperately to lose it all but a name? Is the proposition "Orlando is Orlando" equivalent to Hesperus is Phosphorus? (Kripke 1980). If so, do we recognize Orlando merely as an act of faith, of our giving in, unconditionally, to this universe of truth in which we immerse ourselves by the guiding hand of the author? What does a name carry over the centuries but a thing that can be called to our attention? What is a name but something that vanishes once it has been pronounced?

We are in the business of purging names of the "logic as sublime," as Wittgenstein would put it. A name as a presupposition of use is the going within and beyond any surface. We can only meet things in their use. But we cannot penetrate beneath or inside them without using the very thing we are trying to find out. We always dig our way without noticing that the shovel, the eyesight, the force of the muscles and the command go! are the essence and not what may lie underneath the simple appearance that we are unearthing. We cannot settle the answer of what a name is once and for all, it moves behind and in front of us in its use. It escapes us in the need to use it. If we learned the correct answer, only silence in inaction could follow. But there is nothing out of the ordinary in this, nothing mystifying in saying there is no one answer; simply relish in the possibilities. "Every new day is a little miracle," he thought and fell asleep forever.

A rigid, transcendent description of language, rules, and propositions expels us from the world. Through the definition of words as rules and/or transcendent models we take the word out of any circulation, and by this very same token we arrest all its potentiality. When we rigidly define, we rarely can use the word again; the word becomes of stone; the statute becomes a statue. Henceforth, we must think the decryption of power as tearing down everything that is sublime.

If I were alone, I would not need a name. Hence, we don't use the word "I," or a proposition or name ordinarily as if we were extracting its essence by a very delicate procedure, or if we had to refer only to its essence every time we use these words. To talk is already to talk of language; to talk of language is already to be in the fact of language, in the language game. What remains afar, and thus we must pursue, is the ever-ending capacity of the encryption of power to feast on language games making the opaque seem transparent and the hierarchical flat.

For Deleuze and Guattari, a proper name is the subject of a pure infinitive in a field of intensity (Deleuze and Guattari 1987, 8). Intensity is here opposed to the Cartesian extension where everything is exhausted in its proper place in space, where the Kantian categories can hold every single patch of space in the prison of a formal definition. Intensity knows not of extensive limits; it pours into infinity and explodes space producing multiplicity.

The wave pounds, its water splashes, and the names remain the same. Identity under the guise of a name or an activity of naming is not and cannot become something like a substance to be carried around as a yoke, nor a model that blitzes life and its organization. As we will show, a name is not the ground for logos.

Although it is true that learning a language is learning to use a sequence, it is also true that this sequence has no end point. Some materials could be numbered and limited, the number of letters in an alphabet to begin with. Notwithstanding, the combinations within and beyond grammar and syntaxis but also of musicality and poetry are intense infinities. To say that nothing is new, as in the formula delivered in the Book of Ecclesiastes "What has been will be again, what has been done will be done again; there is nothing new under the sun." That, for example, Beethoven created nothing new in the seventh symphony, that he just rearranged things in a different sequence, or that he gave a diverse order to old things as if he was ordering notes held outside any realm by an archetype (a model) is the stuff of potestas. To hold this would have to mean that we could define at any moment the world as actuality and that the world as actuality is always the "same" (sameness is the key) .... But, the same as what? To itself? Everything is then the same, and no time could be granted. But, then, what does the new consist of? (What is poetry?). If there is no novelty, Beethoven's seventh would be held in some retreated area of the sameness of the world; we could come to it "at any time," but then what role would "at any time" play with the idea of totality? To listen to Beethoven's seventh is to know it changes the very nature of the ordering in space and time of the music. It takes us to a climax and prolongs it deeper and deeper, defying our resistance to intensity, till we are bushed, and nothing else could be expected or wanted but a falling into a dark night. But then, at that moment of a needed collapse, when our body and mind can't cope with more ecstasy, it takes us higher and higher, to new climaxes and new fallings that make space an impossible thing in itself. There are moments we just want to freefall from the music into a gentle instant that is foregone, but the music allows us not but to embrace its climbing vertigo. The seventh makes us hang on the sharp edge of contingency at every note, creating a new order and in the same gest creating the instant from where it is creating it. Beethoven takes the order of tonality to the limit, to a certain type of exhaustion where nothing but silence could follow as a reclaiming of the function of the center, and just at the climax of the production of the model his music de-centers the function and takes it even further, so far, far away, that the model loses all function and has to be re-imagined anew.

Let us take the example of sameness petrified in actuality even further. In a feverish dialogue, the devil mocks Ivan Karamazov for thinking only of sameness as actuality, a frozen picture of time and space lacking any intensity.

> Why, you keep thinking of our present earth! But our present earth may have been repeated a billion times. Why, it's become extinct, been frozen; cracked, broken to bits, disintegrated into its elements, again "the water above the

firmament," then again a comet, again a sun, again from the sun it becomes earth—and the same sequence may have been repeated endlessly and exactly the same to every detail, most unseemly and insufferably tedious. (Dostoyevsky 2005, 598–99)

But the devil also pities himself as the fool that can only think of space as extension and time as a number. As he can only see endless trivial repetition in what every time comes to become anew but is out of the reach of his hands because it is out of his sight.

As I once dreamed, a dying man was condemned to live his life backward instead of dying. Or was it that death was re-living our lives backward? The catch was that in this living backward in time and space, we are condemned to relive every moment, inhabiting a cockpit of flesh, nervous terminals, and moral acuteness from where we feel, see, hear, etc., but cannot intervene. Living an orgasm backward, an illness, a fever, eating, falling, the hand on the stove, crying and the sensations that provoked it, the great encounters, and goodbyes until we die by death by the terminal lust of others, the primal fuck.

In this world of the shadows of actuality, the aim (possibility) of philosophy would only be reduced to liberate difference before the precipice of actuality, to guide it through the labyrinth in order to find a center that holds the truth. Nothing new could ever be brought to light. Are we stretching philosophy to a breaking point? Only if it continues to serve actuality as *Entelecheia*. Otherwise, philosophy could help us humbly, as a light that guides us to difference and out of the oppression of unity-identity-sameness. But then the enigma is reproduced at another scale, what would the antithesis of "I" or of "the one and the same" be? Here, we would not like to talk about antithesis as it rewards us again with the final idea of sameness, as if the world stepped out of itself to look at itself in the coagulated mirror of time. We would like to talk about difference that is namable, but such name is not the burden of a model imposing itself as the only form of life. Therefore, I believe it is already clear why we don't get off the hook simply by saying that things are different, but by letting difference influence our language from its very core of naming, knowing that there is no language without difference.

Returning to the meaning of rigid designators an addition, a correction to Kripke's definition must be made that will become evident as the arguments of the book begin to come together. A rigid designator is the one that denotes or refers to the same thing necessarily in all possible worlds of "contingency." Contingency must qualify the existence of all possible worlds. Let us sharpen the Kripkean description: a rigid designator is a term that serves as the last foundation of reference in all possible worlds. For example, clockwise or counterclockwise is dependent on a decision of a sense in which the clock defines or represents time. In a possible world, counterclockwise (as we know it) could be clockwise (as we know it), but the definition of it is rigid; nevertheless they are both virtual. The rigidity means a last stance of meaning in relation to other meanings. The same thing happens with North and South, etc. For example, "Nixon" refers to the same person in every possible world in which Nixon exists, even if he chose to steal cars instead of elections, and never became president, while "the person who won the United States presidential election of 1968 could refer to Nixon, Humphrey, or any others in the possible position to do so in different possible worlds" (Kripke 1980, 45). There is something necessary and somethings contingent in the name according to what it rigidly designates in each contingent world. The fact of the matter is that contingency does not only open the possibilities of all the worlds but that determines the modality of a name in each world. All names are modal; they jolt in between realities, and they extend and intensify its surroundings as its surroundings compact or dilate the name.

As Kripke extends his theoretical pincers, "Whatever we know about them (rigid designators) determines the referent of the name as the unique thing satisfying those properties" (Kripke 1980, 28). There is then, accordingly, a minimum necessary to name things; this minimum is convention, not essence or nature. Kripke upholds that the necessity of a name, its rigidness within a possible world, obeys to a causal link of uses and traditions against the likes of the theses held by Russell and Frege and by Strawson and Searle. In these latter theories, the name denotes a cluster of concepts (Kripke 1980, 31). They stand near Wittgenstein's family resemblances where a unity of elements is pulled into a vortex of meanings that awards them a significance that is unitary in the sense that it is shared by all elements in a sort of ripple effect.

Against cluster theory, let us ask, how many properties are enough to constitute a cluster? Who determines it? How is this plenty determined as enough? As Kripke insightfully inquires, "Now the question is whether this vote should be democratic or have some inequalities among the properties. It seems more plausible that there should be some weighting, that some properties are more important than others. Strawson, to my surprise, explicitly states that democracy should rule here, so the most trivial properties are of equal weight with the most crucial" (Kripke 1980, 65). But then again, how can we determine cruciality or triviality before the necessity of weighing and before the application of the properties? Determining this is already stipulating the probable, the contingent, and therefore the name of the situation. This is where the cluster theory comes undone. In order to determine the cluster in the way suggested earlier, we would need a model, a certain kind of machine that distributes meaning before the situation, a method that already arranges and thus neutralizes any contingency awarding necessity. Again, the horses are put behind the carriage. Invisibility of the process of choosing the properties of the cluster reigns at full scale. Again, the pre-supposed thwarts any immanent enterprise.

For Russell, it is impossible that the man who taught Alexander did not teach Alexander; that is true of any man who taught Alexander but not of Aristotle. What is necessary is not a cluster of things that are attributable to *x* because they are contingent at every step of the verification through stipulation. Aristotle may have never done any of the things or maybe some, but none of those things are necessary to the name "Aristotle."

In the case of Russell and Frege, imperfection in language is a sin to be redeemed by unitary descriptions that buckle up every meaning of a name. To every unitary description there belongs a unitary name. Until now, the trinity a-priori-necessary-analytic runs down the clock of unity of an intended form of something that is one, that is always the same. Kripke proposes *a-posteriori* necessities, as facts that are necessarily true but that can only be known through empirical findings, such as his classic example of "Hesperus is Phosphorus" or "Cicero is Tully." Through the use of two names that refer to the same object, Kripke is showing us the path to contingency through the plasticity of names imbued in different worlds. As he continues, "Maybe Nixon has moved to the other country and maybe he hasn't, but one is given only qualities. One can observe all his qualities, but, of course, one doesn't observe that someone is Nixon. One observes that something has red hair (or green or yellow) but not whether something is Nixon" (Kripke 1980, 43). The point is well taken but let us take are queue here. Even green, yellow, hair, and of course bachelor are contingent through and through; they cannot be known a-priori or analytically except if we can first propose a world and a context and therefore a network, in which they have meaning. We first learn to use yellow across an array of spectrums where a color palette is not used materially but is made up as we go along the world. Colors appear and disappear from the sample of the color palette; children do not walk around comparing the thing in the leaf of the tree with something inside the color palette. The color palette is the world itself.

If there is contingency, then this world is also contingent and there must be other possible worlds. As Kripke reminds us, "Possible worlds are stipulated, not discovered by powerful telescopes" (Kripke 1980, 45). It is our stipulations that create the possible world, and with it the rules that anyone entering can apply to it. Lamentably, while Kripke opens the door for contingency, he shuts it close with the final stroke of scientific fundamentalism of what composes a rigid designator. According to one of his paramount examples,

> This table is composed of molecules. Might it not have been composed of molecules? Certainly, it was a scientific discovery of great moment that it was composed of molecules (or atoms). But could anything be this very object and

not be composed of molecules? Certainly, there is some feeling that the answer to that must be "no." At any rate, it's hard to imagine under what circumstances you would have this very object and find that it is not composed of molecules. A quite different question is whether it is in fact composed of molecules in the actual world and how we know this. (Kripke 1980, 47)

Must a table in any possible world be composed of molecules? And must such a knowledge be an axiom from stipulating another possible world? But the correct question is truly not only why knowledge, but why "this" knowledge would take center course (eminent modelic transcendence) as the precondition of thinking of possible worlds (that is, of contingency). What is then the element that opens up the possibility of another possible world? Is there an elemental linguistic logical particle to open up the possibility of another world? Is it physical? Whatever it is, it cannot be a model that necessitates its discovery (instead of its stipulation) for opening the other world. If discovery is necessary, then it would mean the end of the possibility itself.

Nevertheless, Kripke continues down the physical path to enliven the rigid designator, "When we think of a property as essential to an object we usually mean that it is true of that object in any case where it would have existed" (Kripke 1980, 48). Thus, a necessary existent can be called strongly rigid. There is more to this than simply names. Is it not rather than what we need is a kind of semirigid contextual character or nuclei of a context as a pliable truth function of the possible world? Not a cluster and its dripping phlegm of truth that engulfs from the center every possible network, but more a family of resemblances. The latter, nevertheless, not of hierarchical affiliation but of alliances and lateral flows of power. We can think of a table without molecules, but could we think of a body without volume? And volume without a context of intensity? For Kripke, first there are rigid designators, *then* there is transworld identity. The confusion of a-prioricity and necessity does not arrive from the definition of rigid designator but due to the dependence to the physical. And here it is problematic because Kripke introduces the concept of definite and formal elementary particles. Notwithstanding, he releases contingency again by declaring that "although we can try to describe the world in terms of molecules, there is no impropriety in describing it in terms of grosser entities" (Kripke 1980, 51). Grosser entities, or rather, the possibility to name any patch of the world is already obstructed and delimited by a previous act of power of definition (elementary particles). Thus, and I cannot emphasize this enough, it is not sufficient to picture and deal with models at macroscopic level, as a legion of kingdoms of obscurity that storm down from heaven. It is as fundamental to think of models in the most micromolecular and discrete level of particles, minute patches that emplace reality, little black holes that swallow difference around them, the miniscule viruses taking hold of a body.

In both cases the force fields they create serve the same purpose, to encrypt power.

Using Kripke's example of gold and the ways of establishing what it is, we must ask simple questions, how does a gold dealer know what gold is? Here there is a multiple scale of forms of understanding drenching the relation. Scientific proof, objectivity, common sense, and common use as well as exchange values. Molecules serve no more than any other given to retrospectively engage the necessity of things. Suppose that we discover or invent a more essential particle, whatever changes the structures of molecules. Then, it was not necessary that in 1970 Kripke said that gold and 79 corresponds to necessity. Another thing would be to leave the meaning of "elementary particle" open as an empty signifier that will always tend toward a minimal configuration of language, but even this, as we will observe, is problematic.

Kripke recognizes the resoluteness of time over language. "One is given, let's say, a previous history of the world up to a certain time, and from that time it diverges considerably from the actual course" (Kripke 1980, 113). Do we construct time as the condition of the circumstances we want to stipulate, or is it history that which we construct? Our thought is here crammed in between the difference of history as narration and time as becoming. History would be here an account of the past until a certain time through a certain means and a certain regard. If we are to conclude that it is a matter of priority, then we must ask who devises it and through what methodical possibility (both political and theoretical). The molecular thesis is self-serving; it attains the objectivity of the object, and it ends up telling us no more than this redundancy "what is molecular is molecular."

Kripke, conscient of the troubles of the molecular thesis, tries to reserve it to a certain form of objects. He concludes that "natural kinds have a greater kinship with proper names than is generally realized. This conclusion holds for certain for various species names, whether they are count nouns, such as 'cat,' 'tiger,' 'chunk of gold,' or mass terms such as 'gold,' 'water,' 'iron pyrites'." (Kripke 1980, 134). But then we must ask if this is due to either an initial baptism or if the relation is fixed as necessary by an act that is plainly retrospective and self-referential. The name "gold" is contingent; it could have been applied to madness. Etymologically, it can be traced to a baptism, but no further than that. Even the sound of the name is arbitrary; the Latin "aurum" means "bright," "shine," "yellow," etc. But these, again, are all exhausted in an etymological line. At the bottom of it, we will find a decision that carries a weight with it, but there is absolutely nothing "molecularly" necessary in the name "gold." It becomes necessary when a bridge is built, hence a "third" term, a third Peircian operation, is needed. We could call gold "element 79," and this would not be necessary at all. The stipulation is fixed. Henceforth, one thing that could pull down names in a sort of necessary fixation is the coherence of language, of the consistency of the name within language: gold, golden, heart of gold, Golden Retriever, golden years, etc., which are all well beyond "element 79." Any derivations are contingently necessary following the rule of coherence of an initial name or condition within a context. We could follow gold as an established atmosphere, but again there is nothing necessary in the origin and the chain of causality; it is simply contingent to multiple uses. Hence, naming would refer not to a cluster of concepts, a molecular necessity, but rather to an organic consistency of something (language) that is finite but unending, finite but incalculable, finite but unlimited. If we look at the problem this way, we begin to understand that *a-priori*, even for Kripke, is a two-step statement, a two-step truth, where the first step consists of establishing a formal realm of logic (possibility) where x is truth only of y (formal realm), and only then does truth become necessarily extracted (where x is necessarily true).

Trying to capture the more particular element, the constitutive particle is not a question of qualities but of contrasting particulars to other particulars within the contingent freedom of naming. When we look for the relation of names and particulars, it is not a matter of choosing the right particular but the correct form of naming that does not privilege any particular as origin or model. When we think of a table before us, we might put it in another world, make it round, smaller, sitting in fewer legs, or change the material it is made of, but how do we know where and when we can still call it a table? Furthermore, we can "stipulate" to call it a turtle, but then all tables must be turtles. If we hold that only molecules rule reality (in all possible worlds) then the word table, is indeed moot, since all reference to objects, as opposed to qualities, has disappeared. It has become the indistinguishable sameness of the model. Besides, with what quality or particle would we begin with? This need for parting from fixated elementary particles as a form of reconstitution of a possible world would necessarily impose the need to reconstitute the actual world bit by bit, phase by phase, and motion by motion, as it cannot avoid the concentration of its particles. There are no particles, singulars, without there being at least two signs and a relation to a third that interprets it.

Kripke replies Wittgenstein's woes of the model meter that it cannot be said to be a meter long, nor that it is not a meter long, by stating, "Part of the problem which is bothering Wittgenstein is, of course, that this stick serves as a standard of length and so we can't attribute length to it" (Kripke 1980, 54). Here, what is at play is Wittgenstein's unmatched role in modern philosophy as the destructor of models and thus the settler of the paradoxical role of models as simply samples. Recently[2] the standard of the kilo that was a thing that stood in the place of the abstract kilo has been changed to a measure. The change from something material (objective) whose shape and weight may vary by the action of time to something ideal—a universal, provides a great example of the reduction of models (universals) to samples. Is any definition of the kilo in itself universal? Neither was the object that previously represented its universality universal, nor the new ideal reference universal (a-priori and analytical) in itself. Both are made so by a decision and the uniformization of said decision throughout a network of users. It is all a matter of "fixing the reference" of the rigid designator. The only advantage of one measurement over the other is that the second, being ideal, is resilient to the march of time (decay) but is still simply a representation, a sample that stands in the place of something else. None of them, as Wittgenstein understood, can be said to be a kilo in weight.

Kripke assumes the defensive

> by stipulating that "one meter" is to be a rigid designator of the length which is in fact the length of S at X. So this does not make it a necessary truth that S is one meter long at x. In fact, under certain circumstances, S would not have been one meter long. The reason is that one designator (one meter) is rigid and the other designator ("the length of S at x") is not. (Kripke 1980, 56)

But could we not reverse the horns of this dilemma? Could it not also be that according to each universe or world the rigid designator varies, it simply must be an element of the proposition or the stipulation that is in a mutual relation of meaning with other elements? In a possible world, the length of S at X defines what a meter is, and so, if it is not stipulated otherwise, this could be carried on to any possible adjacent world. Nevertheless, the distance of S at X could also vary its context of measurement if it is stipulated as such in order to carry it to another world. If in another possible world, we say, "look he is about 1,700 millimeters tall," as odd as it may sound, we are bringing in the metric system as a rigid designator and the complete fixing of a reference in such a possible world.

A fundamental question is how things can be differentiated and at the same time be unique and equal. The question flows between difference and sameness; between uniqueness and equality; between equality and difference; and between sameness and uniqueness.

For Kripke, a name is fixed through causality. Causality is public and social and is linked through a chain of tradition. As he explains, "Someone, let's say, a baby, is born; his parents call him by a certain name. They talk about him to their friends. Other people meet him. Through various sorts of talk, the name is spread from link to link as if by a chain" (Kripke 1980, 91). What is paramount for Kripke is that an initial baptism has taken place. Although this is an empirical picture and it surely can describe how names get around, it does not deliver us into the political milieu of the possibility of naming. Baptism is problematic not only for the religious undertones but also for the redundancy between initial and baptism. Since we are asking for the very possibility of naming, then the problem of the empirical becomes a question not only of parts and wholes but also of politics (who counts). The importance is not so much how a name is acquired or how it is used in timespace but how it can remain within a flat ontology and distribute meaning, affect, and be affected by the neighboring and relational names as well as within a community of users.

Marks as reference could be an initial baptism, but to a certain extent the original baptism is originating but not original. It depends to a degree on a free decision to name; it depends on a freedom and capacity of who names and then spreads (transportation or transduction) with no formula of success of the maintaining of the reference to the name. There are no properties of the references. The name has been passed by tradition from link to link. Nevertheless, as there are hierarchies of subjects, there are hierarchies of traditions.

The initial baptism is problematic even at a descriptive level. For example, were "Ricardo," and its Germanic roots of "rich and hard" taken into consideration when I was named? Have I kept the name alive? At any extent the closest people to me found it easy to call me by that and many other pet names without doubting of the fact that they were always referring to me and without getting into a philosophical helter-skelter in doing so. There is never a traceable originality of proper names as belonging to subjects as agreed by Kripke. Ruth Barcan Marcus speaks of "tags," a much more malleable concept where the meaning of the name, once given, is exhausted by the referential function it begins to have (Barcan Marcus 1961, 309). The importance of tags is that they are in a relation and they establish a soft center over which power re-writes its history over and over again. This division of time between before and after the tag, means that tags do not carry across a heavy descriptive content, but that, rather, they absorb re-inscriptions as they propel its own meaning into the world; they are permanently in a state of symbiosis.

The dispute, again, is who does the tagging and under what circumstances does it occur. Tagging and its consequences are not a free activity; they are encrypted. For Kripke, the important thing of naming is "fixing a reference" (Kripke 107). But here we are getting a direct bitter taste of the political problem of the relation of the thing to itself, of the thing as a sign that means something for a third (Peirce's thirdness) and to the fact that every relation of a thing with itself is a pre-meaning as it is pre-linguistic.

Kripke brings to the floor a discussion of the name as essences and essences as models quoting Timothy Sprigge.

> The internalist [which means the believer that there are some essential properties] says that the Queen must have been born of royal blood. [He means that

this person must have been of royal blood.] The anti-essentialist says there would be no contradiction in a news bulletin asserting that it had been established that the Queen was not in fact the child of her supposed parents, but had been secretly adopted by them, and therefore the proposition that she is of royal blood is synthetic. (Sprigge in Kripke 1980, 110)

Let us observe that here there is essence as long as it has been determined so in a previous configuration (agreed or not, that is, as part of a reciprocal kind of game or a power play). Blood is essential, only insofar as it is deemed essential for x. Henceforth, there is only a necessity when the contingent arbitrator of language determines it so. This is as good example as any to differentiate the magnitudes determined by language games established in flat surfaces of equality and power plays. Think what happens when we come before a football game between almighty Real Madrid and working-class Rayo Vallecano. Both teams are on equal conditions once the referee gives the starting whistle. Eleven players against eleven players, the same rule book applies for all, but, and the big but is, power. Kripke does not ask how it is we got on to such an unbalanced pitch and what this means for naming and necessity. Without it being a question of "how" we got there, and without really highlighting the relations and short-circuits of power, all we are allowed to see is a docile reality that folds peacefully into itself without revealing its true political colors. But we already know this flat surface is bloated and contaminated from within. We are before interconnected spheres that are solid, and that sprout from alternative bases or realities. They are surely interlocking, but they are also multidimensional and laden. What we see through the theory of encryption of power is that the inequality in the interlocking is erased once the last level attains a sort of linguistic certificate of equality of relations of force. Power relations are leveled off in the great scorched earth policy of potestas. Hence, be it true that every form of naming sets forth a set of features, that it ignites a kind of reality, we must add, yes, but this does not tell us if it is encrypted.

MULTIPLE WORLD INTERPRETATION

Through the theory of the rigid designator, Kripke is arriving at a semantics for modal logic. So let us enter this "Garden of forking paths" that is before us. One of the fundamental reaches of modal logic is to reshape the functions of necessity and contingency. Again, the rigid designator illuminates the play at hand. A statement is *possible* if it is true in at least one possible world; a statement is *necessary* when it is true in all possible worlds. Here our guiding concepts of actuality, potentia, virtuality. and extension are also quivering to the core. For example, distinguishing between multiple worlds, for Lewis (1973). is simply a question of indexicality of actuality, that is, we identify the "actual world" from all other worlds by being in it. The world we are in, from where we could imagine or extend the idea of infinite worlds, has only one difference from the others—the fact that we are nominating the others from it. It is the "this" of all other "this and that's." A cockpit of infinity, if you will.

Let us now join the theories of the multiverse, Everett's "Multiple World Interpretation" (MWI), with modal logic and naming. Doing so is not simply a means to liberate our inquiry but to test out our hypotheses. We are not worried about the scientific pedigree of quantum theories of multiverses. It has been noted that it may not be falsified, or as held by the likes of Steinhardt, no experiment can rule out a theory if the theory provides for all possible outcomes (Steinhardt 2014). On the contrary, we delight in the possibility of worlds free of paradigms and inflective theories that capture its movements; we magnify the opportunity granted by them to transgress dull actuality (potestas) from potentia and contingency. The sacred order of the scientific cemetery does not belittle us.

Everett's Many World Interpretation is a first step to thwart Leibniz "best of possible worlds" as the dream of he who teaches us conformity to power as potestas through necessity. Although he is calling the attention of the paradoxical observations of wave functions (ψ) in quantum mechanics (Everett 1973, 5), the effects for philosophy are extensive and intense. Everett is signaling the shortcomings of theories of quantum mechanics that rely on just one observer and thus a single observation method in worlds infested by a multiplicity of sets of observables. To a manifold, a unique observer fails in space and time. Hence, no picture may be given from one perspective (solipsism). As he puts it,

> It is now clear that the interpretation of quantum mechanics with which we began is untenable if we are to consider a universe containing more than one observer. We must therefore seek a suitable modification of this scheme, or an entirely different system of interpretation. Several alternatives which avoid the paradox are: *Alternative* 1: To postulate the existence of only one observer in the universe. This is the solipsist position, in which each of us must hold the view that he alone is the only valid observer, with the rest of the universe and its inhabitants obeying at all times except when under his observation. (Everett 1973, 6)

Consequently, a richer and more congruent observation system arrives only if "Observation processes are to be described completely by the state function of the composite system which includes the observer and his object-system, and which at all times obeys the wave equation" (Everett 1973, 8). Everett's conclusion, that resounds so mightily with our enterprise, is that "All processes are considered equally (there are no 'measurement processes' which play any preferred role)" (Everett 1973, 8). Nevertheless, Everett's thesis is not to be deemed through the flat platform of the Cartesian mind, as if the mind would be capable of splitting, as Buda, in as many universes as it takes for the mind to think. As if the quality and quantity of the worlds depended on the "mirror image" (Rorty) of the mind. Although the Everettean universe is observer-dependent, the upshot is that no object, and indeed no form of observation holds sway to a unique form of truth over any other. As he states, "It is therefore improper to attribute any less validity or 'reality' to any element of a superposition than any other element, due to this ever-present possibility of obtaining interference effects between the elements. All elements of a superposition must be regarded as simultaneously existing" (Everett 1973, 107) The multiple worlds are pure virtuality; their properties are a freeway for the intensive.

Of all the worlds that it takes to make a world, we chose none so we could embrace them all. "Every new day is a little miracle, he thought, and fell asleep forever, below a blade of grass."

From every possible present, a new virtual present is detached as infinite maize from an infinite cob. Infinite universes sprouting in infinite directions. For a way the world is, there is a distinct possibility of another world that is otherwise. Borges' garden as infinite pathways into infinite realities. No present is actual, no future is predestined, and no past is irrevocable. All states may be broken. Borges' labyrinth is a book, the book is a labyrinth, and they are all invisible labyrinths of time. No circularity, no carving the celestial vault of the tower of Babel, as in Chiangs beautiful story (2002), to unearth the same earth on which Babel stands on. No circularity of a book that ends how it begins. As in Borges' story, to choose it all, to choose invisibility "he chooses one and eliminates the others; in the fiction of Ts'ui Pên, he chooses—simultaneously—all of them. He creates, in this way, diverse futures, diverse times which themselves also proliferate and fork" (Borges 1964, 37). One forking path upon the other creating others.

Time to ponder, as only questions may quiet down the frantic march of time. Is the forking a question of time or space? Both? Can these forks diverge infinitely or come back to flood the others? But then, is there an original forking? A center in the spiderweb of time? Time as infinity is the swarming of all becoming where all becoming makes up the stuff of time in the sense that it is indistinguishable from all other becomings. (By the way capitalism has learned an essential sorcery of multiple worlds, it kills itself in one world to resuscitate stronger for its next destructive stint.)

According to Everett's theory, everything that could have happened but did not come to be actual has actually happened in the past of another universe.

Everything that could happen but did not happen happened in another world. Necessity in one world does not imply necessity in the other. Hence, the only true necessity is utter contingency. There is no arbitrariness in this. Many-worlds interpretation assumes realism, while actuality is its founding formal structure.

The hornet's nest of the theory is the use of the concept of actuality. Going back to Lewis' principle of indexicality, it is clear that the actual world is one of the many possible worlds. Henceforth, the name "actual" necessitates the name "now" to be actual—a minimal point in space and time where to slice open the multiplicity of worlds; this spins us off to a new dizzying set of problems. Actuality, as the minimal given, the key to open all possible universes is hugely problematic in itself.

Allow me to problematize the use of actuality through a paradox. If there is an infinity of parallel universes, then it is absolutely necessary that there is a universe where parallel universes are impossible, hence the infinity of parallel universes is limited and thus finite.

Let us dig in further, through other tunnels. Actuality means the need of one universe where we could open up and plunge into the others. Therefore, a "now," an Aristotelean "nun," is needed as the minimal opening for the construction of time-space to do so. As we described in another text, the nun is "a non-temporal particle that affords time existence so that change can hold its substance. The nun is a construction of a name, a graph, as a numbering name that once said is devoured back into the current of time" (Sanín-Restrepo 2018, 194). Ultimately the fundamental Aristotelean name is "nun"; it is the nonbeing of time where time is made possible for beingness, the name that opens up the possibility of being in time. I would like to think the nun as the no-name in a no-time where the possibility of being is conjured from time. But here, the forest thickens the most. If everything is detained, held at a stop in the necessity of "this" universe that measures and compares all the others, then there is a stabilization process that names "what is the case." A funnel to ordain the ripple effect of all the other indexes. Nevertheless, in the acceleration (proper to multiplicity), the visual artifact would allow us to observe that the center of the ripple effect is turned into curvature of the paths of time pulling all universes toward it in a centripetal motion and thus elevating eminence of the "actual world" as a hierarchical vortex. Thus, we could not regard the opening of multiplicity as a "superposition that must be regarded as simultaneously existing," as Everett's aforementioned conclusion. Again, in actuality, everything is detained, held at a stop in the necessity of *the* universe that measures and compares the others. This would suppose the need of one actual universe to create all others. This is nothing but dependence, and at least, ideally, would taint the very possibility of the "alternate" and the "parallel" as uniquely different. There is a stabilization process that names "what is the case," a conduit that ordains the universes under the guise of one of them. Among the infinite possible worlds, there is one that serves as a kind of milieu for all the other worlds.

We are asking a very specific question: what is the time unit needed for the bifurcation? Or is time also senseless? I mean, as the multiverse is not only spatial but temporal, when we plunge into other universes, at what time or ordering of time (*nun*) do we do so? At what expressive form of now is every possible universe bifurcated? What is the value? What is the name? Or, are these questions a form to pull the problem back to the Cartesian mind? But, let us think simply, without invoking the mind problem, that if there is no time unit of bifurcation, then all universes are piled up in space and are undiscernible. To think the latter, we can undo the Cartesian mind. It is not a simple matter of knowledge but of Kripkean stipulation. To think a multiverse, there are infinite times and spaces, nonetheless, to inhabit one and differentiate it from another we need an opening, a link to connect them, but this "*nun*" is never neutral, it is always . . . yes! Also a matter of power.

To the question of what is a now, what is a fact logically follows. What is (the) instant? We must think of the time it takes for a fact to be formed (distinctive fact), but then the problem arrives in the form of what a distinctive fact means or represents, or how it can be named. Are we inside the total dependence of the fact to the relation and the latter as our capacity to dislodge time from itself? Can we only perceive the words "difference" "multiplicity" as they leave our actuality but not their probable outcome in another universe? Let us pay attention to the fact that another world becomes through the exercise of "this" difference and to what it is that is blocked there by a form of identity that we must recognize as coming forth from our world. Taking it up a notch. Is the multiple world interpretation a result or a cause of wave function? Does wave function need the interpretation or is the interpretation the result of wave function? And hence, does wave function demonstrate the many-worlds interpretation or does the many-worlds interpretation explain wave function?

The idea is not to oppose quantum mechanics with the power of poetics but to poetize the former. There is a hard nugget in quantum mechanics that even poetics has a hard time biting on. Accordingly, every time a quantic event occurs the universe is divided into two parallel opposed universes. Hence, whatever happens in one, the exact contrary happens in the other. Certainly, we cannot lose sight that we are speaking of facts, states, objects, and functions. What is bothersome, in taking hold of the MWI, is the idea of the "contrary" when enouncing the possibility of endless parallel universes. Does not "contrary" mean one? Does it mean we must know what the state of affairs are at any given moment in any given space-time, so we declare (prove) that the contrary has happened? "Contrary" necessarily supposes a system of equivalence with a hard identity as its origin. Thence, what is deeply problematic is that the idea of contraries is anchored in binarity, and not any kind of binarity, but one that begs the necessity to decide between normality and exception, between positives and negatives. As if these terms could be adduced from one single identity of states of affairs. If the latter is true, then we would be in the need, every time we break into a new universe, to depart from eminent models, to have them as a launching pad, and therefore cut off any possibility of immanence. This also implies the superposition of finalized forms that cannot be but actual and henceforth necessary.

It is absolutely clear that the jump to an alternate world in quantum mechanics is performed from a stable and fully determinable state. Hence the point of departure is fully known and objective. Nevertheless, from poetics (e.g., critical theory), we cannot know the state from which we begin; this state must be stipulated if we are to talk of immanence and power as constitutively different. Ultimately, critical theory cannot reproduce the instances of the given. It cannot be a mere bizarre copy of the determinable states of normality, of what it is putting on the ledge of criticism. I have been adamant insisting that potestas must be confronted in its own terms, as the producer of the dimensions of our reality, but it cannot be duplicated when we pierce it through critique.

In considering multiple worlds, it is clear that potestas is the world that has no other possible world. It possesses no "contrary" to it, no underworld that would rise to annihilate it. Its most hideous and effective feature is precisely that it has no reflection, no double side; it is a frozen state of identity and oppression. Potestas is thus the paradox of existence. That which cannot exist outside itself, that which is not even different in itself. Accordingly, democracy, as the infinite extension of intense difference, is necessary in all possible worlds.

NOTES

1. To be sure our position is fully against Platonism. As Cooper explains, "Now about the simple elements Plato says not only that they cannot be analyzed into simpler parts but also that if they could be analyzed then they could not only be named but also said" (202a 6-b 2) (Cooper 1990, 156).

2. https://www.theguardian.com/science/2018/nov/16/the-weight-is-over-kilogram-redefined-at-emotional-conference.

Chapter 5

Objects and Social Performances
Seeing as Gathering

THE POWERFUL ILLUSION OF THE SOCIAL

We are coming into the junction of fundamental concepts for our philosophical endeavor. According to Heidegger, objects and performances constitute the social significance of the readiness-to-hand. Social practices are the medium in which the ready to hand are judged and given directionality within a plane of existence. Whatever is ready to hand is responded to through a social practice that defines its "in order to" ("das Um-zu") constituting it either as an object or a performance.

As stated in Being and Time

> Taken strictly, there "is" no such thing as equipment. To the Being of any equipment there always belongs a totality of equipment, in which it can be this equipment that it is. Equipment is essentially "something in-order-to" ["etwas um-zu . . ."]. A totality of equipment is constituted by various ways of the "in-order-to," such as serviceability, conduciveness, usability, manipulability. (Heidegger 2001, 97/68)

Imagine a pastoral, the Heideggerian social practice as the hands that shape the clay of the ready to hand in the sense that it gives it a meaning, a place, and a directionality as objects and performances. Any individuation of objects is achieved through the role it plays within social practices. Consequently, the role awarded by social significance marks the movable relation of its "toward-which." Let us imagine now an industrial pastoral and how capitalisms success depends on creating objects and performances in a massive repetitive scale, re-signifying each of them and pinning them down to exchange value and desire. Imagine, then, how in our days that the hands that knead the clay are algorithms held at an arms-length of a minute elite, but now the clay is not extensive but virtual, and the hands that knead disappear behind a mountain of indecipherable processes and digital highways. Let us keep these images rotating in front of us while we penetrate objects and performances.

It is clear that objects by themselves mean nothing, communicate nothing; only when they are involved in a state of affairs do the obtain meaning. But said meaning is complex and does not limit itself to a definition of objects within a set of exhausting categories. Categories, as the internal working of objects, have no control over the interface of the workings of things within complexes. Internal properties may signal the logical form of objects (as dressing them for the outside world), but the combination of objects in a state of affair is complex because they do not only relate to other objects but form further state of affairs and therefore new performances.

Nevertheless, the first question we must follow is where do social practices come from? Are social practices already set up on their own as a transparent and pacific medium that awards directionality to things within a flat surface? Imagine how, in our three pastorals, society is a blurry and multidimensional compound that is itself the result of colossal combinations of forces. How a thing appears to social practices is already encrypted and destined by power (Artificial Intelligence defining at what rate to feed the social media through algorithms that award the value of visibility to things and how the visibility of theses thing comes around by other algorithms carefully cooked in a laboratory of marketing that reflect and feed our desires).

The second question is regarding the inquiry of contingency and necessity. Any state of affairs that does exist could have been otherwise (contingency). Henceforth, any state of affairs is simply possible but not necessary. Consequently, Heidegger demand that what marks out the ready to hand is a totality of states of affairs (actual and possible) is broken at its seams by the fact that what makes up for reality is always a contingent form of totality. Thus, totality as contingent means that the possibility of said totality is always suspended by an element that is absent in the relation of the state of affairs and the totality. Nevertheless, if a totality could be otherwise, this logically means that reality is not total but open and infinite. Totality and contingency are mutually exclusive.

Now, let us regard this last problem from another perspective. Let us hold that an object is fashioned by internal properties, that these internal properties are the ones that define the possibilities of their combinations, and that these combinations are the states of affairs. If combinations are contingent, what kind of contingency are we speaking of?

Wittgenstein approaches the problem from the elasticity of the uses of language, "But doesn't the fact that sentences have the same sense consist in their having the same *use?*—(In Russian one says 'stone red' instead of 'the stone is red'; do they feel the copula to be missing in the sense, or attach it in *thought?*)" (Wittgenstein 1986, 20). In the "same sense," means "same use," or rather, in the terms of the same use they have the same sense. This view snaps us from the claws of substances and totalities, but it forsakes one essential element, hierarchy, and the role it plays in transforming language and forms of language, as well as syntax and grammar within a language game. In short, it neglects the role of power plays.

If we forsake hierarchies, and the intentions and uses produced and imbued in them, we fail to see the full dimensionality of the game, (linguistic multidimensionality and political intersectionality among others). We are left only with a sound that is strange and intonations that are peculiar. Hierarchies are instilled in the language game, as well as obedience, separations, and possibilities. They are taught in a language game and transmitted through it, but most importantly they are concealed within it. Potestas hides in language like time hides in a clock. This is the vascular system of power.

To get a sharper picture of what it is we are proposing, let us follow Wittgenstein's departure from the dogmatism of the *Tractatus* and from every dogmatism that procures to establish a final and complete theory of it all.

> But how many kinds of sentence are there? Say assertion, question, and command?—There are *countless* kinds: countless different kinds of use of what we call "symbols," "words," "sentences." And this multiplicity is not something fixed, given once for all; but new types of language, new language-games, as we may say, come into existence, and others become obsolete and get forgotten. (Wittgenstein 1986, 23)

And then he goes on to define a language game as follows "Here the term '*language-game*' is meant to bring into prominence the fact that the *speaking* of language is part of an activity, or of a form of life" (Wittgenstein 1986, 73). Let us think again of how ostensive definitions are preceded by a complex training in questioning, commanding, and asserting. A totality of involvements or the inner workings of the object do not come first in learning. It is not the object that irradiates its own light and creates a projection of figures that mark the world as a meaningful something. Rather well, it is the potentiality of the location of the object, its demarcation of a territory, its networking in the face of other objects where we can begin to talk of "in order to." The object is never alone, but neither is society a transparent relation where we can extract the thing as its pure effect. To represent the concept of society as a frame and actor of performances is to afford another name for transcendent models, one that safely hides in disciplines that are desperate to redeem themselves before the tribunal of science. Social performances advance nothing as they are a given, a form of eminence designed to besmirch difference in the name of a mythological consistency of forms. The matter is not to drop a blot of ink in a white paper and see how this creates forces of attractions between colors and forms, but to partake in the language festival that all possible workings can bring about. To regard steadfastly the multiple levels of participation within the event.

PRIVATE LANGUAGES AND THE "VISUAL ROOM"

"Because what they call passion actually is not some emotional energy, but just the friction between their souls and the outside world." (Andrei Tarkovsky's "Stalker")

What happens when we paint a picture, or when we ask a collective to imagine a possible world other than the one (is it one?) we inhabit? The question is not if you can feel like these others or invade their "visual room" to see how they paint their own picture, or even if anyone can think like the others. The question is if we can communicate like these others within the confine of the proposed world. One good example of the gap we are considering is the distance (abyss) between what dreams we have and our capacity to represent them in words to others.

So, you say what you feel is private, then describe to me how it works, how is that you feel. You say the color in your mind is unique? That it is only in there and not out here for all of us? Could we at least try to see in this palette of 1,001 shades of colors which color is the one that comes closer? None? Then, is it not possible that is not a color you are thinking of?

Let us recall Moore's paradox as used in The Philosophical Investigations "I believe that this is the case is used like the assertion 'This is the case'; and yet the hypothesis that I believe this is the case is not used like the hypothesis that this is the case" (Wittgenstein 1986, 190). "It is raining, and I believe it is not raining" is a paradox because one does not contradict the other, because I can say "I believe" in not x while asserting x. "I believe" carries a different meaning if it is an assertion or a hypothesis. I believe x is the case is used as the assertion "this is the case." The hypothesis "I believe this is the case" is also a hypothesis of "this is the case." Wittgenstein's fascination with this paradox is that while what is said appears absurd, it may nevertheless be true, logically consistent, and not contradictory.

"I believe" can never be an assertion only of a state of mind. To believe is to believe in something outside the state of mind. To believe is not belief on its own token, within a vacuum; to believe is to believe in a fact or a performance. Nevertheless, to believe in the fact (right or wrong) is independent of the fact (be it asserted or not). One can mistrust one's own senses, but not one's own belief. That is why we never say, or at least it is absurd to say, "I believe I believe." "I misbelieve" is not the case here, for we would arrive at something like "I misbelieved the believe." We can say "I believe my finger is broken" but not "I believe my finger is in pain." A man that has never been in touch with a society of humans can talk to himself, only it would be impossible for him to discuss what he is saying with us until a common form of communication is garnered through communication itself. This is not to deny that inner processes take place; of course they do, but if they are to exist as language (if they are to be communicated), they must do so in an ordinary (usable or sharable) language. They must convey a knowledge and a sense that lets them speak out. No doubt inner processes take place; the question is that they do not develop a private language. Hence, when the emotion is shared, it has to be so in a public language, in a common space of meaning (*agora* and *polis*). This does not mean a unique form of communication; language never functions in one regular way. It is not about denying that you-remember, it is to avoid that when you say "I remember," then it follows no one else can. We cannot say to the man that is in pain and swears there is nothing like it to look into a palette of pains (as we did with color), but we can say to him, this is a typical pain in cases of appendicitis. To will "will" is absurd; will is as a movement of the arm autonomous of other regimes of mind, actions, and so on. We recognize will within a context that is pregnant of meaning (symbols, attitudes, etc.).

On the other side of this apparent twisted logic, Wittgenstein responds with his de-mystifying arsenal "Don't look at it as a matter of course, but as a most remarkable thing, that the verbs 'believe,' 'wish,' 'will' display all the inflexions possessed by 'cut,' 'chew,' 'run'" (Wittgenstein 1986, 190). To understand that it is illogical to say, "I seem to believe," think of how we don't "cut" in the vacuum, but we cut something, I do not chew vacuum, I chew things.

We come upon one of Wittgenstein's most beautiful "representations," the "visual room." In his words,

> The visual room is the one that has no owner. I can as little own it as I can walk about it, or look at it, or point to it. Inasmuch as it cannot be anyone else's it is not mine either. In other words, it does not belong to me because I want to use the same form of expression about it as about the material room in which I sit. The description of the latter need not mention an owner, in fact it need not have any owner. But then the visual room cannot have any owner. "For"—one might say- "it has no master, outside or in." (Wittgenstein 1986, 398)

As the visual room teaches us, all those things you imagine and you call yours share in bits and pieces of something that belongs to everyone, even the mode you compose those ideas are multiply shared in language through a manifold of representations. Consequently, there is an impossibility of getting rid of methods of representation, this would equate to ridding ourselves from language. Nonetheless, what is paramount is avoiding that no one representation gets enthroned as the transcendent form of communication; what is crucial is then ridding politics, as constituent power, of forms of representation; this difference, I believe is by now perfectly clear.

CAN THE DUCK-RABBIT BE ENCRYPTED?

Here we can bring to our floor another of Wittgenstein's tropes, "noticing an aspect" through his iconic picture of the duck-rabbit. "We are interested in the concept and its place among the concepts of experience" (Wittgenstein 1986, 191). Let us regard the ready to hand as " noticing an aspect." Is there a final form of the duck-rabbit? Can we introduce a deep problematic to the "in order to" of the ready to hand through the duck-rabbit game? Well, we already know its explanatory and heuristic powers. Nevertheless, let us begin the experiment anew.

Take a description: Wittgenstein's idea that the image is definitely of the duck-rabbit. Does this description exhaust the interpretations? Or can it only circumscribe them? Consider the possibility that physically what we are to interpret is not absent or hidden. Rather, what previous circumscriptions of interpretation (encryption) have done with the object is to abscond the multiplicity of possibilities of meaning. The assertions or possibilities of it have been shaven off and reduced. It is thus the possibility of language, and not the image, that has been mystified and absconded. The problem here is not that the object is not an object of visibility (the duck-rabbit is not hidden), but that the availability of the processes of interpretations, the upfront limitations of combinations of words (order) that are possible to apply to it, are made scarce. Think of how in processes of gentrification of art, the mountains of layers of interpretations of experts over the subject serve to conceal and to project an identitary constitution of meanings and to seal them off to any democratic fathoming. "We interpret it" is always under the convention of context, but this convention (circumscription) of context is always encrypted. This is the heart of the matter; we can all see x as one thing or another, but we can only name, describe, and believe (as we chew, run, etc.) in a very particular way, a dissected, directed, and partialized form. Is it not this what our pastorals teach us?

"Now I see this" is a change in my perception. In order to determine the change of perception, there has to be a final judgment as to what the final image truly is. Nevertheless, who holds the truth of the final image? Of the complete picture? How would you know that "seeing x" is simply a perception as it were incomplete of something that you (or someone else) knows is complete? But then again, how do you know it is complete in order to correct my perception? It is a question of a power play. At least we would require a very solid convention that was agreed upon as to the finalized form of certain things. The image, any image, is infinite; we can accord a final point within a context, for example, what are the chemicals, colors, textures, meanings, symbols, and perspectives used in the painting of Picasso's "Old Guitarist"? But if the possibility of imagining the picture is encrypted, what is there left for subalterns to construct in difference other than the crumbs thrown in the air by the hand that rocks the truth?

For Wittgenstein, the object called duck-rabbit remains the same as a particular organization of space. He remarks

> I suddenly see the solution of a puzzle-picture. Before, there were branches there; now there is a human shape. My visual impression has changed and now I recognize that it has not only shape and colour but also a quite particular "organization."—My visual impression has changed;—what was it like before and what is it like now?—If I represent it by means of an exact copy—and isn't that a good representation of it?—no change is shewn. (Wittgenstein 1986, 196)

We must shake off our reverential fears. I see no equivocation in saying "and now it looks like a duck," I am still describing my perception, and it goes just after "I see a rabbit . . . wait, now I see a duck." Does it boil down to a question of time? Perceptions do not exhaust themselves in the act; they are dynamic over a period of time. Wittgenstein recalls the experience to a "changing aspect," but then again, does not everything, in some degree, have a changing aspect? You may believe in anything and this belief has meaning, and it does so as an assertion. The one thing a belief may not hold as an assertion is if it pretends to be a hypothesis. The wall is thus built between what we establish as an assertion and as an opinion, as a hypothesis and as an assertion. But the problem also overflows into authority as the problem of representation that expresses things and in doing so changes the affections of the world, altering its reality. It is raining and I believe it is not raining is a paradox because one does not contradict the other, because I can say "I believe" in not x while asserting x.

Wittgenstein toys with the idea that someone who has never seen a duck, or a rabbit, may describe it as accurately as anyone familiar with the duck-rabbit. And this is a fundamental key for decryption. In this case, both observers need to share some common language and a form of life. Yet the most relevant point made here is that there is no privilege of language for either description, which is to say for either approximation to the things of the world. We have language precisely so that we may communicate difference. And difference in perception, in pictures, in sense impression, and in noticing an aspect are all multidimensional pieces of a puzzle that has no end form. The very possibility to communicate (ontologically) lies in the infinitude of difference.

Sometimes the vision strikes me as x and sometimes as y, but I can always know what x and y are to me in (their) different temporalities. The question is if the temporalities of x and y change due to my "striking as," but also that there is no need to be "always' aware of x or y when we are seeing. We just gather it and put it down and turn away; it becomes part of our world. Is there an urgency, a need or a gamble to decipher it? It depends how it is involved in a language game. If it is just hanging there, it wouldn't excite our attention for too long; we would get rid of it instantaneously as an eye sore that obstructs our clean sight of the world. But, is not precisely something that blocks our way to the world part of the world? Even more so, something that disfigures the completeness of the picture and therefore promises contingency as its bearing?

In familiarity, knowing my way about, as well as seeing, is preceded by a tradition of sight, descriptions, analysis, etc. I never see for the first time as it were. I always see through my language. Seeing is always a composition of language; it is always conceptual, it is always within a tradition. Seeing as gathering and seeing as composition is always within the already existing forms of language. "Regarding as" and "seeing" are didactic. Someone can outline the physical limits of the drawing (of what it is I am supposed to see, and this will carry already a predisposition on my behalf, then the question "what do you see?" is a more open affair). Any didactic tends to establish limitrophe lines of where it is we must look at, but this is no more than questioning. The questioning, as the setting of limits, cannot override a didactic. The danger is turning the didactic into an aesthetic rule. There is a beautiful passage in the Brothers Karamazov. For children, games are the first didactic of art, "young people's games of soldiers and robbers in their playtime are also art in its first stage" (Dostoyevsky 2005, 498). In children's play, the chest as a house, the box as the ship, reflect a need to build representations as close as reality as possible. For children and their sight, not impaired by hierarchies yet, things of the world are all potential representations of other things; significance is infinite. Education is the reduction of this potentiality; emancipation is its inverse. We master the experience of seeing (different from the experience of pain, for example) when we are children. The role of experience is the granting of a form of seeing or a multiplication of meanings. It is an experience of gathering, counting, bringing together, and splitting apart, of relating singularities and basically detecting differentials. As a child we can only be imposed hierarchies once we have gathered life in multiplicity. It all boils down to difference. To truly see is to see difference and only difference. Hierarchies are the simulacra of difference. Seeing is only truly seeing though language (at least rendering a report, you would say—but they are inseparable).

We are thus touching upon promising paths. Seeing as gathering is one of the most intriguing and complex forms of understanding and forming objects and performances. As Heidegger has shown us in his "Introduction to Metaphysics," there is a strong link between seeing and representation. For Wittgenstein, "The concept of a representation of what is seen, like that of a copy, is very elastic, and so *together with it* is the concept of what is seen. The two are intimately connected. (Which is *not* to say that they are alike.)" (Wittgenstein 1986, 198). A concept is a symbolic representation of what is seen. Seen is what is touched upon, what we encounter with our hands, the memory of our smelling, and the repertoires of our hearing. The representation of what is seen is the picture in the mind that is intimately connected to the concept of what is seen. But they are not the same, and, is this not the vortex of the matter? In the necessary split-second between seeing and representation lies the very thing that allows us to uphold equality as the order of difference. We only have linguistic representations of what we see. There is no representation (of an image) without a concept of such a representation, they are both its own elastic measure (as we will soon unearth in the intimate relation with *Aletheia* and *Phusis* in Heidegger's metaphysics). What I see are relations, a network. Do I see a totality of involvements (ready to hand)? For Wittgenstein, that internal relation is not prefixed or held together by one major presupposition. Seeing does not bite properties or categories out of the object. The question is thus reformulated. In Heideggerian terms, is every seeing a form of disclosing? as in *Aletheia* or *Phusis*? (Heidegger 2000.) Or is it something simpler, more direct?

Encryption is all about fixating a "one on one" correspondence between concept and representation in which the appearance of the concept fixes itself axiomatically in a representation. "Every new day is a little miracle,' he thought, and fell asleep forever, below a blade of grass . . . . Don't let the undertaker know we will meet again."

According to the once heir to the biggest fortune in Austria, there is a kind of permanence in seeing an aspect, something that remains the same in the moving of the picture. But then again, how can we define such permanence? To say that the thing remains the same, while the observations vary infinitely, is truly asking for "who" holds the key to the totality of the fact as true. Is it then a matter of time? At any extent, there is an answer moved by the holding onto a final design. I thought I saw only a duck while Ludwig knows that the picture is of a duck-rabbit. If this is true, then we must redefine all language games since they are fixed by an end point, a finality of someone who knows how it all ends up and the possibilities of the totality of engagements. If we wish to avoid reintroducing finality as a transcendent model, we must then agree that there are some games whose purpose is contingently defined by a kind of finality, but at the same time that no finality is the constituent element of the game. As in Heidegger's ready to hand, it is only through a power play that we can arrive at something like the totality of possible relations.

Seeing is an act of gathering in language and constituting a state of things. Within Heidegger's "in order to" seeing and states of things happen at the same time or at best with a split-second in between (seeing as a state and as interpretation). We do not only see with our eyes but seeing is overshadowed and developed by language. Hereunto, the will is the transformation of aspects of reality as they are interpreted by me.

Consequently, our problem is this, every language game would have to be totally defined beforehand, and every outcome calculated from an exteriority of it. Think of a park that has an outer rectangular path of 5km, four inner paths that connect the circumference from north to south, and another four that do the same from east to west. What is it involved in this description? Are we exhausting a picture or creating the possibilities of new ones? Think of all the virtualities created by the paths being ran in counterclockwise by some people and clockwise by others. We can have a frame of things, nevertheless, any truth of the paths only comes around in traveling them, in thinking them, in connecting or disconnecting them, in folding its geometry and inhabiting its materiality (birds, wind, and earth). The description is simply the inner side of an infinite universe of potentialities and actualities interacting virtually, intensely, and extensively. Think of all possible alternate paths and the reports that follow. Think that of all the possibilities of what can be reported. The fundamental question is if every outcome must have to be predetermined in its totality, beforehand, and from an exteriority.

These three aspects (totality, anticipation, and exteriority) are the utter denial of immanent difference. Totality opposes infinity, anticipation opposes simultaneity, and exteriority interiority. To be certain, we must look at the duck-rabbit (and the park we just described) in its heuristic dimension and as a sample of a language game. Nevertheless, as such, we open new possibilities to flatten further our axiom of difference. The game loses all heuristic potential when the "haves" and "musts" of aesthetics break the levee of freedom of the game. The problem is when this "must" escapes the language game and its didactic scheme to convert aesthetics into potestas, and when the "haves" force itself as the only legitimate form of seeing. In either case, we are escalating into a power play.

Wittgenstein touches upon a key political concept—imagination. To see the duck-rabbit over and above itself demands a new composition where imagination clears the skies. What is sayable? What is seeable? Is imagination here deemed as creativity or simply as the capacity to discover hidden forms? As creativity, imagination as seeing things for what they are not necessarily the case (the key is what is not necessarily the case) burns the tip of the fingers of those holding onto necessity. In the case of creativity (even the one that discovers hidden figures), imagination is contingency or better; imagination comes after contingency, as its purest fruit. To conquer the future is to imagine how things could be another way. This outcome impacts at the core of the ready to hand as a totality of involvements; it smashes its strongest tenet, that of totality. And it also contaminates one of its primordial consequences, that of the very possibility of a clean-cut social practice. Imagination is to think contingency. It disallows the possibility of simply thinking the picture as parts of a pre-given world, to fill in the patches of a preformed reality. But even in the latter, in patching the puzzle, there also throbs the potentiality of contingency, of re-writing the rules and thus the potentiality to enliven every eventuality.

Wittgenstein hits the bull's-eye when he eschews a mix-up between states of seeing. "Do not think you knew in advance what the '*state* of seeing' means here! Let the use *teach* you the meaning. There is such an order as 'imagine *this*,' and also: 'Now see the figure like *this*'; but not: 'Now see this leaf green'" (Wittgenstein 1986, 213). In the case of the green leaf, it would seem that we interpret what is not an evident property of the thing. Consequently, it seems that there can never be a perfect and delimited picture of the thing brought on by properties or categories. Even in what Wittgenstein calls "aspect blindness" (a-phantasia, for example someone that is able to see the duck and is incapable of seeing the rabbit), the subject is no less trained to see something as something. Our radical point is to turn on the democratic alarms when this seeing is directed and solidified by forms of encryption.

We can boil it all down to this—we can only experience the meaning of a word, and we can do so because the word has been used; it is in our traffic of meanings and it already suggests a use. We are not caving into the idea that a things name is its properties. Rather, well, what we begin to uncover is that meaning of a word may be represented (as any representation, it is partial, a mere optic device) by a set of arrows that point from a context into the word and from within the word unto to a context ($\leftarrow\rightarrow$). Bear in mind that the representation of these arrows simply stands in the place of something else; they are an extensive representation of something intensive. They do nothing more than represent. Experience or intention may play a part, but they are not constitutive; they are at best secondary. What is primary is the traffic of words within contexts of meaning. Even a word can be its own context: run!, march!, etc. Context is not a matter of size but of regions of applicability of a certain meaning. Against inner language and inner experience detached from the outside world, we must think of the ultimate context, language as a never-ending pool of conversions and divergencies. We are not in the business of diminishing inner experiences or the wealth of intimate worlds. Our business is to help flatten the experience of the world through a language that is open and rich enough for all of us to live and die in. I love the sound of the keyboards in this computer; when I write, they bring, not represent, the rhythm and harmony that I try to convey to whatever I am writing. Sometimes I feel like a graceful percussionist (like Nick Mason at Pompeii), sometimes a careful craftsman piecing a rare thing that has no name, and, yet again, sometimes like an elephant in a crystal shop. The truth of the matter is all wrapped up in this arsenal of signs that are open for all to share.

Motive, certainty, cause, method, and all alike have many different functions and establish diverse networks according to specific language games. Most of Western philosophy (as many other structural disciplines) wants to hijack their meaning, uniform them, and overdetermine every language game with a unidimensional pre-established meaning. Language games are as thick as the power plays that infest them and seize their meaning. This is a very specific kind of encryption that imposes a straitjacket of uses. Think, for example, how it would be impossible for a child to learn what length is if she was shown just one rod, even of the rod is a ruler that represents 30cm. She can only learn measuring by measuring other things with the rod. That is why the same interest birds show for aerodynamics is our interest in the conceptual use of language.

LANGUAGE AS A MODEL: TANGLED UP IN RULES

Think of an order of writing, writing as the result of ordering within time and space. Order as communicability, but also communicability as the deployment of rules. Think of poetics as writing the new, as conceiving of difference. But also think of writing as the conception of a new order with new rules. This is what Li Bai, Joyce, Rulfo, García-Marquez, Borges, Ishiguro, Banksy, and Anzaldua among many have done. But let us strive further. Think of rules as disclosing significations and new languages as languages built on top of old languages and the mere possibility of it.

Let us rain a little more on Dasein's parade of understanding and interpretation, anticipating two objections we will behest on it: simple relationality and idealism. According to Heidegger, "But in significance itself, with which Dasein is always familiar, there lurks the ontological condition which makes it possible for Dasein, as something which understands and interprets, to disclose such things as 'significations'; upon these, in turn, is founded the Being of words and of language" (Heidegger 2001, 121/88). For Heidegger, then, being of the ready to hand equals to involvements whose purchase is definable as a context of assignments or references. Let us retort that the matter at hand has to do with the way entities are set up beforehand in a totality of involvements, where not only the entity may be made inaccessible (obstinate, obtrusive, and impenetrable) but, most importantly, the totality of involvements is maintained hidden. In this second sense, hiddenness, though it is true that the totality of involvements is only revealed through the circumspective use of the entity, when said use is encrypted, it logically follows that the totality of involvements cannot but follow in its encryption. There is no free zone of significance that is not perverted, or at least contaminated by encryption that does not communicate directly with the possibility of understanding. Furthermore, the possibility of understanding is dependent upon the disclosing of significations. One major upshot is that most of humanity is used as ready to hand, a spatiality dismembered and bound up again mass set up against any possible derivative of difference.

We are thus set upon the possibility of language as a transparent thing in which *Dasein* comes freely to disclose things, building its existential core. Hence, we must ask, first, what type of language is this language and what is the part of rule-following within it? Furthermore, how does rule-following constitute language? Wittgenstein's picture of the idling engine takes us to the next level of discussion: the discussion regarding rule-following. "It is not our aim to refine or complete the system of rules for the use of our words in unheard-of ways. For the clarity that we are aiming at is indeed *complete* clarity. But this simply means that the philosophical problems should *completely* disappear" (Wittgenstein 1986, 133). The clarity we are looking for is already in language not in a fantastical superstructure of language that we must build so as to put language easily on top of it. There is not a "thing" on one side of the spectrum that understands and interprets, and an ability, on the other side of the spectrum, that is able to disclose things as "significations." Both things are enmeshed in the same swirl of language they share discourse, they are what is shared. The shared discourse is sharing the unshared, what already is in a co-state of mind but not explicitly. Explicitness only arrives in discourse. In order for Heidegger's premise to show some footing, it would have to suppose a kind of ideal language that makes the relation uniquely transparent and a form of propositional truth that rules others from its hermetic exteriority.

But let us think how the proposition stating what a proposition is, is still just another proposition. In other words, "And to say that a proposition is whatever can be true or false amounts to saying: we call something a proposition when *in our language* we apply the calculus of truth functions to it" (Wittgenstein 1986, 136). We must first know to what truth it is that we are applying the calculus of truth, and this can only manifest itself in other propositions. The settling of what counts as a zone of veracity, where truth may arrive, can only be established by another set of propositions whose privilege is not something uncanny and transcendent but the function it deploys within other propositions. There is no way of establishing truth or false in the absence of a proposition. Wittgenstein considers that to establish the truth function through propositions such as "The king in chess is *the* piece that one can check" is a bad picture. It is a bad picture because it presupposes that we must first establish what is truth and false as absolute values from within a single function of a game, as if this was not also a matter of propositional truths. The relation is thus transversal and not vertical, not the *kitsch* Kelsenian pyramid but interacting networks with no central apparatus that governs over it. Interlocking clouds and not descending waters. The truth not only functions but operates from one proposition to the other, without a single one holding command over the other. The truth of the king depends on the truth of the rook and the pawn as well as the black and white squares and the command to move them. In establishing their mutual truths, no one is propositionally superior to the others. Henceforth, to reach a final proposition is a practical, not a logical, matter. Consequently, a fitting proposition does not entail exact correspondence, but a correspondence that is sound. It is not the coming together of concave and convex, of some things hollow and others bloated, but the coming together in use (as in Bergson's coming together of bodies). It is utter difference, if anything, that they have in common. The propositional form, as the heart of logics (of what is possible or not) presupposes an interaction that must anticipate the existence of the proposition. Hence, the proposition is never first in time though it pretends to be first in logic. The relation of the proposition that fixes the confines of the world and the world it fixes is not triangulated to another third form of legitimacy but is contained within the relation. Any Peircean thirdness comes from the use of the world thus established and not from a hidden form of transcendence.

What a language game is and the general forms of propositions are indissoluble. They move through their mutual fabrics and establish relations of multiplicity within each other's compounds. The ground for things is so movable, so flexible, that it shifts at the rhythm of the things themselves, in other words, it is the things themselves. Ground and things, language games and the general forms of propositions are of the same magnitude and intensity; they are one and the same, and no proposition may alter its own founding zone of creation.

A proposition cannot be enshrined as a general schema. Again, what we have are plausible schemas, and once they assist in fixating a world, they disappear behind it. The schema has to be singled out at the beginning of the game, it must be specified that we are referring to a sample as a schema, because there can be no schema explicating the schema. As we have insisted, models are just particular (samples) elevated (fraudulently) to a schema by power plays. Nevertheless, Wittgenstein asks but might there not be such "general' samples?" Say a schematic leaf, or a sample of pure green?—Certainly there might. But for such a schema to be understood as a schema, and not as the shape of a particular leaf, and for a slip of pure green to be understood as a sample of all that is greenish and not as a sample of pure green—this in turn resides in the way the samples are used. Ask yourself: what *shape* must the sample of the colour green be? Should it be rectangular? Or would it then be the sample of a green rectangle? (Wittgenstein 1986, 74)

Logic, not as the assumed bearer of all transcendent truth but as the clearance into a practical world, shines the most when it is pressed between the ideality of language and common language. The use of a rule seems to be presupposed in every use of language, although we cannot describe it or even name it satisfactorily at every step of its operation. Even if we cannot describe it, it creates a fundamental thing for language, expectations of the outcomes of the use of language. These outcomes are harnessed not only in praxis but fundamentally in ethics. As Rorty has indicted, "Normal discourse (a generalization of Kuhn's notion of 'normal science') is any discourse (scientific, political, theological, or whatever) which embodies agreed-upon criteria for reaching agreement; abnormal discourse is any which lacks such criteria" (Rorty 1979, 11). It is also vital to grasp the way we play with rules, not within them but literally with them. If potestas can be identified by something is its firm grip on the rules but specifically on how to dictate changes in them to comprehend new situations.

A question that is the beating heart at the base of all this architecture is if there is the possibility of making these rules as you go along? And if, consequently, there must be a "constitutional" rule enabling this possibility? Must it be established beforehand? That is, if there is an implicit rule enabling the possibility to alter the rules. The importance of playing by the rules is ethical, and it may be legal. Do we mean linguistically by legally? Yes, the very means of communication is suspended on the capacity to communicate and the availability of interpreting the rules of the language game. This, of course is a pretension of every language game. If it were not the case, then we are directly deposited in the world of encryption. There is a delicate balance here, of liberty within the game, understanding that liberty is the possibility not only to move inside the game but of creating new games, and the very condition of communicability. I mean the form we establish rules must not limit the ways in which we relate to the world and the way we create it, but the lack of them cannot bring language to a standstill of incommunicability. Nevertheless, this is where encryption slips inside the game to grab hold of it. As we remarked in chapter 1: Encryption means surreptitiously establishing sturdy rules that invade the game from nowhere to determine the aesthetical, the poetical, and the religious; to determine once and for all what language is and how it can be assessed, but specifically to obliterate the possibility of creating more games from within the game. To encrypt is to colonize the rest of the world with rules whose creator is outside the language game. It is to control utterly any language game through power plays that control every possible move. Encryption is establishing possible games where the rules are said to anticipate the move but are only knowable in their application after the move (*ex post facto*). This is the beating heart of liberalism.

Poetics is creativity in movement, encryption is controlling the rules of the language games from outside the possible players and after the possible plays are executed. Liberal encryption is the ultimate expansion from legality (normativity) to language. One thing that liberalism excels at is promising that every game it sets before the people is a transparent one, with a heavy set of rules (due process and legality), ruled over stringently (judicial review, etc.) in which the players may duly expect uniform outcomes (rationality and scientific rule-following). Nevertheless, the game is always a frantic deception where the very values within the game, of what counts as subjects, rules, control, and outcomes, vary incessantly and are always exchanged in an *ex post facto* manner by a hidden elite. Just one cherry picked example is how, in the game of human rights, the concept of human is reserved to a handful through precise definitions of humans that exclude the non-national, the non-worker, and the non-white. This is what the lackeys of liberalism gloat with as the "ductility of the law."

The role of logic must be shrunk to a key that opens the possibility of language and not the throne form where it is ruled. The essence of thought is logic; it presents an order. Of what? Of the possibilities of the world. Possible is what is common to world and thought, but this order must be simple, not a super order that supersedes commonality by retrieving the world to a chosen few that understand its workings intimately. Logic is what is common and fully visible; nevertheless, encryption flips it to what is peculiar and opaque. As put beautifully by Wittgenstein. "Whereas, of course, if the words 'language,' 'experience,' 'world,' have a use, it must be as humble a one as that of the words 'table,' 'lamp,' 'door'" (Wittgenstein 1986, 97). Logic is not the harbinger of some magical property that dictates the world and fashions reality all around us; it is ordinary everyday business; it is concomitant to talking, and writing. Therefore, there is not, nor there can be privileged or higher forms of thought. As there are no privileged forms of thought, there are no privileged forms of language. To think thought out of the axis of language goes so far as to ask what time it is in the sun, or if Jupiter is under or above Mars.

If there is sense there is order, but order, not a super order, an ideal order, is of the essence of language. Wittgenstein has thrown logic of its high horse of super order, one that rules over language and life unyieldingly.

But what is also deposed in this revolution is the Fetichization of order. The love of order for the sake of order, the love of the psychiatric hospital, the cemetery, or, worse yet, the shopping mall as the archetype of order. It is rather the sheer simplicity of the order of the world. What is needed for there to be order; Only sense. Or, better yet, order is confined for its existence to its making sense, it is not order that awards the world with sense, but sense gives it into order. So, any endeavor to trace a super order is destined to fail. Maybe through anthropology we could track down the forms and combinations that in history built the order of language. It would be an anthropology of potestas and potentia, of forms of domination and forces of resistance shaping the order of language, giving it its form and sense-order.[1] In other words, only through a continual use of trial and error may we approximate the order of language that renounces any ideal form that should precede it.

But even sense is found in the great outdoors, breathing freely. Any definite sense is not an enclosure; it simply marks the possibility of the interlocutor to say, "and then?" or "go on." "*Entonces*" is the most beautiful word in Castilian, a burning nucleus of meaning much more elastic that any English counterpart. It means "and then what happened" and "go on" or "what comes of it." For me, it marks the most poetic word in any politics; it is the word of sense as order. "*Entonces*" is order as the production of sense; it is alterity to the marrow, order as a permanently open flux of language.

The ideal in reality is not one of purity but one of mere possibility. Once we communicate because there is an order fashioned by sense, don't dare tell logic how it should behave. Order is sense and thus it is a medium, but this medium is language itself. The ideal language is not a language on top of another; it is not building the perfect city on top of the shambles of the old one. The ideal is within language itself (normal quotidian language). In the words of Bakhtin, "A unitary language is not something given [dan] but is always in essence posited" (Bakhtin 1981, 270).

The frenzy of ideal languages as the model of life has always led to doomsday's machines. How do we build the ideal language if not through the ordinary one? Once we built it, we see there is no possibility of its use beyond descending through every cavity and spreading through every nook and cranny of the language that is ordinary. Wittgenstein enacts more than a call to keep it simple; it is a call to keep it in this side of the world. The warning we heed is that trying to build another side of the world, as a model, is simply an illusion plagued with the desire to dominate language and through it every other subjectivity. To build such language is to muddle and confuse, to go amiss with no other way back to the center of your pretensions but sheer hubris. Hence, when the cover is blown, only force and violence remain. The very notion of partitioned vocabularies with whole sets of discursive and referential independence is highly suspicious. As Rorty has put it, "an intentional vocabulary is just one more vocabulary for talking about portions of a world which can, indeed, be completely described without this vocabulary" (Rorty 1979, 207). At the end of ideal languages, we have only recreated an everyday language that is exoteric and whose community is esoteric.

As Wittgenstein has signaled, it is more fruitful to determine an atmosphere than to try to reconstruct the description of events, things, feelings, etc. The atmosphere puts contexts in contact; it overlaps its elements and allows them to interact without losing their traction of the things of life. Our language is as precise as the word precise allows it to be. How could we create a new language without going back on our grammar and lexicon? It would be simply like turning language as the sleeves of a shirt. How can we create a new form of language? Only inside of what already exists, may we aspire to look yonder, to be above or beyond our language.

One of the characters in Ted Chiangs short story "Division by Zero" acidly puts it:

> In the Principia Mathematica, Bertrand Russell and Alfred Whitehead attempted to give a rigorous foundation to mathematics using formal logic as their basis. They began with what they considered to be axioms, and used those to derive theorems of increasing complexity. By page 362, they had established enough to prove "1 + 1 = 2." (Chiang 2002, 74)

Rule-following and rulemaking, sense and order, are all bordered by the importance of building bridges. Hence, examples, intermediate cases, poles of attraction, and zones of veracity are all synergistic properties that constitute language as a flat space-time of equality. Encryption makes us feel permanently tangled up in rules. The idea of foreseeing or calculating attached to a rule is fundamental. It is basically what the rule is for. It throws light on our concept of *meaning* something. For in those cases that things turn out otherwise than we had meant or foreseen we can still make them out within a network, they are not hostile to their environment, that is, unless the rule is mystified, and the outcome encrypted.

Searching for "the order," instead of seeing the order in sense, turns philosophy into dogma. When everything turned to "X" in our language game, we discover that the only way to go ahead is to go back through the memory of our language. What do we find when we go back? Clear forms of distinguishability between orders as vehicles and that orders that appear as transcendent are not language at all but a form of organization that lie hidden behind language. We find that rules are operative when they open up the possibility of communicating and are ethical when they allow the possibility within difference.

Allow us to anticipate something fundamental, as stated by Carlos Fuentes in his masterpiece "La Muerte de Artemio Cruz": "True power is always born of rebelliousness" (Fuentes 2007, 306). What would it the mean to apply rules without guidance? It would mean out of context, out of the interconnecting relation of other rules, of common experience. Rules cannot anticipate every action; if they did, they would itself be the sole action and the world would be indistinguishable in its present, past, and future; everything would be unity and sameness. Rules are spasmodic; they move forth and back according to our capacity to override them through their own use.

It seems we encrypt our own language when we leave our question half the way. We then look back at it and it looks back at us as a mystifying enigma. We therefore elevate it to a place beyond language, a transcendental foundation of all that we may come to understand in order to appease our need of origins and order.

Let us pose the following question: In any form of music is the score a representation of the physical music or the physical music (sound) the representation of the score? Where is the model and where the representation? Are there pure forms of music? Let us complicate this concept so we can simplify our picture. During an iconic concert, Frank Zappa and the Mothers of Invention performed three different representations of a score sheet of "approximate" known as the "Helsinki recording." ("Approximate" is already in itself a complex rhythmical work organized on many semantical levels). In the first part, the musicians play the melody without the lyrics. In the second, they sing it suppressing the melody in the instruments and simply following the rhythm. In the third, they dance to it, suppressing music from the instruments. Three representations of the same score. Which is the true one? According to a major context, a huge language game called "musical appreciation" then it must be number one. But if the language game is theater? Or pantomime? Which one would have precedence, which one could we affirm that comes closer to the truth? And then again what truth? And according to what predefined rules? And yet again, are not all three representations simply one extended presence of an aesthetic game and the creation of new confines of artistic representation? As in a famous aphorism *"duo cum faciunt idem, non est idem,"* if two make the same thing, then it is not the same thing. Take another example, who speaks the truth of Spinoza? His scholars bathed in the incense and myrrh of his works, producing cathedrals of canonical documents or Ivan Fischer's "Translations'? Does not Bob Dylan's "The lonesome death of Hattie Carrol" speak more to the heart of the corruption of the judicial system than all the "cities of paper" produced under the lightbulbs of legal academia. And, isn't the great George Carlin an acuter moral gadfly of our times that an army of TV celeb-soap-philosophers?

Wittgenstein entices us

> Let us imagine the following: The surfaces of the things around us (stones, plants, etc.) have patches and regions which produce pain in our skin when we touch them. (Perhaps through the chemical composition of these surfaces. But we need not know that.) In this case we should speak of pain-patches on the leaf of a particular plant just as at present we speak of red patches. I am supposing that it is useful to us to notice these patches and their shapes; that we can infer important properties of the objects from them. (Wittgenstein 1986, 312).

But there are no "pain" patches in themselves, the patches can be poisonous, or they can be prickly, so they pierce the skin and then *produce* pain. Otherwise, it would be like looking at the teeth of a dog and calling them "pain teeth." Think of a moment when you are not thinking, then, you will understand what it is to think, its beautiful simplicity. Grounds, justifications, frames, and samples are interlocking attitudes and forms of practice within the world. There is no precedence of one over the other, they are employed equiprimordially in living, acting, communicating, loving, etc.

What is important in this whirlwind of rules? Asking for their medium of recognition? And what about a criterion of identity? Wait! Fixing a criterion of identity? We might as well go back to foreshadowing the next move in a machine. Oh! But what if we reserve the concept of "criterion" only to the use? Justifications and grounds, experience and practice, more than induction and programming laws are the stuff of rules. Nevertheless, models and programming do work, and Wittgenstein's indictment that they are queer and useless (that they don't reveal and that they are too stringent) do not stop them cold on their tracks, they still work their way through power as potestas very efficiently. They work because they are tied to one specific form of ruling over language called encryption. Through imposition they become pragmatic. They install themselves within social practices of language until they are naturalized and normalized, or better yet, normativized. It is not that Western philosophy has not found clarity but that it has sold itself to potestas, its workings have always corresponded (exceptions made of the likes of Spinoza and Marx) to forms of governing over logic and language.

Consequently, is there language without rules? Are there games without rules? How limiting are these rules? How versatile must they be to allow "rule-following" and "novelty making"? Can we conceive of a game without rules and/or rules without games?

Wittgenstein delivers us into the eye of the storm, "How is it decided what is the right step to take at any particular stage" (of a language game)?

(Wittgenstein 1986, 186) Are language games always transversal? No lord over them? Or do they hide processes and forms of lordship, hierarchies, etc.? One key conclusion to hold on to is that hierarchies can program consistency and thus detach themselves, or at least hide from the process of rule-following. A *modus operandi* of encryption consists in always reserving the settling of the last and final word of reasoning to an elite, stating at the end of it "it is just as it was meant to be." We have then two key elements of encryption. First, the encryptor has the capacity to program rules within the games that give it a full consistency. The imposition and naturalization of legal regimes, moral architectures, and aesthetic models of selection begin through the giving of consistency to language by power as potestas. And second, potestas always reserves the last word for itself. Although, no one possesses the key to the deployment of rules in time (the key question here is time), the manners the rules are imposed upon a process, are all a matter of training and naturalizing potestas.

As Wittgenstein warns us regarding machines and parts, "We talk as if these parts could only move in this way, as if they could not do anything else. How is this—do we forget the possibility of their bending, breaking off, melting, and so on?' (Wittgenstein 1986, 193). Every problem we have outlined stares dead in our eyes in the problems of parts, design, and order. Think of a problem we began describing before: Does the mill that grinds fresh flour act the same when it is a machine of centralized power (few eat the bread produced by many) to when it is a communal machine of equal distribution? Is it the same machine? Again, do we use the machine when we eat the bread? Can we truly anticipate its action and its meaning from its internal operation? The key to the solution could be in asking, what is the distance between the model of the machine to the actual machine? Never forgetting that in potestas models are samples elevated to transcendence. Wittgenstein pushes the problem further "the machine could also have moved differently it may look as if the way it moves must be contained in the machine-as-symbol far more determinately than in the actual machine. As if it were not enough for the movements in question to be empirically determined in advance, but they had to be really—in a mysterious sense—already *present*" (Wittgenstein 1986, 180). Again, there is a distance from the model of the machine to the actual machine. Here we have a machine as symbolizing the action and language as its movement. This is all too fine, but: why imagine a machine at all?

Allow me to begin to tinker with the image of language as a machine, where the vital idea is the image and not machine. We already began to point out the problem of the image of the machine, the network trouble with parts and engines, with central design systems and rhizomes. Let us suggest another picture, a crossing of different pictures, let us imagine a movie (kinetic pictures) against a still photograph. The possibility of movement seems installed in the machine as model. Movement as transitions between potentiality and actuality is part of the machine. To decrypt a machine is finally to make its model malfunction, and the malfunction in actuality is simply a point of view, "anticipated in some sense" as to how the machine should have behaved. To believe that the movement of a machine is contained in the present is like believing that its use is contained fully in the future. But what if the rigid denominator "anticipated in some sense" is contingent. It cannot be necessary at all; what is present is merely the result of action not its cause.

Against Heidegger's use of the ready to hand we are proving that the potentiality of meaning may lay in a word, but it is only revealed in its use. It is in use as an open relation of fields of forces and interchange where tactics interlock, where meaning appears, not in interpretation that is, as it were, a precondition for any movement. Interpretation is but part of power play; it puts meaning in motion; it attaches a disperse direction to words.

We have then skimmed the problem to the interpretation of rules and rules as interpretation. Obeying a rule and the rule are two separate things, they are not ontologically bonded. Obeying a rule is a thing of practice, from "now I can go on" and "do it," there is no logical accord, no rigid causality, and certainly no necessity. Even for a person to follow something as simple as a signpost, there has to be a tradition of following signposts first. As Wittgenstein formulates it,

> This was our paradox: no course of action could be determined by a rule, because every course of action can be made out to accord with the rule. The answer was: if everything can be made out to accord with the rule, then it can also be made out to conflict with it. And so there would be neither accord nor conflict here. (Wittgenstein 1986, 201)

The paradox stands if we only understand the rule through a process of interpretation. The paradox is dispelled if we grasp the idea that following a rule is a thing of practice and of contingency. The paradox stands if we believe that an interpretation can solve the problem of rule-following, that is, if interpretation becomes a model of rule-following and we award the power of a last word to such interpretation, but then, the need to establish a new rule would immediately follow.

Interpretation cannot be a static action—it cannot depend on the stillness of the model of the machine and the presence of all its possible moves from within the interpretation. If it were, it would become fused (rather confused) with the present of the (ideal) machine. It is a very specific thing to follow a rule. An interpretation can be general, detached; it can cover more than the rule; and it can specify things of the rule that are beyond it, but it is only crystalized in "going through with it." If there is something like an understanding of the rule, an execution, it is solely in its use that language obtains meaning. This use is rule-following and not interpretative, although interpretation is a previous preparative step (of stillness) that may not be favored as the final act on the machine of rule-following. The fundamental thing is contingency, the use of "x" forms of language cannot bear to anticipate "y" forms as a natural follow-up. That is to say, as something already present and that anticipates itself in the use of the present as actuality. No actuality as *Energeia* is perfectly anticipated in potentiality as there is nothing necessary in the contingent use of language. Only in the shadows (something virtual) does anticipation show itself. Following the teachings of Jacques Rancière, the breach between teaching and learning is also the bridge and the excess. I can teach far more than what I myself are able to understand[2] (Rancière 1991).

Interpretation is wide, voluptuous, luscious and incomplete, it ejaculates a myriad of symbols that are open to new interpretations, and it is never exhausted. Contingency in rule-following means creation, it is anchored in potentia and actuality as *Energeia*. The latter means without ends, no qualification, no stratification. Power unstratified is in itself redundant, but we have trouble seeing it. What is contradictory is power in a solid state. Henceforth, every discussion regarding difference and its possibility is in the bottom a discussion about order, on what order means, and if it is or it is not dependent on context and its consequences. We are clear about the difference between chaos and anarchy but not between order and anarchy. Does anarchy suppose an order? Does difference? Let us simply anticipate that anarchy does not mean lack of order but lack of principle as a model of any order. *Energeia* is anarchy as potestas is archy-sm. Like in Fritz Lang's "Metropolis," the heart, not the machine is the intermediary between brain and hands. The means and ends are not to see the symbol behind the symbol, the *Moloch* shadowing the machine but to create the symbol that does away with it.

IMMANENCE AND CONFLICT

Since we have gained our way through a minefield of potestas, let us zoom in again on immanence. For Agamben "the principle of immanence is but a generalization of the ontology of univocity, that excludes all transcendence of being" (2015, 339). Agamben is here following the path through which Deleuze re-institutes immanence to the mobility of life. All of the modes in which being are said are said in one voice, immanence! The modes of one substance in Spinoza. Hence, it is not Plotinus' henology as the counting of the one as one, but the counting of the all of difference as the substance, as the one.

If immanent is said to be immanent to something other than itself, that something is nothing else that transcendence. In immanence, the preposition "between" is superfluous, since things are not immanent between themselves but immanent in themselves. Henceforth, between, is not the measure of a thing of power but the result of a relation of power. Nevertheless, immanence seen under this light still lacks the "to give" "to share," the relation in-between (it is still a thing seen under a single light). Without the "to give," immanent beings would be impossible since immanent is said of the relation of potentialities or, better, it can only "be said" (named) from within a relation. Power as the giving, the sharing, and the affections that mutually nurture life only arise in communication, that is, in an in-between, a relation of immanent things. If within the relation there is a hierarchy, then communication is impossible, and we are before encryption as simulation of relationality. Pure immanence would be incommunicable and hence impotent, not in the sense of lacking the power to do something, but in the sense that no concept of power could be applied to it and hence it could not transit from potentia to actuality. So, the true question of politics is what happens when a pure immanence, a difference in itself and for itself happens to collide with an aberration, with an act of power that exceeds immanence and claims transcendence. That is, when immanence is severed and or limited by something that according to its nature surmounts or rises above it. What if this anomaly claims to be a structure, organized as to produce results? A claimant to immanence that limits life, that qualifies it in order to let it be. Is that not our quotidian experience, is this not the shape of the world? Is it not the world that halts all other possible worlds declaring: "I am the only world?" It is precisely what Foucault and latter Agamben tell us. When life becomes bare, the limit of politics as bio-politics, life and only life as bare becomes the object of politics. This is when the last vestige of potestas becomes the domination of life in its barest form, life reduced to the simpler functions of a body. But, while Agamben takes the road of impotence, we have proven that immanence through *Energeia* is exactly the inversion of qualifications of life; it is the impossibility of conceiving life through qualifications.

ASSEMBLAGES AND RHIZOMES, SOCIETY AND NATURE

Deleuze and Guattari are the mythical figures that perform the work of flattening ontologies. Repeatedly, tactically, and relentlessly, they hammer down any form of transcendence into flat ontologies. They have driven us back to a rich rhizomatic world where difference shines its own light. Flatter! Is the muscular creed against hierarchies. Antoine Bousquet describes assemblages as "any collection of heterogeneous elements that can be said to display some form of consistency and regularity yet remain open to transformative change through the addition or subtraction of elements or the reorganization of the relations between them" (Bousquet 2014, 94). The relations sprouting form an assemblage are multiple immanent networks (a rhizome) rather than an arborescent (hierarchical) structure.

Eduardo Viveiros de Castro reminds us that flat ontology

> prevails, in which the real emerges as a dynamic, immanent multiplicity in a state of continuous variation, a metasystem far from equilibrium, rather than a combinatory manifestation or grammatical implementation of transcendent principles or rules, and as a differentiating relation, which is to say, as a heterogeneous disjunctive synthesis instead of a dialectical (horizontal) conjunction or hierarchical (vertical) totalization of contraries. (Viveiros de Castro 2009, 105)

For Manuel DeLanda, assemblages are hence not totalities since the relation between parts is not logically necessary but only contingently obligatory (DeLanda 2011). The basic pulse of flat ontologies is that there are no totalities and the relation of parts is not necessary (logical) but contingent.

One of the basic footprints of ANT is that it shatters to smithereens the basic structural differences that subsist in social sciences between society (as the origin of the machine, the nuptial bed of all technological progeny) and difference, as heterogenic relations. Thus, the difference between the social and the technological, as the grounds of existence and deployment of machines is rickety. Nevertheless, to rest assure that some remnants of tumorous hierarchies do not remain imbedded in flat ontologies, we must ask: Can we describe a world with machines that is a world without society? And, forthwith, a social world without technology? Are machines social before being technical? Is there human technology before there is a material technology? Well, one is the other, they are interchangeable, not because they are fungible but because they are indistinguishable. Language (word order, power plays) is the first technology, but the use of a stick is no different from it. There is only material technology in human technology.

Against social constructivists that assume a totality of the social (as Present at hand) that is already finalized, ANT proves that society, deemed as such, cannot be construed as something else that transcendence. Latour has proved that there is no totality of the social, only social assemblages that already contain within them bodies, machines, structures, and discourses (Latour 2005, 247). It is the assembling of multiplicities that which constitutes the social and not the other way around. Every factor that can be said belongs to a social situation is on the same level as any other. This realization forces us to do away with the concept of social forces and thus of society, as a peak, as a machine that is self-comprehensive. If the social exists, it is not worth the time or the effort since reconstructing it is simply reconstructing the amalgam of multiplicities that produce it. Society, if it were to exist, is the product and not the cause of multiplicities. As we have dethroned substances and transcendence, we must do the same with society, that is, when it presents itself as the form of substance and the apex of transcendence through which everything else is organized. "Everything is social" is tantamount to "everything is natural"; they are both opposing sides of the dogma, sheer intellectual sloth.

Nevertheless, we come across a template of difficulties between our project and the ANT. These, are nonetheless, very fecund problems. We agree that in seeking out flat ontologies we describe rather that explain. ANT sets out to map relations between material things and concepts. Relations are thus sometimes material and sometimes semiotic (Latour 1996, 375). We agree with this but only in its spirit of heuristics. Notwithstanding, how could we differentiate one from the other before any interaction has taken place? The assertion "the synthesis of proteins needs energy" is in itself material and semiotic. If we could determine the belonging of something to semiotics or materiality in an a-priori fashion, then this mechanism of determinism would be a transcendent form and thus a contradiction with flat ontologies. As we have been taught by Bergson and Peirce there cannot be a clearance of signs that would make signs necessary. The election to call out materiality is semiotic; the sign is invested in every operation but is not derived from it necessarily. Does thinking of the problem through the action of the map and mapping help our situation? The problem of the map and mapping is the idea of the map as a place and a given situation. In Latour's terminology, a thing of "earth" and not of "Gaia" (Latour 2016c). The election of a map is a thing of power. What the simulacra of placing has achieved is to simulate the model of the model. Encryption arbitrarily chooses routes and outlines, directions and forms out of a multiplicity (this is also what art does, but art is anarchic and iconoclastic). Consequently, what is truly arbitrary is not to delineate or to outline but to elevate its action as the correct and identitary image, the unique form to be copied. The Tramp's map in Chaplin's "Gold rush" is the very example of a map, every map has to do with performance. The problem of the map is the idea of the map as place of situation. And, we say all the aforementioned without touching upon the intricate problem of where the sphere (or any other form of representation) begins in order to "orient" oneself or others.

Are we hitting a contradiction? We have been unyielding in saying that potestas cannot be circumvented because it defines the conditions of communicability, that is, of power as relating and understanding the world. This is the truth of the encrypted world through the simulacra of difference. What would the world be without it? Well, the world where there is no hierarchy or structural differences between the ability of technology, humans, and non-humans to produce immanent difference (Latour 2005). Nevertheless, the world of encryption not only weighs on the world but it defines it. We agree in seeking a flat ontology, where *a-priori* nothing has a privilege over anything else. Nonetheless, once in the world of actuality and the circulation of relations, we must distinguish the capacity (actual and material) of things to define reality. Accordingly, in a world defined by potestas, the "ability" (power), which is the key word, does vary substantially. There are grades of abilities defined by potestas, beginning with the power of potestas to make us see a certain world. There is a variation of capacities from thing to thing, this is the stuff of potestas, and we must be attentive to those fluctuations of force. The force field of potestas is to create a filter through which capacities, that are their own potential difference, may be funneled as to input in them a variation of power. Power of expression as well as power to exist are ultimately the same and are separated by potestas who reserves for itself any existence through its own expression. We must, therefore, re-read the stark phenomenon and re-formulate it as "there is no difference in the *potentiality* of *difference* of technology, humans etc." The point is that this potentiality under the rule of potestas is blocked and driven to actuality (as *Entelecheia*). Only through this reconsideration, that seems as a detour but is actually a wormhole, may we speak of an authentic synergy as the lack of any privilege in the description of actants (principle of generalized symmetry). Nevertheless, in order for synergy to exist, we must overthrow potestas first and utmost.

Considering the world of actants in the differentiation between intermediaries and mediators we can grasp a powerful motif of what we are saying. Intermediaries make no difference; they transport without transformation. On the other side, mediators are entities that multiply difference. In the words of Bruno Latour:

> By abandoning the dreams of epistemology, AT (ANT) is not reduced to moral relativism but gets back a stronger deontological commitment: either an account leads you to all the other accounts -and it is good- or it interrupts constantly the movement, letting frames of reference distant and foreign -and it is bad. Either it multiplies the mediating point between any two elements -and it is good- or it deletes and conflates mediators—and it is bad. Either it is reductionism -and that's bad news- or irreductionist—and that's the highest ethical standard for AT. We will see that this touchstone is much more discriminating than the quest for epistemological purity or for foundations or for moral norms. (Latour 1996, 377)

Of course, we are in the world of description. Nevertheless, right here is a distinction in the description of actants. There is a choice, not an empirical hard fact. These choices are political. The only no-choice that would be ontological is the principle of difference. The difference between intermediaries and mediators can only be established by a cut in time that analyses the capacity of one or another thing to communicate difference. Nevertheless, in a world signed by potestas, it cannot be an *a-priori* differentiation. The truth of the matter is that potestas feeds of simulating differences between actants and creating intermediaries that simulate difference. Only a world signed by *Energeia* are there no intermediaries at all; while in a world of potestas as *Entelecheia* the difference is not easy to pick up by any descriptive mechanism if it does not penetrate potestas first.

As Viveiros de Castro specified in Cannibal Metaphysics "Deleuze's thought, at least from Difference and Repetition and the Logic of Sense on, can be taken as an extreme effort to deterritorialize structuralism" (Viveiros de Castro 2009, 104). However, through the insights we have gained, it is high time to ask what is the limit of deterritorialization? Is there not a point where everything, including its principle and its semantic compound simply becomes utter indifference?

What is vital of Deleuze's and Guattari's work on assemblages is that it puts us before the "collapse of the distinction between epistemology (language) and ontology (world) and the progressive emergence of a practical ontology" (Viveiros de Castro 2009, 105). Through it, the common loses any sense as a generic identity and what appears before us, or better yet, where we are immersed in, is a nonhierarchical communication between beings that are different, and thus cannot communicate anything else but difference. "A multiplicity has neither subject nor object, only determinations, magnitudes, and dimensions that cannot increase in number without the multiplicity changing in nature" (Deleuze and Guattari 1987, 8). We will then have to speak of "*a plane of consistency*" of multiplicities that are infinite, always open and incomplete (what is infinite is *per se* incomplete). The infinite nature of the plane of consistency and its relations to incompletion mean that any extending or contracting within the plane is not numerical but intensive; it is not additive but synergic. There is no such thing as a "higher difference." An assemblage is a composite of variables and those variables enter into a relation as a form to change at every step the relation to itself and to the other elements. There is no static category or property in them, they circulate according to new forces that are created from within. It is all presence.

Walt Whitman sings to us:

There was never any more inception than there is now,
Nor any more youth or age than there is now,
And will never be any more perfection than there is now,
Nor any more heaven or hell than there is now.

Encryption is the anti-order of the plane of consistency. Nevertheless, for Deleuze and Guattari, it is a matter of perception. Either we see orders and strata, units that are hierarchical; or we see flat ontologies and rhizomes. But here we must stop and ponder if everything that is the case depends on the mechanisms available to capture and to create reality. And therefore, if the role of encryption is one of founding a perception, of capturing a semblance, of producing an aspect, of guiding it and making any way out "necessarily" impossible, must we scheme a way out of simple perception? When we lift the veil what do we call it? Is it still a veil or has it become a mirror, a pair of glasses? Is it in the skin or in the goosebumps? A virus is also a rhizome. The point is not that a tree is a tree (arborescent), but that it forms rhizomes with the air, the birds, the worms, fungus, the nutrients, at cellular and molecular levels, but also at poetic levels and geographical levels. Now, do the cellular levels speak more of rhizomes than the geographical? Well, think of which of them is more or less a human made division, and thus how it can be composed or decomposed as such. Thence, we must ask what systems of unity do force the tree out of its context (environment) to consider it as a measure of unity and identity (difference within the model of the law of identity). And, thereunto, would it not be more fructiferous to captivate or perceive a rhizome as a way to create it?

SECOND HUMAN NATURE

Our nature is split, deformed. If there ever was one thing called nature it has left us as a plentiful spring of life, it escaped us as a shooting vision. We have built walls around it; we have depleted it and us from it. We have played it as sword, book and mine, as source, mirror and limit. Must of all, we have built a second nature on top of it, multiple natures to say the truth are the Babel sitting on top of a nature that is unrecognizable from our methods of ditching and exploiting it. Our species, of wolf sorcerers, and tricksters of science have nothing but vacuum in between us. Naturalism has become the great structure of homogeneity. Every time humans speak of single, uniform, transcendent nature, a bloodbath usually follows. Nietzsche believed that "Under the magic of the Dionysian, not only does the bond between man and man lock itself in place once more, but also nature itself, no matter how alienated, hostile, or subjugated, rejoices again in her festival of reconciliation with her prodigal son, man" (Nietzsche 1994, 9).

The Dionysian is poetry infused in the fever of contingency and uncertainty; it is ripping apart the scaly layers of knowledge that hold us still in the place of nothing. But, has it not deserted us? Has it not been thinned down to a mimic by science and epistemology? Marx and Webber showed us that certainty is basic, since science embroiled with a specific type of consciousness is a power matrix. As Lefebvre has remarked, "science wants itself to be a science of determinisms, a knowledge of constraints. It abandons to philosophers the exploration of births, of decline, transitions, disappearances" (Lefebvre 2000, 104). Before, was there not a second nature needed as a transcendental axis for the creation of a well-grounded civilization that would overpower and absorb all other semi-civilizations and anti-civilizations? Was this not the work of Hobbes, to second-legally-notarized nature of the contract? And, Adam Smith's second nature as the ruler of political economy? A scathing relation power-knowledge was uncovered by Foucault; nevertheless, what he missed is that philosophy too (not his discrete sciences alone) is executed to give ground to the predominant forms of power. Is there a philosophical theory that is not compromised or that is not the product of a specific form of power? It is high time to begin understanding philosophy from power so we may begin to understand power from philosophy.

The classic division of *techné* and *Diké* is also crossed by this sword. *Diké* is not natural balance or just fitness; it is rather well the production of language and, through this language, in the same act, the act of tearing humans out of nature as nature is baptized and thus created in language all over again. Heidegger intervenes in the realm of second nature through his wager on *Phusis* or being emerging from itself, coming to be, "the coming-into-appearance in such unfolding, and holding itself and persisting in appearance—in short, the emerging-abiding sway" (Heidegger 2000, 46). The ground for being, *Phusis*, is thus the wound of tearing in language. *Techné* is the dominion of knowing and doing that strives to imitate the lost model, what evaporated in inscribing nature as a second nature, a thrust to recover the thing that went awry when it was originally named. Thus, in a world of mere appearances (material and physical), the only way out of this conundrum is the Platonic *Eidos*, an archetype that both *techné* and *Diké* must copy. *Eidos* becomes the model of everything. *Phusis* as a sway of beings is not concealed; it is appearance as a distance between naming and necessity, between logos and ontology, it is the space left out of time. Henceforth, *Phusis* as becoming is reduced to actuality. Becoming, as the change of the thing in time (becoming other through synergy) is spat out through a model of actuality -present at hand- that is, notwithstanding, never present to itself. What accrues to being as becoming within this landscape of the conjuring of being? Becoming is turned into a simple change of place, a physical question of motion, it is compacted to the Cartesian formula of acceleration within space and time.

In building these second-level human natures, there seems to be two phases of encryption. In phase one, there is a stranglehold of human language over things, animals, cells, solar systems, biomes, and photosynthesis. It is a split of internal and external natures in order to fragment them and to cut off any communication between them. As a direct consequence, phase two cuts off any possibility of things to communicate between themselves that does not first triangulate identity to transcendence. In this process we have lost any direct contact with nature, not only jerking ourselves from it but creating a poor substitute in its behalf. Does this not sound farfetched? How can language as a form of human power be able to inhibit natural synthesis? Well, as we are long anticipating the predominance of human actors cannot be underestimated, humans, like it or not, have taken control. A random, chaotic control of nature, not only creating a second nature but spinning the first nature out of any joint of predictability. Science, that was supposed to explain nature meticulously, has created the most horrendous irony; when overcome with technology, it creates a nature it cannot understand or put back on track. Only science destroys the object of its own understanding.

We must recharge our question regarding nature. Bruno Latour offers us a way out of the storm, his opposition between the concept of Earth and Gaia. "Compared to the concept of Nature, the concept of Gaia is *local*. It's a ring of active life forms that have molded their many overlapping niches in such a way that they provide one another a series of envelopes that can in no way be stretched and smoothed in the form of the *res extensa*" (Latour 2016c, 12). Gaia is earth transformed; Gaia is a rhizome as a flat construction of difference through difference. Is it enough to carry us through the thick crusts of nature as transcendence? For we not only named nature but transformed forever its "balance." Hence, we have irremediably changed the course of earth (global warming, etc.) that demands a different kind of political philosophy than simply the praise of difference or the independence of things.

Latour's project liberates Gaia from the laws of Nature. As he makes clear:

> Gaia is not a place for epistemological peace but epistemological warfare. Ask a farmer what he or she thinks of agronomy; an Amazonian Indian what he or she thinks of modern agro forestry; the executive of an oil company what he or she thinks of climate science; the laid off worker of a bank what he or she thinks of the "law of economics"! No discipline any longer has the power to disqualify those claims and transform them into subjective or archaic versions of what really is. (Latour 2016c, 14)

Second natures as transcendent forms of commanding are garnered through disciplinary qualifications, through the hierarchization of disciplines in the dreadful alliance of power-knowledge. What Latour shows us is that Gaia is a fruitful event to flatten discourses where no privilege may be settled upon the description of things and concepts. But, as much as we may gain through Gaia, we still need a differentiation of capacities, faculties, and forces (within potestas) that may effectively flatten the hierarchies of disciplines. The first discipline we must flatten is rather not a discipline, but the monopoly of truth of disciplines (science). Furthermore, we should not speak of disciplines as it is too restrictive; we should speak of experiences (*vivencias*) in order not to favor traditional forms of knowing that also exclude feeling and doing, praxis and poetics as forms of integration of discourses.

The first step is to decrypt the principle of localization. As Latour puts it "When anyone begins to speak of the relations inside which any entity is supposed to 'enter,' *it is too late*. The qualities that the relations bring to the entity were *there all along*, except that they had been cut off by the principle of localization" (Latour 2016b, 315). But there must be a principle of localization, of differentiation or we would be before a principle of flatness that is so flat that we have no notion where is up or down, left or right. It is clear we cannot prefigure the relation and impose it on entities, organisms, or in one word on any actants. Nevertheless, it is still unclear as to how the relations are to be measured, thought, or organized. This is why it is key to take the discussion into an ontological domain, so we may understand it under the principles of *Energeia* and *synergy*.

Feeding on the findings of quantum mechanics regarding realities that are observer dependent, we must ravage our ontological drawers in order to question if our intervention in the world has made it so extreme so as to hold that any postulated natural reality, and our involvement in it, is now utterly observer dependent. As a logical consequence of our previous query, we must then establish if what is needed is the elevation of human mechanics into a metaphysical order from where we can trace its movement, outline its full shape, and determine its content.

NOTES

1. It would be an anthropological enterprise akin to the one done by Pierre Clastres (1987).
2. Miles Davis asked the musicians under his directions to improvise in such a way that they did not play what they knew, but what they didn't yet know.

Chapter 6

Resoluteness (*Entschlossenheit*), Discourse, and Disclosedness

Resoluteness, a key Heideggerian existential attitude, also gets trampled in between the encryption of the ready to hand and its direct relation with the "they." Let us begin with Heidegger definition of "resoluteness" and the central role it plays out in the constitution of being. But on what basis does Dasein disclose itself in resoluteness? On what is it to resolve? Only the resolution itself can give the answer.

> When the call of conscience is understood, lostness in the "they" is revealed. Resoluteness brings Dasein back to its ownmost potentiality for Being-its-Self. When one has an understanding Being-towards-death—towards death as one's ownmost possibility—one's potentiality-for-Being becomes authentic and wholly transparent. (Heidegger 2001, 354/307)

Resoluteness is not a will or a hunger but is the existential attitude that, according to Heidegger, welds the ready to hand and the they in one instantaneous movement revealing the limits of the they and the endless potentialities of the ready to hand. In Heidegger's words,

> Resoluteness, as authentic Being-one's-Self, does not detach Dasein from its world, nor does it isolate it so that it becomes a free-floating "I." And how should it, when resoluteness as authentic disclosedness, is authentically nothing else than Being-in-the-world? Resoluteness brings the Self right into its current concernful Being-alongside what is ready-to-hand, and pushes it into solicitous Being with Others. (Heidegger 2001, 344/298)

Again, we find an arbitrary division between the "they" and the ready to hand. This time it produces an irreparable deviation in resoluteness where the "they" cannot supersede an ever-paralyzed state of actuality while the potentiality of being, the vigor of life, would be exclusive of the ready to hand.

Resoluteness is the disclosing of the potentiality of being, where potentiality becomes positive in the sense that every potentiality is concretely disclosed as indefinite. According to Heidegger the "they" presuppose a closed off amount of potentiality, a limited set of possibilities that are held in captivity by the "they." We can think of it as a game where a player may only move within the scope of the rules determined preemptively by another player. Henceforth, when we are immersed in the "they," there are x (determined) amount of possibilities for being to be. The said possibilities are predefined, ordered, numbered, spatialized, and fractioned by the they. Through resoluteness, being shatters any predictability of an enclosed set of possibilities and contingency is opened anew as an infinity of potentialities for *Dasein*. In short, with resoluteness, the possibilities for authenticity are snatched and liberated from the they. But resoluteness is not exhausted in a machinic plane, it is foremost existential. Resoluteness is the capacity of being to overcome the unflinching facticity of death through a struggle that knows will always end in perpetual loss but strives no less to live and to live to the fullest precisely because it knows the ultimate defeat at the hands of death. As such, resoluteness is the coming to terms with mortality and thrownness (*Geworfenheit*), and is thus the organizing prefiguration of "care."

This is the splitting point. There is only an apparent transparency of the they, *as if* the they had not touched upon the ready to hand or as if the ready to hand remained remote and isolated from any primordial interaction. Dualism at its finest. But beyond this hard-held evidence, how could we decide in what terms and at which moment we are referring to the ready to hand and in what terms and at which moment to the "they." How can we be authentic to life if our recognition of the material boundaries of death run astray? But then again, who else can capture this difference but *Dasein* herself, through herself. We always come too late to ourselves, always in the split second when we are no longer it. The constitution of being is always not being at home in itself, always decentered and riven, (out of joint, as Heidegger quotes Shakespeare). The asking of the question, the longing for the answer attests to the fact that something is already aloof, that a disfigurement has taken hold of change. We cannot creep upon ourselves from the future. The point is that if the ready to hand is not decrypted first, any potentiality of being is also numbered and predetermined, and thus potentiality becomes necessity, and necessity is but actuality—the denial of difference and of being. Henceforth, death sneaks back to beingness, but as a farce—a form of fantasy. In the face of death, *Dasein* conquers authenticity facing it through resoluteness, or so it wrongly believes. If in the mingling of *Dasein* with the things of the world it does not recognize that those things are signed by power games that instill hierarchies and exclusion in them, then authenticity is but the fantasy of a downtrodden being that thinks itself alone in the world. A form of solipsism riding on the back of a bleak shadow of freedom.

A curious being this, that it is running away from the alienation of the "they," but sits comfortably when said alienation is performed to others in the organization of the things of the world. As such, resoluteness does not alter the originality of the ready to hand; it does not decrypt it; it just puts the "they" right alongside it. Resoluteness would not be constitutive but additive: things become in their use as use makes being (interlocking-multilaterally with the they). Resoluteness as "the call" can authenticate the ready to hand, but only if the ready to hand is deprived of encryption in the first place, hence what is primordially disclosed in resoluteness would not hinder or alter the primal encryption; rather, well, it would deepen its fantastical alignment.

Crossing this magnificent bridge of being we find its fault line. Let us keep the picture at arm's length. The actual is in the "they," hence we are before the actuality of the they pitted against a supposed potentiality of being ingrained in the ready to hand. As Heidegger elucidates, "The average everydayness of concern becomes blind to its possibilities, and tranquillizes itself with that which is merely 'actual.' . . . All the same, this tranquillized 'willing' under the guidance of the 'they,' does not signify that one's Being towards one's potentiality-for Being has been extinguished, but *only that it has been modified*" (Heidegger 2001, 239/195. Italics are ours). Very well then, let us ask simply, modified from what? A pure state, something that presupposes the "they" and being? But then again, who can recognize such modification? We must be attentive to the fact that it is not that modification is a simple accident or a deviation; rather, "modification" is what is essential in understanding *Dasein*. But here we run amiss once again. There is no way of knowing such modification because that would presuppose a kind of pure state of *Dasein*, one that is not in the world and hence it would be an a-priori entity, a stuff of another world and not *Dasein* at all. The "they" are substantial for understanding the potentiality of being of *Dasein*; there is no way to reach the potentiality of being that does not share and transit with the "they," if there was, it would be a mere "presence at hand" elevated to the facticity of existentiality. In Heidegger's account, there is a route toward authenticity that is "suspended," or as he says "modified" by the "they." The individual decides to stay in the "they" to tranquilize itself, to protect itself against the risk of taking a step toward authenticity. But the argument, privileging the ready to hand over the "they," would require a sort of Fermat's principle[1] where *Dasein* already knows where such authenticity begins and ends, how and at what speed it will travel to project itself before being, and thus where it knows exactly how to attain perfection before it even exists. It would presuppose that *Dasein* can abstract and detach itself from itself and from the "they" before it has even mingled within the "they," that by this very same token cannot be understood as anything at all. But, if the latter is true, then either (a) There is no true process, no "becoming other" and this would turn out to be a denial of *Dasein*; or (b) A modification would require knowing a "pure" (Kantian) *a-priori* state which is impossible as it negates existentiality. In the case of (b), the modification by the "they" is Heidegger's mortal leap, because, to deem this as such, we would need one of two things: a presupposition of pureness of being (prior to the "they" and thus prior to any being in the world) or an outside observer that perceives from pure neutrality, from an a-modeless model of being, all the drama of life unraveling in an instant (it would require Borges' *Aleph*). Henceforth, the same degree of the capacity to "modify" that is awarded to the "they" must be awarded to the ready to hand as well, or else a catatonic state of being would prevail.

Although this is not the target of the theses of this book, a further issue is that the concealment of being by being should not be deemed as an obstacle to overcome, a finality to reach, but the very state of every being, the phenomenal state that is proper to every being. There is no phenomenology beyond this point. Even though we will not engage here with "temporality," we must bear in mind that resoluteness is the bridge that connects facticity (past), falling (making present), and existentiality (future) as the "*ecstases*" of temporality where uncanniness or "not being at home" *(das Nichtzuhause-sein)* is the existential mode of *Dasein*. Suffice to say that resoluteness, as the righteous attitude produced by anxiety, individualizes being in the world (Heidegger 2001, 235/191). Consequently, it is vital to emphasize the fact that it is not that decryption would make *Dasein* feel at home or that it would heal some kind of original wound, but that the uncanniness would have a direction, a place to begin to disembroil the strangeness of the meaning of being.

Resoluteness is the authenticity of the truth of disclosedness or "care." Thrownness, projection, and fallenness attain their final constituting meaning in care. In resoluteness we have now arrived at that truth of *Dasein* that is most primordial because it is authentic. Only now may we embark in an authentic dealing with the ready to hand, only at this point is "involvement" warranted as ontological. In Heidegger's words,

> Our concernful dealings can let what is ready-to-hand be encountered circumspectively only if in these dealings we already understand something like the involvement which something has in something. Letting things be involved makes up the existential structure of concern. But concern, as Being alongside something, belongs to the essential constitution of care; and care, in turn, is grounded in temporality. If all this is so, then the existential condition of the possibility of letting things be involved must be sought in a mode of the temporalizing of temporality. (Heidegger 2001, 404/353)

Anxiety, as a state of mind, is the potentiality of being. Undisguised anxiety reveals being in the world. That of which we are anxious about is our thrownness, our being unhinged from the world, and this, and only this, is the potentiality of being. Hence, resoluteness bundles up not only anxiety but also falling and thrownness as the facticity of "care." As stated by Heidegger, "Of course, it is essential to every state-of-mind that in each case Being-in-the-world should be fully disclosed in all those items which are constitutive for it-world, Being-in, Self. But in anxiety there lies the possibility of a disclosure which is quite distinctive; for anxiety individualizes'" (Heidegger 2001, 235/191). Potentiality of being is attested by the fact that existentiality is always factical; hence anxiety, as being ahead of itself, cannot be disentangled for the ready to hand, for if one moves or is incomplete it destabilizes the other. If existentiality is always factical, anxiety belongs primordially to the ready to hand as well; its separation would be an enterprise as absurd as to dislodge air from whirlwind. As Heidegger deepens the idea, "To put it otherwise, existing is always factical. Existentiality is essentially determined by facticity. . . . Ahead-of-itself Being- already-in-a-world essentially includes one's falling and one's Being alongside those things ready-to-hand within-the-world with which one concerns oneself" (Heidegger 2001, 236–237/192). Nonetheless, if the ready to hand is afforded a privilege that the "they" are not, this falling would be a simulacrum, a "falling of vacuum in the vacuum," a falling in the wrong way of sorts, as an impossibility (not falling at all but the sensation of falling, a simulacrum of falling) of an existentiale. This simulacrum goes on to rupture the meaning of care at its structural marrow.

We are resolute in the face of death, and death is the unique possibility of the disclosing of being of *Dasein*. Only before death may we be authentic; only in the nudeness of the "absolute nothing" may life become meaningful. And, thus, we may only stare onto the precipice of death when we know life will be carved out of its shape. For Heidegger, this possibility of the meaningful being of life in death is only accomplished when "it has been wrenched away from the 'they .'" Only in the authentic anticipation of death can we rid ourselves of the "they." Lostness is not overcome by anticipation as the ready to hand are unhinged from the beginning of their place and use; so to "understand" and "choose" among the factical possibilities is already a presupposition and an imposition that, if gone unexamined and un-decrypted, will make the anticipation of death inauthentic. At any extent, the choosing and understanding that follows will be based on a false construction of the ontic possibilities of the ready at hand, maxing out existentiality and clinging to it as the only possible experience in the world.

As we anticipated, the question of the "real reality" is ontologically based on *Dasein*, and care is the vortex of its facticity and existentiality, "All access to such entities is founded ontologically upon the basic state of Dasein,

Being-in-the-world; and this in turn has care as its even more primordial state of Being (ahead of itself—Being already in a world—as Being alongside entities within-the-world)" (Heidegger 2001, 246/202). Hence the connection of Dasein to the "Real" is constitutive. As Heidegger continues illuminating, "But even the Real can be discovered only on the basis of a world which has already been disclosed. And only on this basis can anything Real still remain hidden" (Heidegger 2001, 247/203). Notwithstanding, and in the face of what we have proved until now, these statements seem to divide the "world" into two parts: first, there is the world as *res extensa*, a uniformity that is disclosed, an ever-extending thing. And, second, the possibility of there being real or false things within this extensa (singularities); there are things in the thing, as if we could divide space as either being one thing (Descartes) or many things upon many things, as a uniformity set up in patches of referential differences. Could it be that in Heidegger's account the ready to hand would remain undifferentiated if it is not decrypted? The principal work of Heidegger is to disclose. Through decryption we discover that we may only disclose things using them in an average everyday way—but when everydayness means encryption and privation, all the existential formations of *Dasein* logically collapse with it and the representation of one stable presupposition (*res extensa* in this case) arises as the model of potestas.

As Heidegger continues threading, "The making-present, which awaits the 'towards-which' with equal primordiality, is held fast alongside the equipment which has been used, and it is held fast in such a manner, indeed, that the 'towards which' and the 'in-order-to' are now encountered explicitly for the first time" (Heidegger 2001, 406/355). Allow us to recap the constituting elements of the ready to hand. First there is an involvement that precedes circumspection. The said involvement is the existential structure of concern (as being alongside something) that means care and thus the opening into authentic temporality. Involvement is not merely a thematical perception but that which carries to full term the "towards-which" and "in-order-to." For Heidegger, it is an (active) involvement and not a mere experience that forms the thing thematically. Through decryption it has become evident that the latter affirmation, that brings Heidegger's oeuvre together, cannot be so, unless the ready to hand is decrypted. Concern-care-temporality-being fall one after the other in an immediate chain-reaction when the ready to hand goes unexamined by decryption. We could not find neither facticity, nor existentially or any being at all, but only the return to the present to hand in its full-blown power of the denial of ontology. In our language game we would need to turn back to a mere pseudo-experience of the pilling up of entities, or at best, a mangled distribution of things (they and tools) as *res extensa*. To decrypt the ready to hand does not mean that things appear transparent for all of us, as if there would be a primordial meaning in things and their involvement, as if the univocal use of the tool would be inscribed in it as a tag or instruction kit. This is not the case at all. Decrypting the ready to hand means that the possibility of meaning is contingently created in uses through an intense virtuality of difference. Or, in other words, the contingent possibility of enunciation for all precedes the mere existence of something generically called tool. Decryption of the ready to hand means no unity or identity of the things, but the possibility to create new forms of involvements in disobedience of every transcendent order. Being alongside something is never being alone with the thing; the symbiosis is contextual, and hence being along with x means the possibility of renaming it, using it in a novel manner and reconfiguring the context itself.

One of the fundamental angles of the argument is to distance it from an easy "counter-argument" in which it could be suggested that we are demanding a just world or a fair initial distribution of power of the ready to hand. This is not the case at all. Rather, when Heidegger leaves the ready to hand unexamined, he is the one that is presupposing a fair starting point of the world, and, with it, he is not only presupposing fairness but the existence of a world before being. The world is the world of the ready to hand despite any construction on its fairness. But our argument is not one of fairness, it is at root ontological. "The things are the things in their use no matter if the totality of involvements is encrypted" (says the devil's advocate). Demanding a decrypted totality of involvements would be stepping back to Kant and the impossibility of the thing in itself-for itself, or so the argument would go. The problem is not only the nomination of any singularity (thing) that constitutes a ready to hand but the possibility to disentangle one thing form another, the potentiality to name not only things within the firmament of the ready to hand, but to create novel relations beyond any given totality. Heidegger's theory of being lacks a correct examination of how the ready to hand is created and what it creates. Hence, the totality of involvements cannot be lived by *Dasein*; it could not be the world where it could gain moods, understanding, or where it could be fallen (only some would have access to the possibility of being lost). In the ready to hand, the totality of involvements is already predesigned. What is vital to disclose is to what extent politics (as potestas) intervenes to distribute roles and capacities, hierarchies, and possibilities of use but, most importantly, to determine the very nature of use. As we do not know what the body can do, we do not know either what it can do with materials liberated from the yoke of encryption. What can a thing mean? What can it do? Encryption not only hinders the operation of things (depriving and deviating its use) but more importantly it skims the possibility of the use of things. It fouls "what is" and "what ought to be" in one indiscernible heap. Consequently, we are forced into an apparent conundrum of what comes first, the theoretical behavior or the circumspection of the ready to hand. We can safely say they are not two separate things that could be distinguished in space. Circumspection cannot be but of things; it already implies a theoretical behavior. What is encrypted is this territory from where words accrue a certain meaning and from where they can be re-interpreted over and over again.

DISCOURSE, MEANING AND UNDERSTANDING

According to Heidegger "The items constitutive for discourse are: 1. what the discourse is about (what is talked about); 2. what is said-in-the- talk, as such; 3. the communication; 4. and the making-known" (Heidegger 2001, 206/162). Discourse is the articulation of significations of being in the world. For Heidegger, the analytic of *Dasein* is disclosed by discourse (being with) that appropriates the ready to hand that is somehow undisclosed in itself and only there to be used, while in its use it discloses being-with. Heidegger did not worry about the un-disclosing of the ready to hand. Henceforth, if the constitutive items of discourse are simultaneous and we reverse the logic, we would be before discourse in the dark and empty space of the equipment that would only have meaning that is pre-discursive and meta-linguistic. Consequently, we would be before a discourse that is already defined by some unaccounted form and creator. Language would still have meaning, but it would never be disclosed as an *existentiale*; it would be a meaning given in the exact form of the present at hand, that is, as an unquestionable and solid state. Nevertheless, it is not clear what type of meaning we are talking about—for, how can there be a language in a predefined meaning of the use of things even before the thing is used at all? Hence, we would come in contact with things whose use is preestablished and unmovable. Forthwith, the thing cannot be used and therefore would lack any significance at all. If discourse is already shared in being with, what is the discourse really about if the ready to hand is an unexamined given? Discourse, or any possibility of it, would be transcendent and then all of Heidegger's critique of *logos* can be applied to this kind of discourse. Discourse is metaphysical unless the ready to hand is decrypted, if this is so, Heidegger has not taken a step further from the "Greeks inception" (Heidegger 2000) of the *logos* as present at hand.

Interpretation is direct; it is the result of the action as the action itself. Here it is crucial to grasp the difference between two forms of interpretations. Heidegger sets up the limits of the question, "anything interpreted, as something interpreted, has the 'as'—structure as its own; and how is this related to the 'fore' structure? Or do the fore structure of understanding and the as-structure of interpretation show an existential-ontological connection with the phenomenon of projection?" (Heidegger 2001, 191/151). The question is if we only gain the understanding of the world through the tool or if the tool comes already disposed for a kind of understanding, reverberating as it would, a world within it. As if an instruction kit would be germane to the tool, always locked inside it as an essential feature. Do we always have an a-priori understanding of the ready to hand when we use tools? And, therefore, are entities disclosed in their possibilities through a particular detailed use, put in line by the thing itself? Entities are full of meaning before we understand them. When we interpret, the entity is already "as" something, and not because of a machinic essential transparency that belongs to the thing itself. No, nothing so godly, but simply because it has already been used. And, yes, even the design of a thing, the blueprint, the primal idea in someone's head, is its use. As Heidegger rightly sees it, "that which is understood, taken strictly is not the meaning but the entity" (Heidegger 2001, 192–193/151).

Again, we ask, what would meaning, as exclusive to *Dasein*, mean if ready to hand is encrypted? The "as structure" and the "fore" are to be taken as exercises of meaning. The former is an act of appropriation by the *Dasein*, on what things are (as an "as") for it. Hence, the axiomatic principle that meaning only appertains to *Dasein* has to swing with the altogether fun fact that things have meaning before interpretation and understanding. Understanding as the potentiality of being discloses the world in which the possibility of the discovery of nature can be disclosed. But the possibilities are rigged! Why? The temporal short circuit between *Dasein* and meaning, the chicken and egg game, would mean that there are possibilities of meaning from an ontic point of view but not from an existential point of view. Again, the sterile landscape that Hegel warned us about reappears dry as ever, a being projecting itself into a world as vacuum, creating its contours as it falls through it. We must step away from this type of projection that ventures nothing but the vacuum of a super-esteemed being—a godlike figure giving life and meaning only through its touching upon the plants of paradise. Through decryption, we gain the knowledge that projecting is understanding the beings of other entities in terms of the possibilities (potentialities) of being.

Meaning is that which can be articulated in interpretation and more primordially in discourse. Discourse is thus the articulation of meaning. Here we detect a mortal leap in Heidegger between the ready to hand and meaning, and the latter as the existential equiprimordiality of moods and understanding that in turn constitute *Dasein*'s being self within the world. In his words, "That which gets articulated as such in discursive Articulation, we call the 'totality-of-significations' [Bedeutungsganze]. . . . If discourse, as the Articulation of the intelligibility of the 'there,' is a primordial existentiale of disclosedness, and if disclosedness is primarily constituted by Being-in-the-world, then discourse too must have essentially a kind of Being which is specifically worldly" (Heidegger 2001, 204/161). Here we revive the extent of a question we have been drilling at, is language a ready to hand? Heidegger notes that "Language is a totality of words, a totality in which discourse has a 'worldly' Being of its own; and as an entity within-the-world, this totality thus becomes something which we may come across as ready-to-hand" (Heidegger 2001, 204/161). But, then again, if the ready to hand remains encrypted, language remains closed off as a present at hand circling on its own weightless possibilities, directed from above. Henceforth, only a dry theoretical appreciation of language could be possible. The only barren possibility is to use language as it is formulated from a remote hidden place. Speaking, learning, writing, and imagining would be simply filling in the blanks of a figure we ignore but that we know someone, or something, holds at an end point as an imagined perfect figure. Consequently, language loses all possibility of action and transformation, it loses all potentiality and contingency, it is thus powerless.

Nevertheless, we are yet to enter into the den where the creature breathes. Bear in mind that language is a totality as a ready to hand and that discourse is the expression of the intelligibility of being in the world. And here is the quid "Discourse is existentially language, because that entity whose disclosedness it articulates according to significations, has, as its kind of Being, Being-in-the-world—a Being which has been thrown and submitted to the 'world'" (Heidegger 2001, 204/161). This thrownness and submission would be transparent for *Dasein* in Heidegger's terms, but not so if ready to hand remains encrypted, and this is the biting issue. For Heidegger, it is all about discovering the state of thrownness and submission as if it was transparent and already set up with illuminated interiors and measurable dimensions. What encryption shows is that such interiors, if they were to exist, are held within another interior that makes it impossible to reach or create the existentiality of language, and hence to disclose being-in-the world in any term offered by *Dasein*. Language remains present at hand with the grievance that it is thought as a ready to hand, as disclosing discourse while it has not left, and it cannot leave, the plane of the simulacrum.

If understanding is the projecting of the potentialities into the possibilities, this can only be done by a discernment between the present and the ready to hand, but there is no a-priori distinction; the only distinction comes about in learning how to use language in education and transmission. Any ready to hand is already signaled in a certain way by the "they" and power has already established the possibilities (potentialities) of moves and tactics within the world depending on many things like race or gender. In this process, identities are prefixed as also a ready to hand. Awarding meaning and creating discourse is not the paragon of intellectual freedom. To the question, to whom the discourse belongs to, or who dares it, the answer is everyone; it is the child finding its bearings in the world, challenging the weight of his feet and opening up into the world.

Understanding as showing us the possible is a projection of temporality into the possibilities of the things of the world. There is no opposition to potentiality; rather well it is potentiality in its purest form. Nevertheless, if potentiality is reserved for the potentiality of being, *Dasein* and the ready to hand lay there undecrypted, and then the bridge between the potential and the actual may never be crossed. Not because the ready to hand would remain a potentiality but because it would remain a perennial actuality.

Everything that is ready to hand belongs to the "they"; it is produced, delimited and we are trained in the world by them. If we do not decrypt, how can the "they" be deemed as an obstacle/foundation that deals permanently in the ready to hand? It would be absurd to say such a thing, because all we know of the world, we know in the good faith of the lessons of the "they." We have no other view, one that is external, immanent, or above the "they." Without "them" we would suffer form an utter lack of perspective. The creed of phenomenology "to the things themselves" is severed by the impossibility of access to the experience of the things as they belong to the world of encryption that is concealment. In disclosing self, self must first disclose the ready to hand, but this is impossible by one being alone; it needs *synergy*, the potentiality to transform among the infinite many.

And what about the relation between understanding and states of mind? If understanding reduces things to specific forms that can be analyzed just under one light we are before a power play. I understand the *use*, and I say, "now I can go on," but is this "now I can go on" a specific kind of use? A perfect copy of the way it is being asked of me? How ample are the confines of the use of it? But then, is it all an empirical proof that is being asked to attest to the fact that "I understand"? Hence, is "now I can go on" always a kind of perfect understanding? Well, deemed under what light? It must be understanding if the word is not taken in such a reduced manner, but then would it still be understanding? Or, is it then better to talk about interactions (virtual and intense)?

Let us remember Wittgenstein's sound advice "Try not to think of understanding as a 'mental process' at all.—For *that* is the expression which confuses you. But ask yourself: in what sort of case, in what kind of circumstances, do we say, 'Now I know how to go on,' when, that is, the formula *has* occurred to me?" (Wittgenstein 1986, 154). Is there proof of understanding? Only action and reaction. The state of mind is irrelevant; it is the pragmatic use and the empirical verification that matter. Wittgenstein is discussing here something very specific, the proof of understanding. Understanding is not a mental state, or better it does not matter if it is. Only in the use do we verify understanding and understanding becomes equal to the correct use of the rules in a use that conveys meaning. And yet, there are as many forms to exact understanding as there are potentialities of actions. What is left untouched by Wittgenstein are the ways in which the correct use is determined and by whom. In other words, under what kind of authority or under what conditions of a state of affairs and under what truth values (as values set up by power) is understanding construed. Again, the language game is not equalitarian, and this is exactly what determines it! In our actual state of things, encryption is what is definitive for language. We cannot describe or approximate any practice shying away from this extensive "power-base" of language.

In Wittgenstein's example of understanding as "now I can go on" we do not need to exude a method or a system in order to separate understanding from the mere shadow of states of mind. Things are simpler. As Wittgenstein purports, "Suppose, however, that he does not stick to a *single* method of transcribing, but alters his method according to a simple rule: if he has once written *n* for *Ay* then he writes *o* for the next *A, p* for the next, and so on.—-But where is the dividing line between this procedure and a random one?" (Wittgenstein 1986, 163). Think of this in terms of a game of encryption. The encryptor and the intended decryptor must share the rule of decryption; it must be transmitted in a parallel and adjustable manner with the encrypted text, the transmission, holding its bearing above the surface of language.

Now let us think what happens when we describe an experience, any experience, describing not the process but the experience. To say I feel, "attraction," or "causality" are all feelings of an experience; this is how we explain what we feel. A different thing is rule-following. But the feeling regarding the rule-following is an experience as well. Nevertheless, this is a unique experience, not because it is more entrenched in sublime feelings, but because it deforms the rule itself. There is an experience that is not the process of strictly following the rule. Rules are loose, ad-hoc, complementary, overlapping, etc.; we "sense" in them connecting mechanisms and we use the said mechanisms in all sorts of free manners. The experience of the rule is feeling the interactions, and the interaction of that feeling, and how it merges with everything, this is what we call the world.

Both rules as potestas and rules as a free guide through language games create an experience following and understanding that is never the rule itself. It is always open-ended and free flowing. The issue is that "being guided" sets the problem beforehand, it focuses it; another matter would be if we asked what is common to movement or anticipation. Now "I can go on" is the risk of contingency. It is the risk that all potestas has to gamble in order to maintain the simulacrum. It is the undecidability of power. The fundament of it is modeling, indoctrination, imposition, and the outsourcing of the experience to the master. To he who holds the keys of guiding, "now I can go on" is the crack in any language, the promise of the new. It is only here that we may begin to deem the problem of potentiality and actuality, of contingency and necessity through another light, an immanent light. We do not need a tool to liberate us from rules; rules as language are the incision in every system of potestas.

Our critique of Heidegger's concept of understanding and the relation thereof between the ready to hand and language has touched base with our X game of language. The most strenuous point of our X game of language is that it shows us the true magnitude of power as communicability. I mean, though it be true that a certain order of speech and of letters allow a communicability, the possibility of it, the capacities of transmission, are withheld and obscured by power plays. So much so that we must ask, as if it was science fiction, how is that the very nature of language became a thing of imposition? A thing of potestas. In our X game, language as an icon disappears, language as an image disappears, but most importantly, language as fixation and memory vanishes.

Interpretation over interpretation, we have a clearer sky to look at. Decryption is not about finding the hidden meaning; it is about getting around to establish the mechanism by which meaning is fixed and sustained as truth. It does not seek to find the reverse of meaning, a liberating back door of meaning, but rather why in a specific moment an interpretation of the world prevails, and people attach a proper meaning to it.

Measure by measure, *Dasein* is impossible when meaning is not available for all as the decryption of the ready to hand. But the true question beyond this is if an individual *Dasein* is the ultimate question of meaning of meaningfulness or is it rather a collective. May we propose a "we"? Hence, we have two separate but coinciding problems: (a) the impossibility of *Dasein* awarding meaning to itself because the ready to hand is encrypted; and (b) the impossibility of there being an authentic *Dasein* that is not already within a "we" ontological-existential structure.

DISCLOSEDENESESS THROUGH DIFFERENCE

We have got the ready to hand at the crosshairs of decryption. Now let us quickly follow it up with Heidegger's iconic engagement of the "Greck inception" of logos. As he reminds us,

> The Greeks had no word for "language"; they understood this phenomenon in the first instance as discourse. But because the *logos* came into their philosophical ken primarily as assertion, this was the kind of logos which they took as their clue for working out the basic structures of the forms of discourse and its components. this logic was based upon the ontology of the present-at-hand. (Heidegger 2001, 209/165)

Before Plato, Heidegger argues, logos meant disclosure; it meant *Phusis* or being emerging from itself, coming to be, "the coming-into-appearance in such unfolding, and holding itself and persisting in appearance—in short, the emerging-abiding sway" (Heidegger 2000, 46). Coming into being as emerging is complementary to *Aletheia* or coming out of obscurity, showing the self. *Phusis* and *Aletheia* are the cornerstone of disclosedness. While *Phusis* means "coming to presence as self-unfolding" (Heidegger 2000, 64), *Aletheia* means unconcealment, "a struggle for itself forth as the world" (Heidegger 2000, 64). It is vital to remark that *Phusis* is not becoming but the unfolding of the actual.

Disclosedness, as one of Heidegger's most sophisticated concepts, is the axis of all of his metaphysics. Although, as we are aware, it is a profuse concept that crosses the lines of other fundamental concepts such as *Aletheia* and *Phusis*, let us announce it as the existential breaking into the world of *Dasein* that marks the possibility of truth of every assertion. Through the equipmentality of the ready to hand, *Dasein* opens the world anew it discovers a new fundamentality of its place in the world. Through the equipment *Dasein* discloses self, ready to hand and the world in the same swoop of things.

Let us remember we are working within a shortcoming we found within the Heideggerian use of the "they" and the ready to hand that impairs the whole of the Heideggerian philosophy. Hence, what kind of world does *Dasein* disclose when it does not decrypt the ready to hand first? Is decryption implicit in disclosedness? The answer is no. It is not. The huge blind side we are attacking is precisely that if the ready to hand is taken as a given, it supposes a relationality of equality among beings and transparency of tools that, as we proved, does not and cannot exist. Nevertheless, here the downfall is captured at full range. The articulation of something as something in the disclosedness through the ready to hand (that is not decrypted first) truly hides a something that is encrypted but taken as disclosed and transparent (ready to hand) by *Dasein*. When the ready to hand is taken as something given, non-decrypted, this something, whatever it may be, is necessarily tainted in its possibilities, because it has become necessary! It is a stale actuality, and thus it has lost all potentiality for being . . . yes, again, pure immovable potestas. The involvement (totality) of the ready to hand is hindered, not in its ontic level (obtrusive, conspicuous, or obstinate) but in an existential level. That is, its potentiality for being of *Dasein* is turned automatically into a necessary actuality where becoming is impossible, hence *Dasein* is not.

Heidegger continues his bid toward disclosedness "When something is understood but is still veiled, it becomes unveiled by an act of appropriation, and this is always done under the guidance of a point of view, which fixes that with regard to which what is understood is to be interpreted" (Heidegger 2001, 191/150). But when we unveil, we are not unveiling the thing, but the totality of involvements that if encrypted would only unveil the sense it was given to it by the encryptor (an arrangement of things in space). Hence, as we anticipated, every unveiling must be twofold; we must first unveil the circumstances that established the totality of involvements, and only then will the ready to hand be apt to be unveiled in itself.

It is clear, as Heidegger raises the stakes that *Dasein* "only has meaning, so far as the disclosedness of Being-in-the-world can be 'filled in' by the entities discoverable in that disclosedness. Hence, only Dasein can be meaningful or meaningless (*sinnlos*)" (Heidegger 2001, 193/151). In an ontologico-existential way, there is no meaning unless there is *Dasein*. But there cannot be *Dasein* if the possibility of meaning is not available for all beings that produce difference to create meaning. Or, if in this pre-beingness of meaning, the meaning of the ready to hand is astray, thrown off the tracks of inauthenticity, or in a word, encrypted. This would amount to a simulacrum of being. If meaning always belongs proximally and for the most part to a kind or variant of an encryption of the ready to hand, this means that in simple disclosedness, not only authenticity would become impossible but any meaning itself would follow in its path. Hence *Dasein*, as well, would be an impossibility.

The question for authenticity cannot be asked unless ready to hand is disclosed for difference through difference. Difference as the possibility of the new within a boundless connection is the stuff of being, and therefore only through the disclosedness of difference can meaning come forth. Consequently, the ready to hand is not just some paraphernalia that being picks up in his becoming being; it is the medium through which being becomes; it is the multiplicity of life. Here we can begin to propose a form to outgrow Bergson's virtuality and intensity as being something simply for the mind or consciousness and produce these concepts in space itself. (This is the tricky part that I believe Deleuze did not accomplish and buried in tons of purple prose.)

Let us begin to open the meaning awarded by Heidegger to *Aletheia*, as taking entities out of their hiddenness and letting them be seen in their unhiddenness (in their uncoveredness). In the "Metaphysics," Heidegger encloses *Aletheia* as "what shows itself in its sway stands in the unconcealed. The unconcealed as such comes to a stand in showing itself. Truth, as unconcealment, is not an addendum to Being" (Heidegger 2000, 107). *Aletheia* is simply a state of being; it is its transparency; it is evidence that comes out of hiddenness. But *Aletheia* is not a pure state of being; it is not a condition of it, henceforth it requires a process, an asking, or a removing, in short, disclosedness. The extent of the disclosedness is determined by the wingspan of the question being formulated, which, in turn, is already established by the totality of involvements that the use of the ready to hand may uncover. If the totality of involvements is a given, *ergo*, the question (the dimensions of it, its capacity) is already determined. A thing is disclosed only proportionally to the capacity (wingspan) of the question that asks for it. How can I disclose something that I take as a given? In considering the ready to hand, we would be thrown back to the vicious cycle where only what is already there, as a given, allows itself to be disclosed; this disclosure would pass ontic things as ontological, quantities as qualities and so on. As Heidegger continues "Being-true ("truth") means Being-uncovering. But is not this a highly arbitrary way to define "truth"? By such drastic ways of defining this concept we may succeed in eliminating the idea of agreement from the conception of truth" (Heidegger 2001, 262/219) Here Heidegger is speaking of truth as agreement. But then allow us to roll up the question again in a new form: How can you disclose something (ready to hand) when you assume that it is what it is? If this is the case, then you only disclose the intended meaning of the encryptor, and all philosophy is tautological.

Aletheia is a process of coming into disclosedness. Entities show themselves in the "how," the "how" is the key that rotates the being toward *Aletheia*, what brings being into light. Encryption is the clotting of the question for the how. Since there is no one question (a magic how), then we are before the incapacity to even raise the possibility of "the how of things" which is not posited by a presupposition. Encryption is the impossibility of the how. Without decryption, the "how" is going through the motions, describing an outline, overshadowing movement, missing the mark of the question that could make being transparent.

Heidegger continues down the same road, "Assertion communicates entities in the 'how' of their uncoveredness. The assertion which is expressed is about something, and in what it is about [in ihrem Worüber] it contains the uncoveredness of these entities. This uncoveredness is preserved in what is expressed. What is expressed becomes, as it were, something ready-to-hand within-the-world which can be taken up and spoken again" (Heidegger 2001, 266/224). Here we are before the ready to hand as the expression of uncoveredness. When we perform an assertion over a thing, it becomes unbound from its thingness and becomes a ready to hand. But even this sleight of hand cannot avoid the trepidation with which the ready to hand is encrypted. It irremediably falls into a vicious cycle because the expression of the ready to hand is tainted from the beginning. Uncovering something that has been covered in a different way that is not asked upon because the possibilities of the question are already directed in a certain form and not another is simply going around in logical circles. It is simply obeying. Following in Heidegger's example (2001, 260/217), "Is the picture askew" is the only question that can be posed.[2] We disclose the ready to hand in the uses that were predetermined by a force that remains covered up, and, to be sure, what remains covered up (unaccounted for) becomes the presupposition of being . . . sheer transcendence, utter impossibility of truth. There is no internal structure of truth within an assertion, which could be said to be independent of being in the world nor disclosedness of entities as being in the world. Truth is not a question of correspondence between judgment and things; it is the disclosedness of being by being. But the truth we are seeking corresponds to difference that has been encrypted in the ready to hand.

Let us approximate the problem from a convergent wrinkle of power. We have already thoroughly settled the boundaries of the problem of *Energeia* and *Entelecheia*. Hence, in lieu of the divergent form of finalities, when is a symphony complete? Or when can we say a thing is unfolding or becoming? When this unfolding or becoming already presupposes a finished form that anticipates, controls, and commands the act of unfolding, that is, when it is "modeled," then we are before *Entelecheia*. Henceforth, the blossoming of a rose already presupposes a model "eidos" of a rose. Finality always presupposes "presence." Something that must become "presence as present" presents itself in the presence; the presenting is what constitutes the temporality of the present, non-being is eschewed in the coming to be. Notwithstanding, the "coming to be" is simply the modal component, where the prerogative is of the present. It also supposes that the principle of identity is previous to the becoming. A thing (being) must first be individuated in order to count as becoming, so something other must be added to the definition of *Phusis* and *Aletheia* or else subtracted from its structure.

NOTES

1. "Light travels between two points along the path that requires the least time, as compared to other nearby paths."

2. "Let us suppose that someone with his back turned to the wall makes the true assertion that 'the picture on the wall is hanging askew.' This assertion demonstrates itself when the man who makes it, turns round and perceives the picture hanging askew on the wall. What gets demonstrated in this demonstration? What is the meaning of 'confirming' [Bewhrung] such an assertion? Do we, let us say, ascertain some agreement between our 'knowledge' or what is known and the Thing on the wall? Yes and no, depending upon whether our Interpretation of the expression what is known' is phenomenally appropriate. If he who makes the assertion judges without perceiving the picture, but merely represents' it to himself, to what is he related? To 'representations,' shall we say? Certainly not, if 'representation' is here supposed to signify representing, as a psychical process. Nor is he related to 'representations' in the sense of what is thus 'represented,' if what we have in mind here is a 'picture' of that Real Thing which is on the wall" (Heidegger 2001, 260/217).

Conclusion

If we can only deem becoming from *Energeia*, then, are we not before a power that is beyond both actuality and potentiality? A horizontal and immanent power that is the order of both? A third order of power? If this is so, then everything is contingent, and contingency means that only when beings exist, not as a necessity, is the meaning of being necessary.

Bibliography

Agamben, Giorgio. 1998. *Homo Sacer: Sovereign Power and Bare Life*. Stanford: Stanford University Press.
Agamben, Giorgio. 2015. *A Potência do Pensamento (ensaios e conferencias)*. Belo Horizonte: Autêntica Editora.
Aristotle. 2015 *Metaphysics*. Perseus Digital Library. http://www.perseus.tufts.edu/hopper/.
Aristotle. 2015. *Nicomachean Ethics*. Perseus Digital Library. http://www.perseus.tufts.edu/hopper/.
Austin, John L. 1975. *How to Do Things with Words*. Oxford: Oxford University Press.
Bakhtin, Mikhail Mikhailovich. 1981. *The Dialogic Imagination Four Essays*. Austin/London: University of Texas Press.
Baldwin, James. 1993. *The Fire Next Time*. New York: Vintage International.
Barcan Marcus, Ruth. 1961. "Modalities and intensional languages." *Synthese 13* (4):303–322
Bergson, Henri. 2002. *Key Writings*. Edited by Keith Ansell Pearson and John Mullarkey. New York: Continuum.
Borges Jorge Luis. 1964. *Labyrinths Selected Stories & Other Writings*. New York: Directions Publishing Corporation
Borgwaldt Susanne R. and Terry Joyce. 2013. *Typology of Writing Systems*. Philadelphia: John Benjamins Publishing Company
Bousquet, Antoine. 2014. "Welcome to the Machine: Rethinking Technology and Society through Assemblage Theory." In *Reassembling International Theory: Assemblage Thinking and International Relations*, edited by Acuto, Michele and Simon Curtis. Basingstoke: Palgrave Macmillan.
Brandom, Robert. 2005. "Heidegger's Categories in Being and Time". In *A Companion to Heidegger*, edited by Dreyfus, Hubert L., and Mark A. Wrathall. Hoboken: Blackwell Publishing Ltd.
Buber, Martin. 1996. *I and Thou*. New York: Simon & Schuster.

Cervantes, Miguel de. 2010. *Don Quijote de la Mancha*. Kindle Edition. Guttenberg.net

Césaire, Aimé. 2000. *Discourse on colonialism*. New York: Monthly Review Press.

Chiang, Ted. 2002. *Stories of Your Life and Others*. New York: Knopf Doubleday Publishing Group.

Clastres, Pierre. 1987. *Society Against the State*. New York: Zone Books.

Conley, Verena. 2010. *The Deleuze Dictionary*. Revised edition edited by Adrian Parr Edinburgh: University Press.

Cooper, James. 1990. *Plato's Theaetetus*. London/New York: Routledge.

Coulmas, Florian. 2003. *Writing Systems. An Introduction*. Cambridge: Cambridge University Press.

Daniels, Pete and William Bright (eds). 1996. *The World's Writing Systems*. Oxford: Oxford University Press.

DeLanda, Manuel. 2008. "Meshworks, Hierarchies and Interfaces." In *Zero News Datapool. World-Information Institute*. 2008. http://www.t0.or.at/delanda/meshwork.htm.

DeLanda, Manuel. 2011. *Philosophy and Simulation: The Emergence of Synthetic Reason*. London/New York: Continuum.

Deleuze, Gilles and Felix Guattari. 1987. *A Thousand Plateaus: Capitalism and Schizophrenia*. Minneapolis: University of Minnesota Press.

Dostoyevsky, Fyodor. 2005. *The Brothers Karamazov*. New York: Dover.

Dreyfus, Hubert L. and Mark A. Wrathall. 2005. *A Companion to Heidegger*. Hoboken: Blackwell Publishing Ltd.

Everett, Hugh. 1973. The Many-Worlds Interpretation of Quantum Mechanics. *The Theory of the Universal Wave Function*. Quantum Mechanics, Princeton NJ: Princeton University Press. https://www-tc.pbs.org/wgbh/nova/manyworlds/pdf/dissertation.pdf

Fischer, Steven Roger. 2001. *The History of Writing*. London: Reaktion.

Foucault, Michel. 1978. *The History of Sexuality Volume I: An Introduction*. New York: Pantheon Books.

Fuentes, Carlos. 2007. *La Muerte de Artemio Cruz*. Ciudad de México: Penguin Random House, Alfaguara.

Griffiths, A.J.F., Miller, J.H. and Suzuki, D.T. et al. 2000. *An Introduction to Genetic Analysis*. New York: W. H. Freeman.

Heidegger, Martin. 2000. *Introduction to Metaphysics*. New Haven/London: Yale Nota Bene.

Heidegger, Martin. 2001. *Being and Time*. Oxford: Blackwell.

Kripke, Saul. 1980. *Naming and Necessity*. Cambridge: Harvard University Press

Latour, Bruno. 1996. On actor-network theory. A few clarifications plus more than a few complications. *Soziale Welt 47*:369–381.

Latour, Bruno. 2005. *Reassembling the social: An Introduction to Actor-Network-Theory*. Oxford/New York: Oxford University Press.

Latour, Bruno. 2016a. "Life Among Conceptual Characters." New Literary History 47, 2–3 on *Latour and the Humanities*. 149 NLH Felski Symposium. Edited by Stephen Muecke and Rita Felski.

Latour, Bruno. 2016b. "Onus orbis terrarum: About a possible shift in the definition of sovereignty." *Millennium: Journal of International Studies* 44(3):305–320.

Latour, Bruno. 2016c. "On a possible triangulation of some present political positions". Paper given as the *Mosse Lecture, Zukunftswissen Humboldt University*, Berlin, 12th of May 2016.

Lefebvre, Henri. 2000. *Writings on Cities*. Translated and edited by Eleonore Kofman and Elizabeth Lebas. Oxford: Blackwell Publishers Ltd.

Leibniz, G. W. 1989. *Philosophical Essays*. Edited by R. Ariew and D. Garber. Indianapolis: Hackett, 1989.

Levinas, Emmanuel. 1979. *Totality and Infinity: An Essay on Exteriority*. The Hague: Martinus Nijhoff publishers and Duquesne University Press.

Lewis, David. 1973. *Counterfactuals*. Malden: Blackwell Publishers.

Maldonado-Torres, Nelson. 2007. 'On the coloniality of being'. *Cultural studies*, 30, Vol 21, Nos 2-3, pp 240–270.

Marx, Karl. 1973. *Grundrisse: Foundations of the Critique of Political Economy*. Harmondsworth: Penguin.

McDonald, Angus. 2018. The Equivocation that Lies Like Truth. In *Decrypting Power*, edited by Ricardo Sanín-Restrepo. London: Rowman & Littlefield International.

Meillassoux, Quentin. 2008. *After Finitude. An Essay on the Necessity of Contingency*. Translated by Ray Brassier. London: Bloomsbury Academic.

Mignolo, Walter. 2001. *Cosmopolis: el Trasfondo de la Modernidad*. Barcelona: Península.

Nancy, Jean-Luc. 2000. *Being Singular Plural*. Stanford: Stanford University Press.

Negri, Antonio. 2003. T*he Savage Anomaly: The Power of Spinoza´s Metaphysics and Politics*. Translated by Michel Hardt. Minneapolis: University of Minnesota.

Nietzsche, Friedrich. 1994. *The Birth of Tragedy. Out of the Spirit of Music*. London: Penguin Books

Peirce, Charles Sanders. 1878. 'How to Make Our Ideas Clear'. In *Popular Science Monthly,* vol. 12, pp. 286–302. Reprinted widely, including Collected Papers of Charles Sanders Peirce (CP) v. 5, paragraphs 388–410.

Peirce, Charles Sanders. 1905. *Pragmatismo*. Traducción castellana de Sara Barrena. Fuente textual en MS 318. Grupo de Estudios Peirceanos (Gep). Departamento de Filosofía Universidad de Navarra E-31080 Pamplona, Spain.

Peirce, Charles Sanders. 1940. *The Philosophy of Peirce: Selected Writings*. Edited by Justus Buchler. London: Routledge and Kegan.

Plato. 1992. *Theaetetus*. Indianapolis: Hackett Classics.

Prigogine, Ilya. 1980. *From Being to Becoming: Time and Complexity in the Physical Sciences*. London: W. H. Freeman and Company.

Quijano, Aníbal. 2001. *Colonialidad del Poder, Globalización y Democracia*. Caracas: Instituto de Estudios Internacionales Pedro Gual.

Ramberg, Bjørn. 2009. Richard Rorty. *The Stanford Encyclopedia of Philosophy* (Spring 2009 Edition). Edited by Edward N. Zalta. https://plato.stanford.edu/archives/spr2009/entries/rorty/.

Rancière, Jacques. 1991. *The Ignorant Schoolmaster Five Lessons in Intellectual Emancipation*. Stanford: Stanford University Press.

Rorty, Richard. 1979. *Philosophy and the Mirror of Nature*. Princeton: Princeton University Press.

Sachs, Joe. 2005. 'Aristotle: Motion and Its Place in Nature'. Internet Encyclopedia of Philosophy. http://www.iep.utm.edu/aris-mot/#H2.

Said, Edward. 1978. *Orientalism*. New York: Vintage Books.

Sanín-Restrepo, Ricardo. 2016. *Decolonizing Democracy: Power in a Solid State*. London: Rowman & Littlefield International.

Sanín-Restrepo, Ricardo (ed.). 2018. *Decrypting Power*. London: Rowman & Littlefield International.

Sanín-Restrepo, Ricardo. 2020. 'Decrypting the City'. In: *The Built Environment in Emerging Economies: Cities, Space and Transformation*, edited by Amira Osman. BEinEE book series. Pretoria: Tshwane University of Technology (In Press).

Santos, Boaventura de Sousa. 2010. *Para Descolonizar Occidente: Más Allá del Pensamiento Abismal*. Buenos Aires: Clacso.

Steinhardt, Paul. 2014. 'Big Bang blunder bursts the multiverse bubble.' *Nature 510* (7503):9. doi:10.1038/510009a.

Tlostanova, Madina and Mignolo, Walter. 2009. '*Global coloniality and the decolonial option*'. *Kult 6, Special edition*. Roskilde University.

Viveiros de Castro, Eduardo. 2009. *Cannibal Metaphysics*. Minneapolis: Univocal Publishing.

Vonnegut, Kurt. 1997. *Slaughterhouse Five*. New York: Random House.

Wallerstein, Immanuel. 1999. *El Moderno Sistema Mundial*. Madrid: Siglo XXI de España Editores.

Whitman, Walt. 1995. "Leaves of Grass". In *The Complete Poems of Walt Whitman*. London: Woodsworth Editions.

Winkler, Rafael. 2006. 'Husserl & Bergson On Time and Consciousness'. *Logos of Phenomenology and Phenomenology of the Logos. Book Three. Analecta*

Wittgenstein, Ludwig. 1986. *Philosophical Investigations*. Translated by G. E. M. Anscombe. Oxford: Basil Blackwell.

Woolf, Virginia. 1965. *Orlando: A Biography*. New York: A Harvest Book, Harcourt Inc.

Index

Actor Network Theory (ANT), 3, 11, 44–45, 121–23, 127
actuality. *See Energeia*; *Entelecheia*
Agamben, Giorgio, 14, 16–17, 19–21, 54, 120
Aletheia, 40–41, 67–68, 105, 142–45
Alexander, the great, 84
Antigone, 73
anxiety. *See* Dasein, anxiety
Anzaldúa, Gloria, 108
apparatus, 69–70
arborescent systems, 45, 120, 125
Aristotle, 84; actuality. *See* actuality; definition of being. *See Energeia*; *Entelecheia*; *Eudaimonia*, 19; *Ousia*, 15, 27–28; *Thaten*, 75; virtue, 19–20
assemblages, 3, 57, 73, 120–21, 123–25, 128
assertions, 100–103, 144, 145n2
Austin, John, 10, 58

Bakhtin, Mikhail, 10, 56, 113
Baldwin, James, 65
Banksy, 108
Barcan Marcus, Ruth, 89
Basquiat, Jean-Michel, 10
becoming, 29, 126, 132, 142, 145, 147
Beethoven, Ludwig van, 81

being. *See* difference; *Energeia*
being in the world. *See* Dasein, being in the world; ready to hand, the, being in the world
being–one's–self. *See* resoluteness (*Entschlossenheit*)
being there. *See* Dasein, falling
being with. *See* Dasein, being with
being within the world. *See* Dasein; ready to hand, the, being within the world
Bergson, Henri, 11, 34n2, 37, 79, 110, 122, 143
Borges, Jorge Luis, 92, 108, 132
Borgwaldt Susanne R, 8
Bousquet, Antoine, 120–21
Brandom, Robert, 29
Bright, William, 8
Buber, Martin, 39

Carlin, George, 116
categories, 23, 28–29, 80, 98, 144
Césaire, Aimé, 24
Chaplin, Charles, 122
Chiang, Ted, 92, 114
circumspection (*Umsicht*). *See* ready to hand, the, circumspection (*Umsicht*)
Clastres, Pierre, 128n1
cluster theory of concepts, 83–87

153

concern (*Besorgen*). *See* ready to hand, the, concern (*Besorgen*)
Conley, Verena, 58
consciousness. *See* co–states of mind (*mitbefindlichkeit*)
contingency: of being, 147; and change, 3, 75, 119, 126; definition, 2–4, 16, 98, 147; as democracy, 4, 21; and necessity, 3–4, 52, 72, 93, 147; and novelty, 52, 82, 116, 119, 134–35, 140; and orders, 52, 119; and potentiality, 16, 119, 147. *See also* potentia; and power, 4; third order of power, 6, 139, 147; and transitions, 4, 21, 75, 77, 79
Cooper, James, 95n1
co–states of mind (*mitbefindlichkeit*), 68–70, 100, 133, 139
Coulmas, Florian, 8
Culkin, John, 62–63

Daniels, Pete, 8
Dasein: ahead–of–itself, 133–34; analytic of, 136; anxiety, 41–42, 132–33; authenticity, 32, 36, 39–40, 130–32, 141, 143; as becoming, 126, 132, 141–42; being already in the world, 134; being in the world, 27–28, 41, 129, 134, 136, 138. *See also* ready to hand, the, being in the world; being within the world, 28–29, 36, 133. *See also* ready to hand, the, being within the world; being with the world, 28–29, 36, 136. *See also* ready to hand, the; care (*sorge*), 29, 130, 132–33; collective, 141; decryption of, 29, 36–37, 39, 41–42, 47, 67–68, 132, 134, 140–42; ecstases, 132; everydayness. *See* they, the, everydayness; existential attitudes, 28; *existentialles*, 29, 41, 133; facticity, 41–42, 132–33; falling, 41–42, 132–33; impossibility of, 37–38, 41–42, 47, 66, 140–43; as meaning, 29, 133, 140–41, 143. *See also* meaning; meaningless (*sinnlos*), 143; modes of beings, 28, 38; moods, 137; not–being at home, 130, 132; ontic properties, 23, 28–29, 98, 144; out of joint, 130; real, the, 134; and resoluteness. *See* resoluteness (*Entschlossenheit*); solicitude, 29; temporality, 28, 132; they, the (with–others), 35–36, 38, 141–45. *See also* they, the; ready to hand the; das Man. *See* Dasein; ready to hand, the; they, the

Davis, Miles, 128n2
decryption of power, theory of. *See* theory of encryption of power (TEP)
DeLanda, Manuel, 44–45, 121
Deleuze Gilles, 3, 11, 45–46, 50–51, 56–59, 73, 80, 119, 120, 124–25, 143
Descartes, 27, 75, 80, 94, 126, 134
deseverance (*ent–fernung*), 66–67, 109, 130–31
difference, 1, 3, 13, 30, 38, 74–75, 123, 142–43, 147
Diké, 126
disclosedness (*erschliessen*), 39, 60, 105, 133, 136–37, 141–45
discourse: definitions, 136; encrypted, 136, 138; explicitness, 109; indirect, 58; and language, 138; making known, 136–37; and thrownness (*Geworfenheit*), 138; totality–of–significations (*Bedeutungsganze*), 137–38; as transcendent, 136, 138; as understanding, 136–37, 139
dissipative systems, 45
Dostoyevsky, Fyodor, 81, 104
Dreyfus, Hubert L, 48
duck–rabbit, the. *See* noticing an aspect
Dylan, Bob, 115

Ecclesiastes, Book of, 81
Eidos, 23, 71, 126, 145
empty signifiers. *See* names, as empty signifiers
encryption. *See* theory of encryption of power (TEP)

Energeia: and being, 15, 145, 147; being at work, 18, 20–21; definition, 14–19, 21, 119, 123, 145, 147; etymology, 17–18; finality. *See Entelecheia*, as finality; and immanence, 65, 75, 119, 124, 145, 147; and non–being, 15; as non–qualified actuality, 20–21, 119, 147; as open infinity, 21, 47, 54, 69, 104, 108, 147; as privation, 16, 18, 134; redundancy, 18, 20, 119; as synergy, 20–21, 47, 65, 75, 139, 145, 147; as unstratified power, 119, 145

Entelecheia: definition, 14–19; etymology, 18; final cause, 17, 19, 61, 145; as finality, 13, 17–18, 20, 49, 55, 61, 82, 123, 145; and immanence, 120, 145; as perfection, 18–20; primacy of, 16, 18, 82; as qualified life, 19–20, 120; theory of causes, 16–17

equipment. *See* ready to hand, the, as equipment

Everett, Hugh, 3, 91–94

Excalibur. *See* names, Excalibur, example

existential analytic. *See* Dasein, falling

existentialles. *See* Dasein, *existentialles*

facticity. *See* Dasein, facticity; potestas

falling. *See* Dasein, falling

family resemblances, 83, 85

Fischer, Ivan, 115

Fischer, Steven Roger, 8

flat ontologies, 5, 74, 76, 89, 120–21, 123

forms of life, 111

Foucault, Michel, 5, 120, 126

Frege, Gottlob, 83–84

Fuentes, Carlos, 115

García–Márquez, Gabriel, 108

Griffiths, AJF, 46

Guattari, Felix, 3, 11, 45–46, 50–51, 56–59, 73, 80, 120, 124–25

Heidegger, Martin: *Aletheia*. *See Aletheia*; care (*sorge*). *See* Dasein, care; circumspection (*Umsicht*). *See* ready to hand, the, circumspection (*Umsicht*); Dasein. *See* Dasein; deseverance. *See* deseverance (*ent-fernung*); Greek inception, 23, 74, 136, 141; metaphysics, 6n2, 142; pastorals, 97, 98; ready to hand. *See* ready to hand, the; resoluteness. *See* resoluteness (*Entschlossenheit*); understanding. *See* understanding

Heraclitus, 73

hidden people, the: as actuality, 21; as alterity, 40; definition, 13, 26n7; exceptionality, 26n7, 38; as excess, 39; as excrement, 13; as infinity, 13, 21; paradox of sovereignty, 26n7; as potentiality, 21; as ready to hand, the, 109; as synecdoche, 13, 109; as totality, 13, 39; as virtual others, 38–40

hierarchies, 12, 38, 47, 51

Hobbes, Thomas, 26n7, 126

Hume, David, 54

Humphrey, Hubert, 83

Husserl, Edmund, 28

ideal languages, 5–6, 109, 113–14

identity, 55, 72, 74, 76, 82, 125

imagination, 100–12

immanence, 12–13, 47, 55, 65, 78, 119–20, 145, 147

infinity, 12, 56, 104, 106, 108, 124

in order to (Um-zu). *See* ready to hand, the, in order to

intensity, 11, 30, 34n2, 38, 60, 80, 106, 134

interpretation, 52, 118–19, 136–37

Ishiguro, Kazuo, 108

Joyce, Terry, 8

Kant, Immanuel, 27, 74–75, 80, 132, 135

Kelsen, Hans, 58, 110

Kripke, Saul, 3, 11, 79–94
Kuhn. T. S, 111

Lang, Fritz, 119
language: as apparatus, 70. *See also* apparatus; atmosphere, 114; clarity, 109, 116; and contingency, 52, 78–79, 119, 138, 140; definition of, 49, 78; encryption of, 13, 60, 70, 101, 103, 106, 136–38; and experience, 53–54, 116, 140; formal, 58; grounds of, 53, 78, 116; hierarchies of, 46–47, 51, 60, 103; impenetrability, 13, 138; as infinity, 108, 116; and logic, 51, 54, 141; making sense, 54, 70, 101, 113, 116; metalanguage, 58; as model, 108, 138; objective, 53, 58, 73; ordinary, 58, 70, 112–13, 116; as present at hand, 138; private languages. *See* private languages; as a ready to hand. *See* ready to hand, the, and language; and repetition, 57, 82; and representation, 105, 145n2; as sequence, 81; as technology, 121, 123; and time, 86–87, 103; and transcendence, 53, 138; transmission, 56, 138; undecidability of, 53, 140; univocal, 53; as use, 51, 103; veracity, 51, 109; words, 107
language games, 5, 49, 53, 61–62, 75, 99, 106, 111, 117, 140
Latour, Bruno, 11, 45, 55, 121–23, 127–28
Lefebvre, Henri, 46, 126
Leibniz, Gottfried Wilhelm (von), 4, 72, 91
Levinas, Emmanuel, 39
Lewis, John, 91, 93
Li bai, 108
liberalism, 23, 112
life, 19–21, 120
localization principle, 128
logic, 50–51, 54–55, 75, 83, 87, 90, 110–12, 141
logos, 23, 74, 136, 141–42

machine, the, 56, 70, 116–17
Maldonado–Torres, Nelson, 23, 25
Marx, Karl, 66, 116, 125–26
McDonald, Angus, 13, 25n2
meaning, 55, 61, 72, 76, 107, 118, 133, 137, 140–41, 145n2
Meillassoux, Quentin, 3, 9, 11, 54, 78
Méndez–Hincapíe, Gabriel, 64, 70n4
Meshwork, 44–45, 51. *See also* Actor Network Theory (ANT)
Mignolo, Walter, 23–24
model of meter, 87
models: function, 77, 85, 116–17, 145; and language. *See* language, as model; and machines, 117. *See also* machine, the; as micromodels, 85. *See also* transcendent models; as representation, 77, 87–88; as samples, 77, 87–88, 110–11, 117. *See also* transcendent models
Moore´s paradox, 100, 103
Multiple Worlds Interpretation (MWI): and actuality, 93; and contingency, 91–93; and the contrary, 94–95; and immanence, 92; indexicality, 91; and modal logic, 91; multiverse, 94; and naming, 91; and necessity, 93, 95; nun, 93–94; observer dependent, 91, 128; parallel universes, 93–95; poetization of, 94–95; and quantum mechanics, 91–92, 94; state of affairs, 94–95, 98; virtuality, 92; wave functions, 91–92, 94. *See also* possible worlds
multiplicity, 14, 43–44, 57, 75, 104, 121, 124

names: as arch–factuality, 78; and context, 73, 76, 78; definitions, 78, 80; descriptivist theories. *See* cluster theory of concepts; and difference, 72, 74, 88; as empty signifiers, 86; as essence, 89–90; Excalibur, example, 71–72; function, 71, 74; and hierarchies, 74; ideal,

71, 79; as identity, 72, 76, 80, 82; indestructible, 77; as individuals, 73; as meaning, 72, 84; as modals, 83; as primary element, 72, 75, 84, 87; relationality, 78, 89; 'this' function, 72, 75, 91; transcendent meaning, 71; as use, 80, 89. *See also* naming

naming: and causality, 88; as classifying, 74; composition/decomposition, 73–75, 77, 79; and contingency, 58, 72–74, 79, 84, 87, 89; and difference, 78, 88; encryption, 89–90; gold example, 86–87; molecular thesis, 86; and natural kinds, 86; and necessity, 72, 86, 89; original baptism, 86, 88–89; a priori, 84, 88; tags, 89

Nancy, Jean-Luc, 39

Negri, Antonio, 14, 16, 19

Nietzsche, Friedrich, 21–22, 125

Nixon, Richard, 83–84

noticing an aspect, 102–7

ontology, 5, 28. *See also* Dasein; flat ontologies

order, 51–52, 56–58, 113–14, 119, 141

order-word, the, 42, 44, 50–51, 56–59, 99

ostensive definitions, 48–49, 60–61, 70nn2–3, 99

paradox, 4, 95

Peirce, Charles, Sanders, 11, 51–52, 64–65, 122

people, the, 13, 26n7

phenomenology, 28, 48, 72, 132, 139

phusis: and *Aletheia*, 142, 145. *See also Aletheia*; and appearance, 126, 141–42; as becoming, 126, 132, 141–42, 145, 147; and *Diké*, 126; as gathering, 74, 105, 141–42; as sway, 126, 142, 145; and *techné*, 126

Picasso, Pablo, 103

Plato, 19–20

Plotinus, 119

Poetics, 4, 93, 95, 112, 128

Politics, 13, 18–21

possible worlds, 82–85, 87, 94

potentia: as ability, 123; acquired, 16; and actuality. *See* actuality; as capacity, 123, 135; as contingency, 16, 107, 119, 139; definition, 14–21; and difference, 4, 47, 120, 139; and impotence, 17, 20–22, 120; natural, 16, 18–19; rational, 19; potentiality for being, 131–32, 139

potestas: definition, 4–5, 13, 41; and Dasein, 41. *See also* Dasein, *existentialles*; as domination, 13, 19, 120, 141; as facticity, 41, 78, 123; final word, 117; impossibility of, 95; and language, 51, 57, 59, 78, 99, 139–41. *See also* language; and necessity, 4, 52, 79, 123; obstinacy, 5, 62, 123; as reality, 21, 123; and simulacrum, the, 4–5; as stratification, 13, 51, 79, 120

power play, 5–6, 13, 58, 62, 66, 71, 75, 79, 99, 103, 108, 112, 140–41

present at hand. *See* ready to hand, the

Prigogine, Ilyia, 45

private languages, 100–104

propositions, 109–11

Protagoras, 73

Quijano, Anibal, 23

Quixote, Don, 76

Ramberg, Bjørn, 73

Rancière, Jacques, 119

ready to hand, the: being along something, 134; being in the world, 28, 42, 129, 134, 138; being within the world, 28, 35–37, 133, 138. *See also* Dasein; they, the, being within the world; concern (*Besorgen*), 38, 129, 132, 134; connectedness, 38, 135; circumspection (*Umsicht*), 31–32, 109, 134, 136–37; and Dasein, 27, 36, 42, 45, 109, 132–33,

138, 141–43. *See also* Dasein; decryption of, 31–32, 37, 41, 44–45, 109, 118, 130–31, 133–36, 140–43; definition, 27, 29, 37; directionality, 31, 66, 109, 135. *See also* deseverance; encryption of, 32, 36, 41, 45, 60, 66–67, 109, 112, 130–31, 133, 136, 138, 143–44; enworld, 40, 47–48; as equipment, 29, 42, 61, 97, 118, 134–35, 137–38, 142; as equiprimordiality, 137; and existentiality, 133, 135, 137–38; as false totalities, 32, 37, 130, 135, 138; and Fermat's principle, 131; as a given, 60, 142, 144; hierarchies, 38, 51, 61, 99, 135; as infinity of involvements, 43, 108, 134–35, 137; in order to (Um–zu), 64–65, 97, 99, 102, 134; instrumentality, 31, 36, 135; intensive virtuality, 135, 143; interactions, 75–76, 117–18, 130, 139; and language, 40, 61; living labor, 21, 27, 31, 66; as metaphysics, 6n2, 105, 143; objects and performances, 97–98; obtrusiveness (*aufdringlichkeit*), obstinacy (*aufsässigkeit*), conspicuousness (*auffälligkeit*), 30–31, 109; occurrentness, 29; as potentiality of being, 29, 42, 118, 130–33, 135, 137, 139. *See also* potentia; and present at hand, 28–29, 36, 59–60, 130–31, 136, 138. *See also* present at hand; as relation of power, 29, 31, 33, 36, 41, 77, 109, 131; as resource, 63–64; scarcity, 32, 102; and they, the, 36–38, 42, 130, 133, 138–39; as totality of involvements (*Bewenden*), 29, 32–33, 36–37, 42–44, 47–48, 66, 97–99, 105, 109, 118, 130, 134. *See also* towards which; towards this, 43, 97, 131; and transcendent models, 43, 60, 99, 118; transparency, 30, 35–36, 38, 66, 106, 130, 142. *See also* deseverance; utility, 29–30,

39; worldhood, 28, 38, 47, 135; repetition, 57, 82
representation, 39, 64, 102, 107
resoluteness (*Entschlossenheit*), 129–31, 141–44
rhizomes, 45, 56, 117, 120, 125
rigid designator, 82–90
Rorty, Richard, 11, 59, 73–74, 92, 111, 114
rule following, 50, 62, 66, 108–11, 114–16, 119, 136, 140–41
Rulfo, Juan, 108
Russell, Bertrand, 72–73, 114

Sachs, Joe, 18
Said, Edward, 25
Santos de Sousa, Boaventura, 23
science, 126–28
Searle, John, 83
second human nature, 125–27
seeing, 104–6
Shakespeare, William, 130
sign: Cartesianism dualism, 64; and context, 59, 87, 98, 102, 104–5, 108; encryption of, 54, 104. *See also* theory of encryption of power (TEP); as *Energeia*, 65, 108. *See also Energeia*; and hierarchies, 65, 122; and ideas, 64; and immanence, 65; as indicating, 64, 87; as mapping, 122; mediation, 52. *See also* interpretation; and necessity, 122; in Pearce, 64, 122; and power, 65; and the ready to hand, 59, 134–37; as reference, 64; and representation, 65, 102, 104–5, 108, 115; semiotic monism, 64; and signifying, 66, 87, 108; thirdness, 65, 87, 89, 110; and totalities, 59, 66
signification: assignation, 66; definition, 59; encryption, 66, 109, 135–37; familiarity, 65; final, 66, 105, 109, 137; in Heidegger, 60, 109, 135–37; and language games, 60, 107, 140; as meaning something by

something, 62, 71, 104, 108, 137; in Wittgenstein, 60, 104. *See also* ready to hand, the
simples and composites, 73–76
simulacrum, the, 4, 13, 65, 143
simultaneity, 106
singulars, 73–75, 134–35
Smith, Adam, 126
social, the, 97–98, 100, 121–23
Socrates, 72–73
solicitude. *See* Dasein, solicitude
Sophocles, 73
Sovereignty, 26n7
speculative turn, 3, 11, 76
Spinoza, Baruch, 26n6, 115–16, 119
Sprigge, Timothy, 89–90
Steinhardt, Paul, 91
Strawson, P. F., 83
striking as. *See* noticing an aspect
synergistic properties, 45, 47, 76, 128
synthesis, 75

tags. *See* naming, tags
Tarkovsky, Andrei, 100
techné, 126
Technology, 63, 126
telos. *See* Entelecheia, final cause
temporality. *See* Dasein, temporality
theory of encryption of power (TEP): consistency of the encrypted, 117; definition, 11–13, 102, 111–12, 141; and democracy, 13; and difference, 125, 141. *See also* difference; final word, 117. *See also* potestas, final word; as fixing a meaning, 141; ex post facto decisions, 53, 66, 112; as hiding, 11, 13, 99, 102, 138–39, 141; and interpretation, 102; and language, 12–13, 46, 53, 56, 106, 115, 136–41. *See also* language; and language games, 106, 108, 112, 115–17, 140–41; and modernity, 23–24; spiritual, the, 68; as stratification, 12, 141

they, the: as actuality, 131; authenticity, 32, 35, 130–31; definition, 37, 40, 139; encryption of, 32, 36–37, 130–31, 138; everydayness, 131, 134; fascination with, 36; idle talk (*Gerede*), 41; as inauthenticity, 35–36, 130–31; phenomenological fallacy, 36; and ready to hand, the, 35, 37, 130–31, 136–38. *See also* ready to hand, the; representation (*Vorstellungen*), 39
third order of power. *See* contingency, third order of power
thrownness (*Geworfenheit*), 132–38
Tlostanova, Madina, 23–24
tools. *See* ready to hand, the, as equipment
totalities, 12–13, 55–56, 61, 71, 98, 105, 122
towards which, 47, 97–99, 134. *See also* ready to hand, the, as totality of involvements
transcendent models, 12, 23–24, 43–44, 81, 122, 126, 144–45
transduction, 46–47, 50–51, 67, 89
transmission. *See* language, transmission

unconcealment. *See* Aletheia
understanding, 54, 108, 137, 139–40
universals, 75. *See also* transcendent models
unveiling. *See* Aletheia

virtuality, 34n2, 60, 92, 106, 143
virtue, 19–20
visual room, the, 2, 101–2
Viveiros de Castro, Eduardo, 121, 124
Vonnegut, Kurt, 26n6

wave functions. *See* Multiple World Interpretation (MWI), wave functions
Weber, Max, 126
Whitehead, Alfred North, 114
Whitman, Walt, 124

Wittgenstein, Ludwig: family resemblances. *See* family resemblances; language games. *See* language games; Moore's paradox. *See* Moore's paradox; and names. *See* names; naming; noticing an aspect. *See* noticing an aspect; ostensive definitions. *See* ostensive definitions; philosophy of language, 3; propositions. *See* propositions; private languages. *See* private languages; rule following. *See* rule following; and samples. *See* models, as samples; propositions; signification. *See* signification; understanding. *See* understanding; visual room. *See* visual room, the

Woolf, Virginia, 79

world, the, 12–13

worldhood. *See* ready to hand, the, worldhood

Wrathall, Mark A, 48

writing, 108

written system, 8

X game of language, the, 2, 8–10, 114, 141

Zappa Frank, 115